Apache Ignite Quick Start Guide

Distributed data caching and processing made easy

Sujoy Acharya

BIRMINGHAM - MUMBAI

Apache Ignite Quick Start Guide

Commissioning Editor: Amey Varangaonkar
Acquisition Editor: Reshma Raman
Content Development Editor: Roshan Kumar
Technical Editor: Shweta Jadhav
Copy Editor: Safis Editing
Project Coordinator: Hardik Bhinde
Proofreader: Safis Editing
Indexer: Rekha Nair
Graphics: Alishon Mendonsa
Production Coordinator: Nilesh Mohite

First published: November 2018

Production reference: 1301118

Published by Packt Publishing Ltd.
Livery Place
35 Livery Street
Birmingham
B3 2PB, UK.

ISBN 978-1-78934-753-1

www.packtpub.com

`mapt.io`

Mapt is an online digital library that gives you full access to over 5,000 books and videos, as well as industry leading tools to help you plan your personal development and advance your career. For more information, please visit our website.

Why subscribe?

- Spend less time learning and more time coding with practical eBooks and Videos from over 4,000 industry professionals

- Improve your learning with Skill Plans built especially for you

- Get a free eBook or video every month

- Mapt is fully searchable

- Copy and paste, print, and bookmark content

Packt.com

Did you know that Packt offers eBook versions of every book published, with PDF and ePub files available? You can upgrade to the eBook version at `www.packt.com` and as a print book customer, you are entitled to a discount on the eBook copy. Get in touch with us at `customercare@packtpub.com` for more details.

At `www.packt.com`, you can also read a collection of free technical articles, sign up for a range of free newsletters, and receive exclusive discounts and offers on Packt books and eBooks.

Contributors

About the author

Sujoy Acharya works as a Principal Engineer with Cerner. While growing up, he pursued his interests in the fields of computer science and engineering. His hobbies are watching movies and sitcoms, playing outdoor sports, and reading books.

Sujoy likes to research upcoming technologies. His major contributions are in the fields of TDD, building scalable applications, cloud services, and the Spring Framework.

He has authored four books for Packt, namely, *Test-Driven Development with Mockito*, *Mastering Unit Testing using Mockito and JUnit*, *Mockito Essentials*, and *Mockito for Spring*.

At the time of writing this book, I was fortunate to work with an excellent team at Packt, whose contributions vastly improved the presentation of this book. I would like to thank my technical reviewers, proofreaders, and my colleagues for their thorough reviews and insightful comments. I was able to incorporate some of the knowledge and wisdom they have gained over their many years in the software development industry. This book was possible because they provided valuable feedback. The entire process of writing a book requires a huge number of lonely hours. I would like to thank my wife, Sunanda, and my son, for their patience and endless support.

About the reviewer

Deepak Kumar Sahu is a big data technology-driven professional with extensive experience in data gathering, modeling, analysis, validation, and architecture/solutions design to build next-generation analytics platforms. He has a strong analytical and technical background with good problem-solving skills for developing effective complex business solutions. He enjoys developing high-quality software and designing secure and scalable data systems. He has written several blogs on machine learning, data science, big data management, and blockchain. He can be reached at deepaksahu092@gmail.com and on LinkedIn at deepakkumarsah.u.

I would like to thank my parents, and my family, who supported and backed me throughout my life, and my friends for being precisely that. Thanks to Packt Publishing for selecting me as one of the technical reviewers on this wonderful book. It is my honor to be a part of this book.

Packt is searching for authors like you

If you're interested in becoming an author for Packt, please visit authors.packtpub.com and apply today. We have worked with thousands of developers and tech professionals, just like you, to help them share their insight with the global tech community. You can make a general application, apply for a specific hot topic that we are recruiting an author for, or submit your own idea.

Table of Contents

Preface

With the advent of microservice architecture, the software innovation life cycle became much faster. We are now able to build small, cohesive services that communicate with each other and be scaled and developed independently. Some of the key non-functional requirements of this style are scalability, availability, and high performance. In-memory distributed data fabrics play a key role in fulfilling these requirements.

Apache Ignite is a stable, feature rich, and distributed in-memory platform designed to scale and process large volumes of data. It can be integrated with both microservices as well as monolithic systems—and, for that matter, can also be used as a scalable, highly available, and highly performant deployment platform for microservices.

This book is a comprehensive guide that lets you explore all the advanced features and use cases of Apache Ignite, taking you through why you should explore Apache Ignite; in-memory technologies; installation and clustering of Ignite nodes; caching topologies; and various caching strategies, such as caching aside, read-through and write-through, and write-behind. You'll delve into detailed aspects of Ignite's data grid, including web session clustering and querying data. You will also obtain hands-on experience of processing large volumes of data using Compute Grid and Ignite's MapReduce and Executor Service. Furthermore, you'll gain experience with the memory architecture of Apache Ignite, monitoring memory and cache, complex event processing, event streaming, and time series prediction of opportunities and threats. Additionally, this book covers off-heap and on-heap caching, swapping, native and third-party persistence, and Spring Framework integration with Apache Ignite.

By the end of this book, you will have mastered the features of Apache Ignite 2.x and be able to build an efficient, high-performance, scalable, and high-availability system architecture.

Who this book is for

This book is for anyone who is familiar with Java and wants to build a high-performance, scalable, and high-availability system architecture. However, no prior knowledge of caching is required.

What this book covers

Chapter 1, *Getting Familiar with Apache Ignite*, explains why Apache Ignite is important and how adding a new tool to your tech toolbox can help solve different problems. You will also get to look into various rich features of Apache Ignite, explore Apache Ignite use cases, and understand refactored traditional architecture building blocks using Apache Ignite support.

Chapter 2, *Understanding the Topologies and Caching Strategies*, looks at Apache Ignite clustering, caching topology, and caching strategies. This chapter also explores the caching modes for distributing data. This chapter will gets into local, partitioned, and replicated caching modes, and how scalability, availability, and read/write performance can be tuned using the caching modes.

Chapter 3, *Working with Data Grids*, covers Apache Ignite data grid concepts. You'll start with the JSR 107 specification, learning about cache configuration, cache events, listeners, and filters. You will also explore how Hibernate L2 cache can be stored in Apache Ignite in order to improve application performance. This chapter also explores web session clustering with Apache Ignite.

Chapter 4, *Exploring Compute Grid and the Query API*, covers two important components of Apache Ignite architecture: Apache Ignite Query API and distributed computing using Apache Ignite Compute Grid. This chapter concludes with Compute Grid and distributed computation using the following APIs: MapReduce and ForkJoin, ExecutorService, job scheduling APIs.

Chapter 5, *Building Microservices with Service Grid*, explains the concepts of service grid and microservices deployment with Apache Ignite. You will also look into the core service grid APIs, the Service and IgniteServices interfaces, and how a service can be defined, deployed, and canceled. This chapter also covers complex event processing, event data streaming APIs, and continuous queries.

Chapter 6, *Sharpening Ignite Skills*, will cover the art of building an ACID-compliant, high-performance, scalable, and highly available system. You will also learn about the need for data persistence and how to persist data to a commonly used RDBMS or NoSQL datastore, such as MySQL or Cassandra.

Chapter 7, *Deploying to Production*, covers the nitty-gritty of fine-tuning our Apache Ignite application for production deployment. You will also explore the various features and use cases of Apache Ignite. This chapter will also take you through Apache Ignite, in-memory technologies, the installation and clustering of Ignite nodes, caching topologies, and various caching strategies.

To get the most out of this book

You will need basic knowledge of the following technologies:

- Java 8
- Eclipse
- Apache Ignite 2.5
- ZooKeeper 3.4
- MySQL 8.0.11
- MySQL Workbench
- Postman
- Apache Cassandra 3.11

Download the example code files

You can download the example code files for this book from your account at www.packt.com. If you purchased this book elsewhere, you can visit www.packt.com/support and register to have the files emailed directly to you.

You can download the code files by following these steps:

1. Log in or register at www.packt.com.
2. Select the **SUPPORT** tab.
3. Click on **Code Downloads & Errata**.
4. Enter the name of the book in the **Search** box and follow the onscreen instructions.

Once the file is downloaded, please make sure that you unzip or extract the folder using the latest version of:

- WinRAR/7-Zip for Windows
- Zipeg/iZip/UnRarX for Mac
- 7-Zip/PeaZip for Linux

The code bundle for the book is also hosted on GitHub at https://github.com/ PacktPublishing/Apache-Ignite-Quick-Start-Guide. In case there's an update to the code, it will be updated on the existing GitHub repository.

We also have other code bundles from our rich catalog of books and videos available at `https://github.com/PacktPublishing/`. Check them out!

Download the color images

We also provide a PDF file that has color images of the screenshots/diagrams used in this book. You can download it here: `https://www.packtpub.com/sites/default/files/downloads/9781789347531_ColorImages.pdf`.

Conventions used

There are a number of text conventions used throughout this book.

`CodeInText`: Indicates code words in text, database table names, folder names, filenames, file extensions, pathnames, dummy URLs, user input, and Twitter handles. Here is an example: "Mount the downloaded `WebStorm-10*.dmg` disk image file as another disk in your system."

A block of code is set as follows:

```
pojoCacheConfig.addCacheEntryListenerConfiguration(new
MutableCacheEntryListenerConfiguration<>(cacheEntryCreatedListenerFactory,
filterFactory, true, true));
```

When we wish to draw your attention to a particular part of a code block, the relevant lines or items are set in bold:

```
System.out.println("Find max, min salary of players group by club");
 fieldQry = new SqlFieldsQuery("select c.name , max(p.salary),
min(p.salary) from SoccerPlayer p, \"" + CLUB_SQL_CACHE + "\".SoccerClub c
where p.clubId = c.id group by c.name");
```

Bold: Indicates a new term, an important word, or words that you see onscreen. For example, words in menus or dialog boxes appear in the text like this. Here is an example: "Select **System info** from the **Administration** panel."

Warnings or important notes appear like this.

Tips and tricks appear like this.

Get in touch

Feedback from our readers is always welcome.

General feedback: If you have questions about any aspect of this book, mention the book title in the subject of your message and email us at `customercare@packtpub.com`.

Errata: Although we have taken every care to ensure the accuracy of our content, mistakes do happen. If you have found a mistake in this book, we would be grateful if you would report this to us. Please visit `www.packt.com/submit-errata`, selecting your book, clicking on the Errata Submission Form link, and entering the details.

Piracy: If you come across any illegal copies of our works in any form on the Internet, we would be grateful if you would provide us with the location address or website name. Please contact us at `copyright@packt.com` with a link to the material.

If you are interested in becoming an author: If there is a topic that you have expertise in and you are interested in either writing or contributing to a book, please visit `authors.packtpub.com`.

Reviews

Please leave a review. Once you have read and used this book, why not leave a review on the site that you purchased it from? Potential readers can then see and use your unbiased opinion to make purchase decisions, we at Packt can understand what you think about our products, and our authors can see your feedback on their book. Thank you!

For more information about Packt, please visit `packt.com`.

Getting Familiar with Apache Ignite

1

As software practitioners, we review different technologies and frameworks. They are nothing but a tool. A toolbox contains many tools for different purposes. The challenge for us while picking a tool is to know which is the right one to apply to the situation. If we pick up a hammer and try to use it for everything, we will probably end up with a mess. The art of designing software is knowing its purpose, and when to use each tool. Apache Ignite adds another tool to our toolbox that we can pick up when the right situation arises. When you learn a new concept or framework, you should always ask: why do I need a new framework?

The *why* explains the purpose, *how* tells you about the process, and *what* talks about the result of *why*.

As technologists, we can adhere to Simon Sinek's *Golden Circle* theory that people don't buy what you do, they buy why you do it. Our clients don't care about our technology stack, they care about business functionalities.

Let's explore the *why* of Apache Ignite. The following topics are covered in this chapter:

- Why Apache Ignite?
- Exploring the features
- Refactoring the architecture
- Installing Apache Ignite
- Running `HelloWorld`
- Classifying Apache Ignite

Why Apache Ignite?

Apache Ignite is an open source **In-Memory Data Grid** (**IMDG**), distributed database, caching and high performance computing platform. It offers a bucketload of features and integrates well with other Apache frameworks such as Hadoop, Spark, and Cassandra.

So why do we need Apache Ignite? We need it for its **High Performance** and **Scalability**.

Of course, the phrase *high performance* might be very popular in our industry, but it's equally ambiguous. There's no established numerical threshold for when regular performance becomes high performance, just as there's no clear threshold for when data becomes Big Data, or when services become Microservices.

Fortunately, culture tends to generate its own barometers, and in computer science, the term high performance generally refers to the prowess possessed by supercomputers. Supercomputers are used to achieve high throughput using distributed parallel processing. They are mainly used for processing compute-intensive tasks such as weather forecasting, gene model analysis, big-bang simulations, and so on. High performance computing enables us to process huge chunks of data as quickly as possible.

Following the supercomputers analogy, we can stack up many virtual machines/workstations (form a grid) to process a computationally intensive task, but in traditional database-centric applications, parallel processing doesn't scale linearly. If we add 10 more machines to the grid, it **will not** process 10 times faster. At most, it can gain 2-4% in performance.

Apache Ignite plays a key role here to achieve a 20-30% linear performance improvement. It keeps data in RAM for fast processing and linear scaling. If you add more workstations to the grid, it will offer higher scalability and performance gains.

 NoSQL databases were introduced to mitigate RDBMS scalability issues. There are four types of NoSQL databases, used to handle different use cases, but still, a NoSQL database cannot help us to scale our system to handle real high volume transactional data. Apache Ignite offers caching APIs to process a high volume of ACID-compliant transactional data.

If you need to process records in a transactional manner and still need a 20-30% performance gain over a traditional database, *Apache Ignite can offer you high performance improvement, linear scalability, and ACID compliant transactions with high availability and resiliency.*

Apache Ignite can be used for various types of data sources, from high volume financial service transaction data to streams of IoT sensor data. Ignite stores data in RAM for fast processing throughput but for resiliency, you can persist the data in a third-party data store as well as in the native Ignite persistence store. We will explore each of them later.

Ignite offers an ANSI SQL query API to query data, an API to perform CRUD on caches, ACID transactions, a compute and service grid, streams, and complex event processing to Machine Learning APIs.

NoSQL and NewSQL
NoSQL came into the picture to solve the RDBMS scalability bottleneck, they are eventually consistency and follows the CAP theorem of distributed transaction. Doesn't offer transactional consistency, relational SQL joins but scales many times faster than the RDBMs. NewSQL is a new type of databases offer the ACID complaint distributed transaction that can scale. Apache Ignite can be termed as a NewSQL db

Exploring the features

Apache Ignite is a feature-rich, open source, in-memory platform. In this section, we are going to explore Apache Ignite's features and use cases. Later, we will deep dive into each topic.

In-Memory Data Grid (IMDG)

One of the key features of Apache Ignite is the In-memory Data Grid. You can consider IMDG as a distributed Key-Value pair store; the key and value both must implement the *serializable* interface as they get transferred over the network. Apache Ignite stores objects in off-heap and on-heap memory (and on disk when native persistence is enabled). Apache Ignite's data grid operations, such as **Create, Read, Update, and Delete** (**CRUD**), are many times faster than RDBMs operations as the traditional databases store data in a filesystem (B+ tree), whereas IMDG data is stored in memory.

Apache Ignite IMDG has the following capabilities:

- It supports distributed ACID transactions. You can perform more than one cache operation in a transactional manner.
- Adding more Ignite nodes can store more data and scale elastically.

- It can store data in off-heap storage and also provides capabilities to persist data in RDBMS, HDFS, and NoSQL databases.
- JCache (JSR 107)-compliant cache APIs.
- Supports Spring Framework Integration. You can annotate your Java methods with a Spring cache annotation to access data from the Ignite cache. As we know, SQL summation is a costly time consuming database operation; the following code snippet calculates total PTO hours for a department and stores it in an Apache Ignite cache. Now, if you again invoke the `retrieveTotalPaidTimeOffFor` method with the same `departmentId`, it will be served from the cache instead of performing a costly database aggregation:

```
@Cacheable("ptoHours")
public double retrieveTotalPaidTimeOffFor(int departmentId) {
    String sql =
        "SELECT SUM(e.ptoHrs) " +
        "FROM Employee e " +
        "WHERE e.deptId= ?";

    return jdbcTemplate.queryForObject(sql, Double.class,
    departmentId);
}
```

- Hibernate can be configured to store an L2 cache in a Data Grid.
- Web Session Data clustering for high availability.

We will cover the IMDG in Chapter 3, *Working with Data Grids*.

In-Memory SQL Grid (IMSG)

Apache Ignite SQL Grid is a distributed data grid where you can execute ANSI SQL-99-compliant SQLs (SELECT, UPDATE, INSERT, MERGE, and DELETE queries) to manipulate a cache. The Apache Ignite cache API provides you with the get/put/remove methods (and variants) to interact with the cache, but the SQL API offers you more flexibility; for instance, you can execute a SELECT query to fetch objects or update a few specific records using a where clause, or delete objects from a cache.

Applications developed in different languages can interact with the Ignite platform with their native APIs and ANSI SQL-99 syntax through Apache Ignite's JDBC and ODBC APIs. Suppose you want to store student information in a database table called *student*. In the in-memory world, you can create a student cache to store data. The student cache will store the student ID as the key and the student object as the value. If you know the student id, you can easily fetch the student details by calling `cache.get(studentId)`. SQL grid APIs enable you to query the student using its fields—such as you can query:

```
SELECT * FROM student WHERE firstName = 'john'
```

The student class needs to be serializable. The following is the `Student` class code snippet. Some fields are annotated with `@QuerySqlField` to make them queriable. You can write an SQL query to fetch students data with `studentId`, `firstName`, or `lastName`. We will cover the indexing in SQL section:

```
public class Student implements Serializable {
    private static final long serialVersionUID = 1L;
  @QuerySqlField(index = true)
  private Long studentId;
  @QuerySqlField(index= true)
  private String firstName;
  @QuerySqlField(index= true)
  private String lastName;
    ...
}
```

Compute Grid

Apache Ignite Compute Grid is a distributed in-memory MapReduce/ForkJoin or Splitter-Aggregator platform. It enables the parallel processing of data to reduce the overall processing time. You can offload your computational tasks onto multiple nodes to improve the overall performance of the system and make it scalable. Suppose you need to generate the monthly student dues of a class. This includes accommodation charges, electricity usage, internet bills, food and canteen dues, library fees, and so on. You can split the processing into multiple chunks; each task computes a student due and finally the parent job sums up the dues of all students. If we have 10 nodes/threads and 100 students, then we can do 10 parallel processing.

Compute grid sends the tasks onto different worker nodes; each node performs a series of expansive calculations such as joining caches/tables using SQL queries. As a result, if we add more nodes the job will scale more.

The following diagram explains the compute grid architecture. We have to calculate bills for M students and already have N Apache Ignite nodes. Provided M > N, we can split the job into M/N chunks (if M = 101 and N=10, then we will end up with 101/10=10 + 1= 11 chunks) and send each chunk to a worker node. Finally, we aggregate the M/N chunks and send the result back to the job. It will reduce the overall computational time by N * number of loops times:

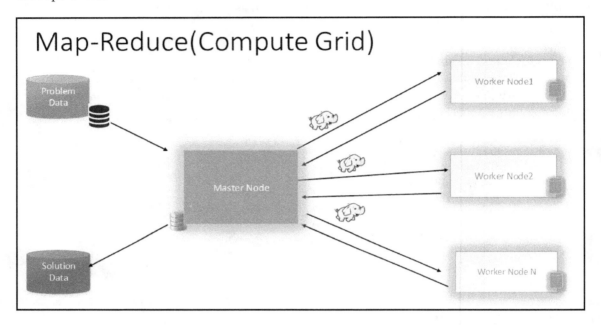

Ignite compute grid supports distributed closure and SQL joins. We will cover them in Chapter 4, *Exploring the Compute Grid and Query API*.

Service Grid

What if we get the ability to deploy our service to a MySql/MS SQL or Oracle database? The service will collocate with the data and process DB-related computational requests way faster than the traditional deployment model. Service grid is a nice concept where you can deploy a service to an Apache Ignite cluster.

It offers various operating modes:

- Microservice-type multiple service deployment
- Singleton deployment: Node singleton, cluster singleton, and so on
- High availability: If one node goes down, another node will process the requests
- Client deployment and node startup deployment
- Anytime service removal

The following diagram represents a cluster-singleton service grid deployment. Only one node is active in the grid cluster:

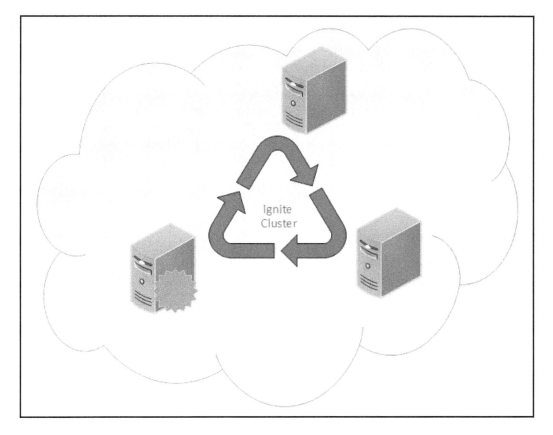

Service grid and compute grid look similar but in compute grid, a computational closure is sent to a node and it needs to have peer class loading enabled, whereas for service grid, the service and its dependencies need to be present in all the cluster node's classpath.

Streaming and Complex Event Processing

Before we look at streaming and complex event processing, let's explore the concept of OLTP and OLAP databases. **OLTP** stands for **Online Transaction Processing**. OLTP supports online transactional operations such as insert, update, and delete, and stores data in normalized form. Normalization is cleaner easier to maintain and changes as it minimizes the data duplication—for example you may store student name and student address in to tables. If you need to update the address or add two addresses for a student, you can do it efficiently without touching the student table. But to query a student's details, one needs to join the student and address tables.

OLAP stands for **Online Analytical Processing**. It processes historical or archived data to get business insights. In OLAP generally, data is denormalized or duplicated in multidimensional schemas for efficient querying. Here, you don't have to join ten tables to get an insight. OLAP is the foundation of **business intelligence** (**BI**).

ETL (**Extract, Transform, and Load**) is a process to pull data from OLTP to OLAP. ETL is not a real-time process, jobs are generally executed at the end of the day. The ETL/OLAP model, or the typical business intelligence architecture, doesn't work when we need to process a stream of transactional data and provide business insights or detect threats or opportunities (business insights) in real time. For example, you cannot wait for a few hours to detect fraudulent credit card transaction.

Complex event processing enables real-time analytics on transactional event streams. It intercepts different events, then computes or detects patterns, and finally takes action or provides business insights.

Apache Ignite has the capability to stream events from disparate sources and then perform complex event processing. The following diagram explains Apache Ignite's complex event processing architecture:

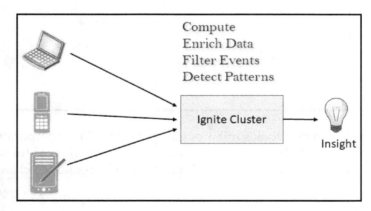

Ignite File System (IGFS)

Apache Ignite has an in-memory distributed filesystem interface to work with files in memory. IGFS is the acronym of Ignite distributed file system. IGFS accelerates Hadoop processing by keeping the files in memory and minimizing disk IO.

IGFS provides APIs to perform the following operations:

- **CRUD (Create, Read, Update, and Delete Files/Directories)** file operations
- Perform MapReduce; it sits on top of **Hadoop File system (HDFS)** to accelerate Hadoop processing
- File caching and eviction

We'll explore IGFS and Hadoop MapReduce acceleration in later chapters.

Clustering

Apache Ignite can automatically detect when a new node is added to the cluster, and similarly can detect when a node is stopped or crashed, transparently redistributing the data. This enables you to scale your system as you add more nodes. The coolest feature of this sophisticated clustering is that it can connect a private cloud's Ignite node to a public cloud's domain cluster, such as AWS. We will look at clustering in detail in Chapter 2, *Understanding the Topologies and Caching Strategie*s.

Messaging

Messaging is a communication protocol to decouple senders from receivers. Apache Ignite supports various models of data exchange between nodes.

The following messaging types are supported:

- Cluster-wide messaging to all nodes (pub-sub)
- Grid event notifications, such as task execution
- Cache events such as a cache updating in local and remote nodes

Distributed data structures

Apache Ignite allows you to create distributed data structures and share them between the nodes. One really useful data structure is the ID generator. In many applications, ID generation is handled using a UUID or custom stored procedure logic, or by configuring tables to generate `seq ids`. A distributed ID generator residing in an in-memory grid is orders of magnitude faster than traditional ID generators.

The following distributed data structures are supported till version 2.5:

- Queue and Set
- Atomic Types
- `CountDownLatch`
- ID Generator
- Semaphore

We'll explore each of the preceding data structures in later chapters.

Refactoring the architecture

We looked at various aspects of Apache Ignite. In this section, we are going to explore different system architectures and how Apache Ignite can be integrated into our existing system to help us build a scalable architecture.

Achieving High Performance

In traditional web application architecture, we deploy our application into multiple nodes and each node connects to a relational database to store data. The following diagram depicts the traditional system architecture; different clients (desktop, mobile, tabs, laptops, smart devices, and so on) are communicating with the system. There are multiple JVMs/nodes to handle the traffic (the load balancer is removed for brevity), but there is only one database instance to store data. DB operations are relatively slow as they interact with the file IO, so this architecture may create a bottleneck if the client requests come faster than the DB prepossessing rate. The database ensures data atomicity, consistency, transaction isolation, and durability, we just cannot run multiple DB instances or replace it:

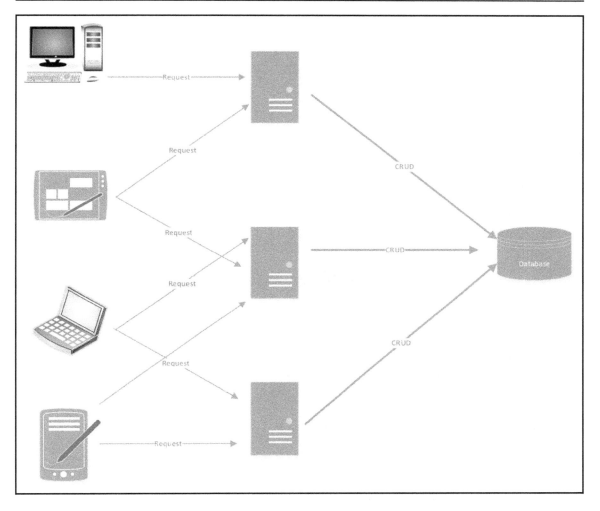

Adding a new Apache Ignite in-memory data grid layer to the existing N-tier architecture can improve the performance of the system many times over. The in-memory cluster can sit between the JVMs and the database. The JVMs/nodes will interact with the Ignite in-memory grid instead of the database, since the CRUD operations will be performed in-memory the performance will be way faster than direct database CRUDs. Data consistency, atomicity, isolation, and durability, and the transactional nature of operations, will be maintained by the Ignite cluster.

This new architectural style reduces the transaction time and system response time by moving the data closer to the application:

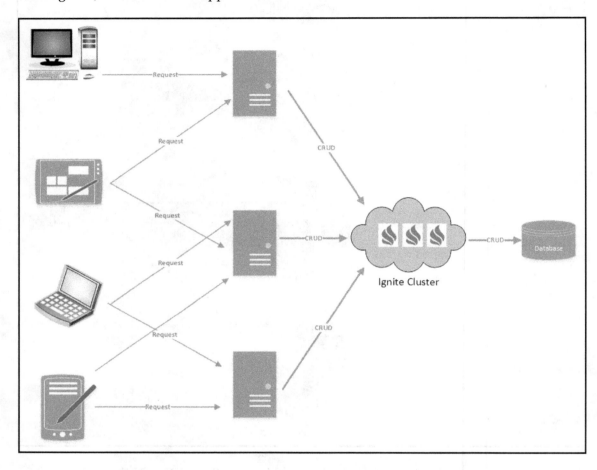

In Chapter 2, *Understanding the Topologies and Caching Strategies,* we will explore how to write code to interact with an in-memory data grid and then sync up data with a relational database.

Addressing High Availability and Resiliency

Load balancers are used to distribute user loads across the JVMs/nodes of an enterprise application. Load balancers use sticky sessions to route all the requests for a user to a particular server, which reduces session replication overhead. Session data is kept in the server; in the case of server failures, the user data is lost. It impacts the availability of the system. Web session clustering is a mechanism to move session data out of application servers, to the Apache Ignite data grid. It increases system scalability and availability; if we add more servers, the system can handle more users. Even if a server goes down, the user data will still be intact.

The following diagram depicts web session clustering with the Apache Ignite in-memory data grid:

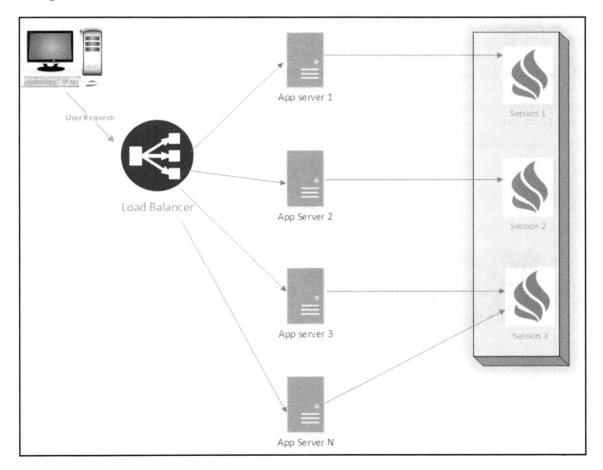

A **Load Balancer** can route user requests to any server based on the load on the server; it doesn't have to remember the server-session affinity mapping as the user sessions are kept in the Ignite grid. Suppose a user's requests were being processed by **App server 3**, and his session is kept in the Apache Ignite session grid **Session 3** in the previous diagram. Now, if **App server 3** is busy or down, then the load balancer can route the user request to **App Server N**. **App Server N** can still process the user request as the user session is present in the Ignite grid.

You don't have to change code to share user sessions between servers through the Apache Ignite grid. We will configure web session clustering in `Chapter 3`, *Working with Data Grids*.

Sharing Data

Cache as a Service (**CaaS**) is a new computing buzzword. CaaS is used to share data between applications and it builds a common data access layer across an organization. In the healthcare domain, **Charges & Services**, **Claims**, **Scheduling**, **Reporting**, and **Patient Management** are some of the important modules. Organizations can develop them in any programming language the team is comfortable with, in a Microservice fashion. The applications can still share data using Apache Ignite's in-memory data grid. There is no need to create a local caching infrastructure for each application:

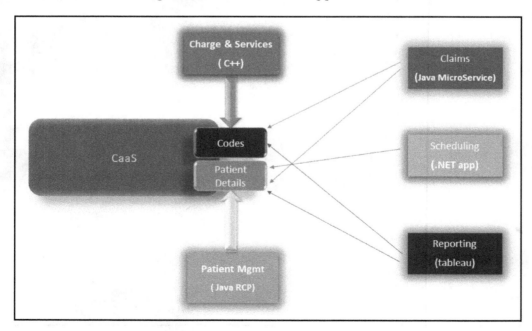

Moving Computation To Data

Microservices offer so many advantages over a traditional monolithic architecture. One of the main disadvantages of distributed Mircoservice-based deployment is service-to-service communication for data access. Apache Ignite provides a mechanism to move applications closer to the data and process requests faster. Microservices can be deployed directly to Apache Ignite nodes as it works faster than an app server filesystem-based deployment.

We are going to cover many more in-memory grid architecture refactoring styles and use cases in details.

Now, it is time for getting your hands dirty with Apache Ignite.

Installing Apache Ignite

Apache Ignite requires a Java 8 or higher runtime environment. You can download the source or binary version of Apache Ignite from `https://ignite.apache.org/` to start working with the Apache Ignite grid.

There is no magic in installation; as of June 2018, the latest version is 2.5.0. Download the `apache-ignite-fabric-2.5.0-bin.zip` binary and extract the content and do the following:

1. Browse to the installation directory and open the `bin` folder:

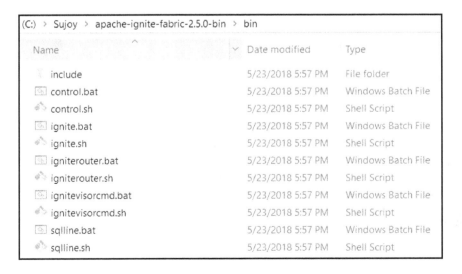

2. Run the `ignite.bat` file in a Windows operating system or the `ignite.sh` file in macOS/Linux:

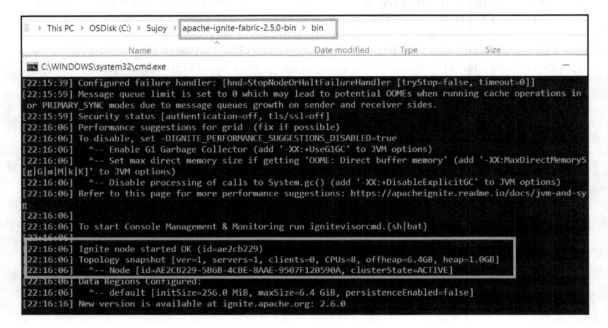

3. Run Apache Ignite as a Windows service using `NSSM.exe`. Download `NSSM.exe`
4. Copy `NSSM.exe` into the `bin` folder
5. Open a command prompt and run the following commands, replacing `{IGNIT_INSTALL_DIR}` with the original Ignite installation directory path:

```
nssm install ignite-poc {IGNIT_INSTALL_DIR}\bin\ignite.bat
nssm set ignite-poc AppDirectory {IGNIT_INSTALL_DIR}
nssm set ignite-poc AppStdout {IGNIT_INSTALL_DIR}\logs\sysout.log
nssm set ignite-poc AppStderr {IGNIT_INSTALL_DIR}\logs\syserr.log
nssm set ignite-poc AppStdoutCreationDisposition 2
nssm set ignite-poc AppStderrCreationDisposition 2
nssm set ignite-poc AppStopMethodSkip 6
```

6. Open the Windows `services.msc` file and notice that a new service, `ignite-poc`, was created

Congratulations! You have successfully launched an ignite node and installed Ignite as a Windows service.

Running HelloWorld

You have successfully installed Apache Ignite, now it's time for fun. Let's connect to the Apache Ignite node and create a cache. The following are the steps to create a new Ignite cache:

1. Open your favorite IDE and create a new Gradle project, `hello-world`
2. Edit the `build.gradle` file with the following entries:

```
implementation 'com.h2database:h2:1.4.196'
compile group: 'org.apache.ignite', name: 'ignite-core', version:
'2.5.0'
compile group: 'org.slf4j', name: 'slf4j-api', version: '1.6.0'
compile group: 'org.apache.ignite', name: 'ignite-spring',
version: '2.5.0'
compile group: 'org.apache.ignite', name: 'ignite-indexing',
version: '2.5.0'
compile group: 'log4j', name: 'log4j', version: '1.2.17'
```

3. Create a new Java class, `HelloWorld`
4. Add the following lines to create a cache, `myFirstIgniteCache`, put values into the cache, and then retrieve values from the cache:

```java
public class HelloWorld {
  public static void main(String[] args) {
    try (Ignite ignite = Ignition.start()) {
      IgniteCache<Integer, String> cache =
ignite.getOrCreateCache("myFirstIgniteCache");

      for (int i = 0; i < 10; i++)
        cache.put(i, Integer.toString(i));

      for (int i = 0; i < 10; i++)
        System.out.println("Fetched [key=" + i + ", val=" +
cache.get(i) + ']');
    }
  }
}
```

The `Ignition.start()` starts an Ignite instance in memory. A cache stores key-value pairs like `java.util.Map`. `IgniteCache<Key, Value>` represents a distributed cache where Key and Value are serializable objects. Here, we are asking Ignite to create (or get, if already created) a cache `myFirstIgniteCache` to store an integer key and String value, then store 10 integers in the cache, and finally ask the cache to get the values:

1. Add the import statements and run the program.
2. It will start a server node and add it to the existing cluster. You can see the topology snapshot indicating `version=2` and `servers=2`:

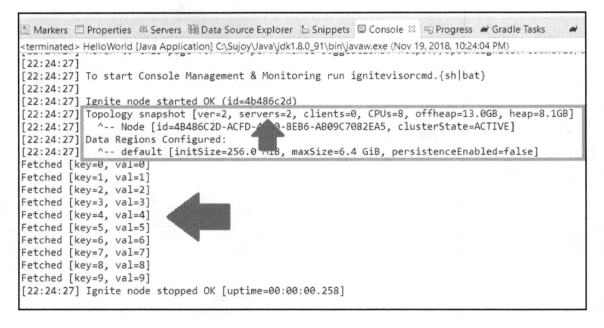

Don't panic if the code doesn't look familiar; we will explore it step by step in `Chapter 2`, *Understanding the Topologies and Caching Strategies*.

Classifying Apache Ignite

In this section, we will compare Apache Ignite with other open source frameworks. First, we will look at what an in-memory database is.

IMDB versus IMDG

In-memory databases are fully functional good old RDBMS that store data in memory (RAM). When you make a database query to fetch records or you update a row, you access the RAM instead of the filesystem. RDBMS accesses the disk to seek data and that's why IMDBs are faster than the RDBMS.

Although IMDBs store data in RAM, your data will not be lost when the machine reboots. You can configure an IMDB to recover from machine restarts/crashes. Typically stores data in memory but keeps a transaction log for each operation. The log appends transaction details at the end of the file. When the machine restarts, it reloads data from the transaction log and creates a snapshot, that's it!

So, for each update or insert operation, it writes a transaction log to disk; shouldn't it slow down the performance? Not really. It is like writing logs for your Java application using Log4j; sequential disk operations are not slow as the disk spindle doesn't move randomly.

Then how is an IMDG different than an IMDB? An IMDG also keeps the data in-memory and has capabilities to recover from failures, as it keeps transaction logs. An IMDB is fully ANSI SQL-compliant but IMDG offers limited support for ANSI SQL; rather, IMDG recommends key-value pair or MapReduce access. IMDB lacks parallel processing of distributed SQL joins. IMDB cannot scale like IMDG; if we add more IMDG nodes, then it can scale more and store more data. IMDG offers ACID compliant DB access and many other features.

YugaByte DB

YugaByte DB is a transactional, high-performance, planet-scale database and is very useful to achieve ACID-compliant high-volume distributed transactions. YugaByte doesn't have the mechanism to deploy microservices, CaaS, Hadoop Accelerator, or compute grid.

Geode, Hazelcast , Redis, and EhCache

Apache Geode is the oldest in-memory data grid. Indian and China Railways re-architected their legacy system to handle 36% of the world population's ticketing demands using the commercial version of Geode. But the Apache Geode APIs are ancient and lack readability; the documentation is also not easy to understand.

Hazelcast, Redis, EhCache, Infispan, and other in-memory data grids are not as feature-rich as Apache Ignite. Especially the service grid, IGFS and Hadoop MapReducec play a key role in choosing Apache Ignite. Key-value pair and SQL query performance are also faster in Apache Ignite.

Summary

This chapter started with explaining why you need Apache Ignite and how adding a new tool to your tech toolbox can help you solve different problems. We looked at the rich features of Apache Ignite, explored Apache Ignite use cases, and refactored traditional architecture building blocks using Apache Ignite support.

We then installed Apache Ignite on Windows and Mac, created a Hello World program to access an Ignite cache, and finally compared Apache Ignite with other frameworks.

In Chapter 2, *Understanding the Topologies and Caching Strategies,* we will explore caching strategies and Ignite clustering.

References

- https://ignite.apache.org/features/
- https://apacheignite.readme.io/docs

2
Understanding the Topologies and Caching Strategies

In `Chapter 1`, *Getting Familiar with Apache Ignite*, we learned about various features and the architecture of Apache Ignite; this chapter covers the bare bones of Apache Ignite. We'll look at Apache Ignite clustering, caching topology, and caching strategies. Clustering, caching topology, and caching strategies solve different enterprise architecture problems. In this chapter, we are going to cover the following topics:

- CAP theorem and Apache Ignite
- Clustering architecture
- Caching topology
- Clustering strategy

CAP theorem and Apache Ignite

Apache Ignite supports distributed transactional cache operations, and at the same time it is highly available. Supporting both ACID transactions and high availability is a big ask for any distributed data store. Distributed data stores follow the CAP theorem. Computer scientist Eric Brewer proposed the CAP theorem, and it says that a distributed data store cannot offer more than two of the following three capabilities:

- **Consistency**: You will always get the latest and greatest data. Suppose you have two nodes, A and B, and someone is updating a document/record in node B and you are reading that same record from node A. You should get the latest update made to the record in node B.
- **Availability**: You should always get a response; it may not be the latest data, but it should not throw an error.
- **Partition tolerance**: This means that if you remove the network connection between the nodes (A and B, in our case), the system should still operate.

Distributed data stores cannot escape from network failures; CAP theorem states that in the case of network partitions, a node can either be consistent or available.

What does that mean? In our example, we have two nodes, A and B. Suppose someone chops the network cable and disconnects A and B. Someone may make changes to node B after that network partitioning. If you are connected to node A, you can get old data or A may stop responding to your queries. If A returns you data, that means your distributed system is available but not consistent as you are getting stale data, which is not consistent. If A stops responding to you, that means your data store system is consistent but not available, as it is not giving you any stale data and at the same time has stopped responding to you.

Any distributed network data store can either be **CA**, **CP**, or **AP**. Let's explore the characteristics of each system:

- **CA system**: Here, the data store supports consistency and availability but doesn't support network partitioning, so this architecture is not scalable. To provide ACID transactions and high availability, it sacrifices network partitioning. All RDBM data stores are CA systems.
- **CP system:** This system architecture supports consistency and partition tolerance, but sacrifices availability. In the case of network outage, some nodes stop responding to queries to maintain consistency. Some data is lost.
- **AP system:** The distributed data store is always available and partitioned. This system architecture sacrifices consistency in the case of network partitioning.

The following diagram depicts the CAP abilities:

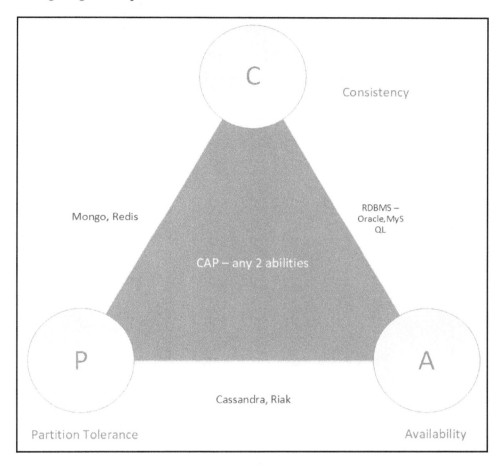

Apache Ignite is a distributed data store, so it must adhere to the *CAP theorem* and support any two of the following three capabilities: **C**, **A**, or **P**. Apache Ignite supports ACID-compliant distributed transactions with partition tolerance and also offers high availability when the network is partitioned, so it's a **CP** and **AP**, but not **CA**, as it is scalable and supports network partitioning. But how in the world can a distributed network data store support both consistency and availability during a network outage? It must adhere to CAP and support either availability or consistency. The catch is that the Apache Ignite cache API supports two cache modes for cache operations:

- Atomic mode
- Transactional mode

In *atomic* mode, Apache Ignite supports AP, high availability, and sacrifices consistency when the network is partitioned. In *transactional* mode, Apache Ignite supports consistency (ACID-compliant cache operations) and sacrifices high availability.

The following diagram explains the Apache Ignite cache modes:

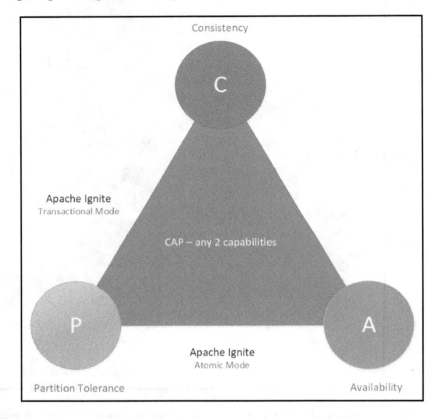

The consistency or transactional behavior is achieved through two-phase commit and locking. We will write code to verify both cache modes. Later in this chapter, we will explore optimistic and pessimistic locking, isolation levels, and two-phase commit in detail.

Next, we are going explore the cluster topology of Apache Ignite.

Clustering architecture

Apache Ignite offers an out of the box clustering mechanism and APIs to perform various caching activities. This section is going to cover the following clustering features:

- Node discovery
- Node deployment
- Cluster grouping

Node discovery

Apache Ignite is designed to scale elastically by adding more nodes to the cluster. The addition of a new node or removal of a node is transparent to the cluster. It depends on inter-node communication and doesn't rely on a master node to maintain the cluster. As of version 2.5, Apache Ignite supports two types of node discovery:

- TCP/IP discovery
- ZooKeeper discovery

We will explore both of these discovery types.

TCP/IP discovery

The default cluster discovery type is TCP/IP, and it is recommend for a 100-200-node deployment. Apache Ignite's DiscoverySpi is used to discover the nodes, as shown in the following screenshot. TcpDiscoverySpi is the default implementation:

`TcpDiscoverySpi` needs to know about IPs to discover the nodes.

The `TcpDiscoveryIpFinder` implementation is used to configure the TCP/IP finder. The following is the default implementation of `TcpDiscoveryIpFinder`:

Apart from JDBC, SharedFile, VM, and multicast IP finders, there are a couple of custom IP finders from the vendors. Some of the popular implementations are as follows:

- ZooKeeper IP finder
- Kubernetes IP finder
- Google Cloud Storage IP finder
- Amazon S3 IP finder
- Amazon ELB IP finder
- Apache jCloud IP finder

We will be interested in exploring the multicast and VM IP finders, as they cover most of the use cases. The multicast IP finder is the default IP finder; we don't need to change any configuration to discover nodes using IP multicast, but multicasting always has an overhead.

The following code snippet creates a `TcpDiscoverySpi`, which will instantiate a `TcpDiscoveryMulticastIPFinder` and sets the `multicastGroup` with a multicast IP address. You can find the multicast address by running the following command in a DOS prompt, that is, `netsh interface ip show joins`:

```
package com.packt;

import org.apache.ignite.Ignite;
import org.apache.ignite.Ignition;
import org.apache.ignite.configuration.IgniteConfiguration;
import org.apache.ignite.spi.discovery.tcp.TcpDiscoverySpi;
import
org.apache.ignite.spi.discovery.tcp.ipfinder.multicast.TcpDiscoveryMulticas
```

```
tIpFinder;

public class Multicast {
  public static void main(String[] args) throws InterruptedException {
      TcpDiscoverySpi spi = new TcpDiscoverySpi();

      TcpDiscoveryMulticastIpFinder ipFinder = new
TcpDiscoveryMulticastIpFinder();

      ipFinder.setMulticastGroup("239.255.255.250");

      spi.setIpFinder(ipFinder);

      IgniteConfiguration cfg = new IgniteConfiguration();

      // Override default discovery SPI.
      cfg.setDiscoverySpi(spi);
      cfg.setIgniteInstanceName("The Painter");
      // Start Ignite node.
      try(Ignite ignite =Ignition.start(cfg)){
          System.out.println("Node name "+ignite.name());
          Thread.sleep(9999999);
      }
    }
}
```

It will print the following log in the console:

```
 Markers    Properties   Servers   Data Source Explorer   Snippets   Console 
Multicast [Java Application] C:\Sujoy\Java\jdk1.8.0_91\bin\javaw.exe (Nov 19, 2018, 11:48:31

[23:48:59]
[23:48:59] To start Console Management & Monitoring run ignitevisor
[23:48:59]
[23:48:59] Ignite node started OK (id=6ad99d0b, instance name=The
[23:48:59] Topology snapshot [ver=1, servers=1, clients=0, CPUs=8,
[23:48:59]   ^-- Node [id=6AD99D0B-19AD-437D-8E3A-59CB9FB9ADD0, clus
[23:48:59] Data Regions Configured:
[23:48:59]   ^-- default [initSize=256.0 MiB, maxSize=6.4 GiB, persi
Node name The Painter
```

Now, run another instance of the same code but change the multicast group IP. Comment out the `setMulticastGroup` to use the default multicast IP address:

```
//ipFinder.setMulticastGroup("239.255.255.250");
```

It will create a separate cluster and not join the old cluster:

```
Multicast [Java Application] C:\Sujoy\Java\jdk1.8.0_91\bin\javaw.exe (Nov 19, 2018, 11:52:38 PM)
[23:53:02]
[23:53:02] To start Console Management & Monitoring run ignitevisorcmd.{sh|bat}
[23:53:02]
[23:53:02] Ignite node started OK (id=dd6adf7a, instance name=The Painter)
[23:53:02] Topology snapshot [ver=1, servers=1, clients=0, CPUs=8, offheap=6.4GB, heap=7.1GB]
[23:53:02]    ^-- Node [id=DD6ADF7A-7DE5-   0-B2A6-7BAE7ADEF6D1, clusterState=ACTIVE]
[23:53:02] Data Regions Configured:
[23:53:02]    ^-- default [initSize=256.0  B, maxSize=6.4 GiB, persistenceEnabled=false]
Node name The Painter
```

Now, uncomment the `setMulticastGroup` line and rerun the program. It will join the old cluster. You can find `vers=2` and `servers=2` in the console log:

```
Multicast [Java Application] C:\Sujoy\Java\jdk1.8.0_91\bin\javaw.exe (Nov 19, 2018, 11:56:34 PM)
[23:56:58] Refer to this page for more performance suggestions: https://apacheignite.readme.io/doc
[23:56:58]
[23:56:58] To start Console Management & Monitoring run ignitevisorcmd.{sh|bat}
[23:56:58]
[23:56:58] Ignite node started OK (id=e1f9ea06, instance name=The Painter)
[23:56:58] Topology snapshot [ver=2, servers=2, clients=0, CPUs=8, offheap=13.0GB, heap=14.0GB]
[23:56:58]    ^-- Node [id=E1F9EA06-995D-4  9-A6DB-34D7C3B1B227, clusterState=ACTIVE]
[23:56:58] Data Regions Configured:
[23:56:58]    ^-- default [initSize=256.0  B, maxSize=6.4 GiB, persistenceEnabled=false]
Node name The Painter
```

To work with a set of static IP addresses, you need to create a new class with the following code snippet. The `TcpDiscoveryVmIpFinder` serves the static IP discovery task. This class has a method, `setAddresses`, to pass a list of static IP addresses:

```
package com.packt;

import java.util.Arrays;
import org.apache.ignite.Ignite;
import org.apache.ignite.Ignition;
import org.apache.ignite.configuration.IgniteConfiguration;
import org.apache.ignite.spi.discovery.tcp.TcpDiscoverySpi;
import
org.apache.ignite.spi.discovery.tcp.ipfinder.vm.TcpDiscoveryVmIpFinder;
```

```java
public class StaticIp {
  public static void main(String[] args) throws InterruptedException {
      TcpDiscoverySpi spi = new TcpDiscoverySpi();

      TcpDiscoveryVmIpFinder ipFinder = new TcpDiscoveryVmIpFinder();

      // Set initial IP addresses.
      // Note that you can optionally specify a port or a port range.
      ipFinder.setAddresses(Arrays.asList( "127.0.0.1:47500..47509"));

      spi.setIpFinder(ipFinder);

      IgniteConfiguration cfg = new IgniteConfiguration();

      // Override default discovery SPI.
      cfg.setDiscoverySpi(spi);

      cfg.setIgniteInstanceName("The Painter");
      // Start Ignite node.
        try(Ignite ignite =Ignition.start(cfg)){
          System.out.println("Node name "+ignite.name());
          Thread.sleep(9999999);
        }
      }
   }
}
```

When you run this program, the console log will look as follows:

```
StaticIp [Java Application] C:\Sujoy\Java\jdk1.8.0_91\bin\javaw.exe (Nov 20, 2018, 12:02:36 AM)
[00:03:03] Refer to this page for more performance suggestions: https://apacheignite.readme.io
[00:03:03]
[00:03:03] To start Console Management & Monitoring run ignitevisorcmd.{sh|bat}
[00:03:03]
[00:03:03] Ignite node started OK (id=     ccd8, instance name=The Painter)
[00:03:03] Topology snapshot [ver=1, servers=1, clients=0, CPUs=8, offheap=6.4GB, heap=7.1GB]
[00:03:03]   ^-- Node [id=DE1DCCD8-AFBF-48BA-B580-952CC027FE9A, clusterState=ACTIVE]
[00:03:03] Data Regions Configured:
[00:03:03]   ^-- default [initSize=256.0 MiB, maxSize=6.4 GiB, persistenceEnabled=false]
Node name The Painter
```

Rerun the same program; the old program is still running as it has a `thread.sleep`. It will join the old cluster:

```
Staticlp [Java Application] C:\Sujoy\Java\jdk1.8.0_91\bin\javaw.exe (Nov 20, 2018, 12:06:52 AM)
[00:07:20]    ^-- Disable processing of calls to System.gc() (add '-XX:+DisableExplicitGC' to JVM
[00:07:20] Refer to this page for more performance suggestions: https://apacheignite.readme.io/d
[00:07:20]
[00:07:20] To start Console Management & monitoring run ignitevisorcmd.{sh|bat}
[00:07:20]
[00:07:20] Ignite node started OK (id=1d8a288c, instance name=The Painter)
[00:07:20] Topology snapshot [ver=2, servers=2, clients=0, CPUs=8, offheap=13.0GB, heap=14.0GB]
[00:07:20]    ^-- Node [id=1D8A288C-815D-4446-B35E-7CD245E9C809, clusterState=ACTIVE]
[00:07:20] Data Regions Configured:
[00:07:20]    ^-- default [initSize=256.0 MiB, maxSize=6.4 GiB, persistenceEnabled=false]
Node name The Painter
```

We looked at how static and multicast IP finders work. Next, we will look at the most efficient ZooKeeper way of clustering.

ZooKeeper discovery

ZooKeeper discovery is recommended for 1000-2000-node deployments and linear scalability. ZooKeeper discovery needs a ZooKeeper cluster. The Apache Ignite nodes connect to the ZooKeeper cluster to build a star topology where discovery events go through the ZooKeeper server cluster. It is recommended to use more than one ZooKeeper server for high availability, so if one ZooKeeper server goes down, the Apache Ignite nodes can still exchange discovery events through the other instance.

To work with the ZooKeeper topology, you need to install ZooKeeper. Download Apache ZooKeeper from the following link:
`https://www.apache.org/dyn/closer.cgi/zookeeper/`:

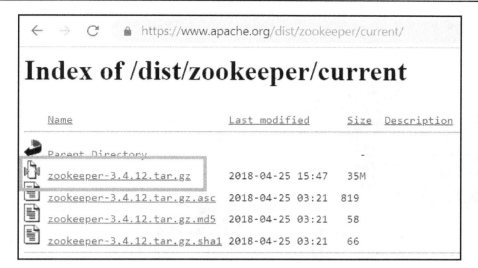

Follow these steps to configure ZooKeeper:

1. Extract the `tar` file to a directory such as `C:\apache-zookeeper-3.4.12`.
2. Go to the `bin` directory and create a file, called `zoo.cfg`.
3. Edit the file and add the following lines:

```
# The number of milliseconds of each tick
tickTime=2000

# The number of ticks that the initial
# synchronization phase can take
initLimit=10

# The number of ticks that can pass between
# sending a request and getting an acknowledgement
syncLimit=5

# the directory where the snapshot is stored.
dataDir=C:\\apache-zookeeper-3.4.12\data

# the port at which the clients will connect
clientPort=2181
```

4. Now, start `zkServer.cmd` or `zkServer.sh` based on your operating system. The console will look as follows:

```
C:\WINDOWS\system32\cmd.exe                                              —
2018-11-20 00:12:49,818 [myid:] - INFO  [main:Environment@100] - Server environment:java.compiler=<NA>
2018-11-20 00:12:49,819 [myid:] - INFO  [main:Environment@100] - Server environment:os.name=Windows 10
2018-11-20 00:12:49,820 [myid:] - INFO  [main:Environment@100] - Server environment:os.arch=amd64
2018-11-20 00:12:49,820 [myid:] - INFO  [main:Environment@100] - Server environment:os.version=10.0
2018-11-20 00:12:49,821 [myid:] - INFO  [main:Environment@100] - Server environment:user.name=
2018-11-20 00:12:49,821 [myid:] - INFO  [main:Environment@100] - Server environment:user.home=C:\Users\
2018-11-20 00:12:49,821 [myid:] - INFO  [main:Environment@100] - Server environment:user.dir=C:\apache-zookeep
bin
2018-11-20 00:12:49,835 [myid:] - INFO  [main:ZooKeeperServer@835] - tickTime set to 2000
2018-11-20 00:12:49,835 [myid:] - INFO  [main:ZooKeeperServer@844] - minSessionTimeout set to -1
2018-11-20 00:12:49,836 [myid:] - INFO  [main:ZooKeeperServer@853] - maxSessionTimeout set to -1
2018-11-20 00:12:49,893 [myid:] - INFO  [main:ServerCnxnFactory@117] - Using org.apache.zookeeper.server.NIOSe
ctory as server connection factory
2018-11-20 00:12:49,895 [myid:] - INFO  [main:NIOServerCnxnFactory@89] - binding to port 0.0.0.0/0.0.0.0:2181
```

Now, our ZooKeeper server is up and running, and waiting for connections on port `2181`.

Apache Ignite needs a client jar to connect to Apache ZooKeeper. Open the Java project that we created in Chapter 1, *Getting Familiar with Apache Ignite*. Modify the `build.gradle` file to include the `ignite-zookeeper` dependency:

```gradle
build.gradle ✕
 1 apply plugin: 'java-library'
 2
 3 repositories {
 4     jcenter()
 5 }
 6
 7 dependencies {
 8     api 'org.apache.commons:commons-math3:3.6.1'
 9
10     implementation 'com.google.guava:guava:20.0'
11     implementation 'com.h2database:h2:1.4.196'
12     compile group: 'org.apache.ignite', name: 'ignite-core', version: '2.5.0'
13     compile group: 'org.slf4j', name: 'slf4j-api', version: '1.6.0'
14     compile group: 'org.apache.ignite', name: 'ignite-spring', version: '2.5.0'
15     compile group: 'org.apache.ignite', name: 'ignite-indexing', version: '2.5.0'
16     compile group: 'log4j', name: 'log4j', version: '1.2.17'
17     compile group: 'org.apache.ignite', name: 'ignite-zookeeper', version: '2.5.0'
18
19     testImplementation 'junit:junit:4.12'
20 }
21
```

Refresh the project to update the dependency graph. It will download `zookeeper.jar` and its dependencies:

```
🔏 Markers  ⬜ Properties  🖧 Servers  🗐 Data Source Explorer  🗋 Snippets  🖵 Console ⌗  🖳 Progress  ⚡ Gradle Tasks  ⚡ Gradle Executions
[Gradle Model Retrievals]
|
CONFIGURE SUCCESSFUL in 7s
Download  https://jcenter.bintray.com/org/apache/ignite/ignite-zookeeper/2.5.0/ignite-zookeeper-2.5.0.jar
Download  https://jcenter.bintray.com/org/apache/ignite/ignite-zookeeper/2.5.0/ignite-zookeeper-2.5.0-sources.jar
Could not resolve: org.apache.ignite:ignite-log4i:*
> Task :Chapter3:session-clustering:cleanEclipseWtpComponent
```

We need to configure `ZookeeperDiscoverySpi` to connect to ZooKeeper. The `ZookeeperDiscoverySpi` needs to know two things, `zKConnectionString` and `sessionTimeout`. `zKConnectionString` is a comma-separated ZooKeeper server IP and port list, and `sessionTimeout` is required to tell the ZooKeeper cluster how soon it will close an Ignite node session if the node gets disconnected from the ZooKeeper cluster. This value should be greater than the ZooKeepr's `tickTime * syncLimit` defined in `zoo.cfg`. ZooKeeper sends a tick to its nodes every `tickTime` (here, this is 2,000 milliseconds) and waits for `syncLimit*tickTime` before declaring a node as disconnected and closing the session. In our case, the `sessionTimeout` should be greater than `2000*5 = 10,000` milliseconds.

The following code snippet will configure the `discovery spi`. Check that the session timeout is set to `30,000` and that ZooKeeper's server URL is set to `127.0.0.1:2181`. The Zookeeper's client connection port is `2181` (we configured it in the `zoo.cfg` file):

```
ZookeeperDiscoverySpi zkDiscoSpi = new ZookeeperDiscoverySpi();
zkDiscoSpi.setZkConnectionString("127.0.0.1:2181");
zkDiscoSpi.setSessionTimeout(30_000);
zkDiscoSpi.setZkRootPath("/apacheIgnite");
zkDiscoSpi.setJoinTimeout(10_000);
```

Now, create an Ignite configuration and pass `zkDiscoSpi` as `discoverySpi`:

```
IgniteConfiguration cfg = new IgniteConfiguration();
// Override default discovery SPI.
cfg.setDiscoverySpi(zkDiscoSpi);
```

Pass the config to the `start` method to start an ignite instance:

```
try (Ignite ignite = Ignition.start(cfg))
```

The following is the full code snippet:

```java
public class HelloWorld {
    public static void main(String[] args) throws InterruptedException {
        ZookeeperDiscoverySpi zkDiscoSpi = new ZookeeperDiscoverySpi();
        zkDiscoSpi.setZkConnectionString("127.0.0.1:2181");
        zkDiscoSpi.setSessionTimeout(30_000);
        zkDiscoSpi.setZkRootPath("/apacheIgnite");
        zkDiscoSpi.setJoinTimeout(10_000);

        IgniteConfiguration cfg = new IgniteConfiguration();
        // Override default discovery SPI.
        cfg.setDiscoverySpi(zkDiscoSpi);

        try (Ignite ignite = Ignition.start(cfg)) {
            IgniteCache<Integer, String> cache =
ignite.getOrCreateCache("myFirstIgniteCache");
            for (int i = 0; i < 10; i++)
                cache.put(i, Integer.toString(i));
            for (int i = 0; i < 10; i++)
                System.out.println("Fetched [key=" + i + ", val=" +
cache.get(i) + ']');
            //sleep few seconds
            Thread.sleep(999999999);
        }
    }
}
```

Now, run the program. It will connect to the ZooKeeper server:

```
HelloWorld (1) [Java Application] C:\Sujoy\Java\jdk1.8.0_91\bin\javaw.exe (Nov 20, 2018, 12:33:22 AM)
[00:33:46] To start Console Management & Monitoring run ignitevisorcmd.{sh|bat}
[00:33:46]
[00:33:46] Ignite node started OK  (id=9fb9c0b9)
[00:33:46] Topology snapshot [ver=1, servers=1, clients=0, CPUs=8, offheap=6.4GB, heap=7.1GB]
[00:33:46]    ^-- Node [id=9FB9C0B9-E89B-4    -B5A7-7ED07B3AAE5E, clusterState=ACTIVE]
[00:33:46] Data Regions Configured:
[00:33:46]    ^-- default [initSize=256.0       maxSize=6.4 GiB, persistenceEnabled=false]
Fetched [key=0, val=0]
Fetched [key=1, val=1]
Fetched [key=2, val=2]
```

Check the ZooKeeper console:

```
2018-11-20 00:12:49,836 [myid:] - INFO  [main:ZooKeeperServer@853] - maxSessionTimeout set to -1
2018-11-20 00:12:49,893 [myid:] - INFO  [main:ServerCnxnFactory@117] - Using org.apache.zookeeper.server.NIOServerCnxnFa
ctory as server connection factory
2018-11-20 00:12:49,895 [myid:] - INFO  [main:NIOServerCnxnFactory@89] - binding to port 0.0.0.0/0.0.0.0:2181
2018-11-20 00:33:45,494 [myid:] - INFO  [NIOServerCxn.Factory:0.0.0.0/0.0.0.0:2181:NIOServerCnxnFactory@215] - Accepted
socket connection from /127.0.0.1:56269
2018-11-20 00:33:45,499 [myid:] - INFO  [NIOServerCxn.Factory:0.0.0.0/0.0.0.0:2181:ZooKeeperServer@948] - Client attempt
ing to establish new session at /127.0.0.1:56269
2018-11-20 00:33:45,500 [myid:] - INFO  [SyncThread:0:FileTxnLog@213] - Creating new log file: log.1
2018-11-20 00:33:45,512 [myid:] - INFO  [SyncThread:0:ZooKeeperServer@693] - Established session 0x10002f462280000 with
negotiated timeout 30000 for client /127.0.0.1:56269
```

The program is still running as we put a `thread.sleep` at the end.

Now, launch the same program again. It will try to connect to the ZooKeeper cluster and log information to the ZooKeeper console:

```
ctory as server connection factory
2018-11-20 00:12:49,895 [myid:] - INFO  [main:NIOServerCnxnFactory@89] - binding to port 0.0.0.0/0.0.0.0:2181
2018-11-20 00:33:45,494 [myid:] - INFO  [NIOServerCxn.Factory:0.0.0.0/0.0.0.0:2181:NIOServerCnxnFactory@215] - Accepted
socket connection from /127.0.0.1:56269
2018-11-20 00:33:45,499 [myid:] - INFO  [NIOServerCxn.Factory:0.0.0.0/0.0.0.0:2181:ZooKeeperServer@948] - Client attempt
ing to establish new session at /127.0.0.1:56269
2018-11-20 00:33:45,500 [myid:] - INFO  [SyncThread:0:FileTxnLog@213] - Creating new log file: log.1
2018-11-20 00:33:45,512 [myid:] - INFO  [SyncThread:0:ZooKeeperServer@693] - Established session 0x10002f462280000 with
negotiated timeout 30000 for client /127.0.0.1:56269
2018-11-20 00:40:08,172 [myid:] - INFO  [NIOServerCxn.Factory:0.0.0.0/0.0.0.0:2181:NIOServerCnxnFactory@215] - Accepted
socket connection from /127.0.0.1:56613
2018-11-20 00:40:08,174 [myid:] - INFO  [NIOServerCxn.Factory:0.0.0.0/0.0.0.0:2181:ZooKeeperServer@948] - Client attempt
ing to establish new session at /127.0.0.1:56613
2018-11-20 00:40:08,180 [myid:] - INFO  [SyncThread:0:ZooKeeperServer@693] - Established session 0x10002f462280001 with
negotiated timeout 30000 for client /127.0.0.1:56613
```

The Program console will tell you that the new ignite node is connected to the old ZooKeeper cluster:

```
HelloWorld (1) [Java Application] C:\Sujoy\Java\jdk1.8.0_91\bin\javaw.exe (Nov 20, 2018, 12:39:46 AM)
[00:40:08]
[00:40:08] To start Console Management & Monitoring run ignitevisorcmd.{sh|bat}
[00:40:08]
[00:40:08] Ignite node started OK (id=2ef28179)
[00:40:08] Topology snapshot [ver=2, servers=2, clients=0, CPUs=8, offheap=13.0GB, heap=14.0GB]
[00:40:08]   ^-- Node [id=2EF28179-2085-4F?A-BE0A-9A4743647DC3, clusterState=ACTIVE]
[00:40:08] Data Regions Configured:
[00:40:08]   ^-- default [initSize=256.0     , maxSize=6.4 GiB, persistenceEnabled=false]
Fetched [key=0, val=0]
Fetched [key=1, val=1]
```

After the `sessionTimeout` time, in our case, set to 30,000 milliseconds, the ZooKeeper terminates the session if there is no communication between an Apache Ignite node and the ZooKeeper:

```
2018-11-20 01:05:48,645 [myid:] - INFO [NIOServerCxn.Factory:0.0.0.0/0.0.0.0:2181:NIOServerCnxn@1040] - Closed so
cket connection for client /127.0.0.1:56613 which had sessionid 0x10002f462280001
2018-11-20 01:06:11,912 [myid:] - INFO [SessionTracker:ZooKeeperServer@354] - Expiring session 0x10002f462280001,
timeout of 30000ms exceeded
2018-11-20 01:06:11,912 [myid:] - INFO [ProcessThread(sid:0 cport:2181)::PrepRequestProcessor@487] - Processed se
ssion termination for sessionid: 0x10002f462280001
```

Node deployment

Apache Ignite nodes exchange events that are used to discover each other and communicate. There is no special node to mediate discovery and cluster management. In our node discovery examples, we created Apache Ignite nodes to use TCP/IP or ZooKeeper-based discovery. These nodes are data nodes or server nodes by default. A server node is capable of storing data, caching, hosting services, participating in data streaming, and many other activities. In a sense, a server node offers all the capabilities of an in-memory Ignite grid.

There is a second type of node called a client node; it can create, modify, or delete cache entries sitting on a server node. Generally, the purpose of a client node is to retrieve cache entries from the server nodes or put entries into a server cache. It doesn't participate in computational tasks unless you are writing code to utilize the client nodes. We will write code to utilize the client nodes in the *Cluster Grouping* section.

To enable a client mode, you need to set the client mode flag either in the configuration or in *Ignition*. It is recommended to use `IgniteConfiguration`, `TcpDiscoverySpi`'s, and `setForceServerMode`.

The following code snippet uses `IgniteConfiguration` to enable the client:

```
package com.packt;

import org.apache.ignite.Ignite;
import org.apache.ignite.Ignition;
import org.apache.ignite.configuration.IgniteConfiguration;
public class ClientMode {
public static void main(String[] args) throws InterruptedException {

    IgniteConfiguration cfg = new IgniteConfiguration();
    //Set the client mode true
    cfg.setClientMode(true);
```

```
    try(Ignite ignite = Ignition.start(cfg)){
        System.out.println("Node name "+ignite.name());
    }
  }
}
```

Run the program. It will wait and retry every 2 seconds to connect to a cluster:

```
Configured failure handler: [hnd=StopNodeOrHaltFailureHandler [tryStop=false, timeout=0]]
Message queue limit is set to 0 which may lead to potential OOMEs when running cache operations in FULL_ASYNC or PRIMARY_SYNC modes due to message queues growth
Security status [authentication=off, tls/ssl=off]
REST protocols do not start on client node. To start the protocols on client node set '-DIGNITE_REST_START_ON_CLIENT=true' system property.
IP finder returned empty addresses list. Please check IP finder configuration and make sure multicast works on your network. Will retry every 2000 ms. Change
```

Now, kill the Java program and start a new instance of an Apache Ignite server from the installation directory's `bin` folder, such as `C:\Sujoy\apache-ignite-fabric-2.5.0-bin\bin`:

```
[10:43:35]
[10:43:35] Ignite node started OK (id=2175e84f)
[10:43:35] Topology snapshot [ver=1, servers=1, clients=0, CPUs=8, offheap=6.4GB, heap=1.0GB]
[10:43:35]    ^-- Node [id=2175E84F-B5A4-4CDA-9525-8729D1AED63C, clusterState=ACTIVE]
[10:43:35] Data Regions Configured:
[10:43:35]    ^-- default [initSize=256.0 MiB, maxSize=6.4 GiB, persistenceEnabled=false]
[10:43:45] New version is available at ignite.apache.org: 2.6.0
```

Look at the topology snapshot, `servers=1`, `clients=0`. Now, rerun the program and look at the program console. It will show `clients=1`:

```
[10:47:22] Refer to this page for more performance suggestions: https://apacheignite.readme.io/
[10:47:22]
[10:47:22] To start Console Management & Monitoring run ignitevisorcmd.{sh|bat}
[10:47:22]
[10:47:22] Ignite node started OK (id=bc4c3cd4)
[10:47:22] Topology snapshot [ver=2, servers=1, clients=1, CPUs=8, offheap=6.4GB, heap=8.1GB]
[10:47:22]    ^-- Node [id=BC4C3CD4-6F57-4057-8C8D-9EB4220D08BE, clusterState=ACTIVE]
Node name null
```

The Ignite console will tell you about the topology's history. Initially, `ver=1` had only one server and no clients. `ver=2` shows one server and one client, and when our client program ends, `ver=3` shows `servers=1, clients=0`:

```
C:\WINDOWS\system32\cmd.exe
[10:43:35] To start Console Management & Monitoring run ignitevisorcmd.{sh|bat}
[10:43:35]
[10:43:35] Ignite node started OK (id=2175e84f)
[10:43:35] Topology snapshot [ver=1, servers=1, clients=0, CPUs=8, offheap=6.4GB, heap=1.0GB]
[10:43:35]   ^-- Node [id=2175E84F-B5A4-4CDA-9525-8729D1AED63C, clusterState=ACTIVE]
[10:43:35] Data Regions Configured:
[10:43:35]   ^-- default [initSize=256.0 MiB, maxSize=6.4 GiB, persistenceEnabled=false]
[10:43:45] New version is available at ignite.apache.org: 2.6.0
[10:47:21] Topology snapshot [ver=2, servers=1, clients=1, CPUs=8, offheap=6.4GB, heap=8.1GB]
[10:47:21]   ^-- Node [id=2175E84F-B5A4-4CDA-9525-8729D1AED63C, clusterState=ACTIVE]
[10:47:21] Data Regions Configured:
[10:47:21]   ^-- default [initSize=256.0 MiB, maxSize=6.4 GiB, persistenceEnabled=false]
```

Broadly, there are two types of deployment topologies:

- Your program starts a client node to access the server caches
- Your program starts a server node and participates in caching and computational work

Next, we will look at how can we group Apache Ignite nodes to efficiently segregate computational tasks.

Cluster grouping

Cluster grouping is the process of building logical groups of Apache Ignite nodes to perform some computational work. For example, you may only want to access the client nodes or remote nodes or just the local node. We will look at the following grouping techniques:

- All nodes
- Remote nodes
- Cache nodes
- Attributes
- Node age

- Local nodes
- Client and server nodes
- Custom nodes

All nodes

The Apache Ignite clustering API provides a class, `ClusterGroup`, for the logical grouping of cluster nodes. Let's start with broadcasting a task to all the nodes of a cluster. Create a new class and add the following lines:

```
package com.packt;
import org.apache.ignite.Ignite;
import org.apache.ignite.IgniteCompute;
import org.apache.ignite.Ignition;
import org.apache.ignite.configuration.IgniteConfiguration;
public class BroadcastAll {
    public static void main(String[] args) {
        IgniteConfiguration cfg = new IgniteConfiguration();
        cfg.setPeerClassLoadingEnabled(true);
        try (Ignite ignite = Ignition.start(cfg)) {
            //Get a compute task
            IgniteCompute compute = ignite.compute();

            //broadcast the computation to all nodes
            compute.broadcast(() -> {
                System.out.println("Broadcasting to all nodes");
                });
        }
    }
}
```

The program starts with a configuration setting `peerClassLoadingEnabled=true`, then gets a compute object from ignite and broadcasts the computation to all the nodes of your cluster.

Open the `default-config.xml` file under the `config` directory of the Ignite installation folder. The ignite servers start up with this default configuration file. We need to enable the `peerClassLoadingEnabled` flag to send a computational task to a server node. Add the `peerClassLoadingEnabled` flag value:

```
<bean id="grid.cfg"
class="org.apache.ignite.configuration.IgniteConfiguration">
    <property name="peerClassLoadingEnabled" value="true"/>
</bean>
```

Start two Ignite server instances:

Run the program, and check the two ignite server consoles and the program console:

Remote nodes

To send tasks to all remote nodes, you need to get the remote cluster group and then create a compute object from the remote compute group. The code will look as follows, but you need a remote Apache Ignite server instance to verify the code's execution:

```java
package com.packt;
import org.apache.ignite.Ignite;
import org.apache.ignite.IgniteCluster;
import org.apache.ignite.IgniteCompute;
import org.apache.ignite.Ignition;
import org.apache.ignite.cluster.ClusterGroup;
import org.apache.ignite.configuration.IgniteConfiguration;

public class RemoteNodes {
  public static void main(String[] args) {
      IgniteConfiguration cfg = new IgniteConfiguration();
      cfg.setPeerClassLoadingEnabled(true);
```

```
try (Ignite ignite = Ignition.start(cfg)) {
    IgniteCluster cluster = ignite.cluster();

    //Get remote server group
    ClusterGroup forRemotes = cluster.forRemotes();

    //Get a compute task for remote servers
    IgniteCompute compute = ignite.compute(forRemotes);

    //broadcast the computation to remote nodes
    compute.broadcast(() -> {
        System.out.println("Only remote nodes");
    });
}
}
}
```

Cache nodes

You can logically group together nodes that are storing cache *data* or all client nodes accessing the data cache. We will look at affinity and cache grouping in Chapter 4, *Exploring the Compute Grid and Query API*.

Create a client to access cache *data* in an infinite loop:

```
package com.packt;
import org.apache.ignite.Ignite;
import org.apache.ignite.IgniteCache;
import org.apache.ignite.Ignition;
import org.apache.ignite.configuration.IgniteConfiguration;

public class ClientAccessCache {
 public static void main(String[] args) throws InterruptedException{
    IgniteConfiguration cfg = new IgniteConfiguration();
    cfg.setPeerClassLoadingEnabled(true);

    //Client mode is ON
    cfg.setClientMode(true);

    try (Ignite ignite = Ignition.start(cfg)) {
     //Access the 'data' cache
     IgniteCache<Long, String> cache = ignite.getOrCreateCache("data");

        //infinite get/put cache operation
        while(true) {
            long longValue = System.currentTimeMillis();
```

```
        cache.put(longValue, String.valueOf(longValue));

        System.out.println(cache.get(longValue));
        Thread.sleep(1000);
      }
    }
  }
}
```

Start the program; it will keep putting objects into the cache *data*:

```
[11:05:59] Ignite node started OK (id=8cc259bd)
[11:05:59] Topology snapshot [ver=5, servers=2, clients=1, CPUs=8, offheap=13.0GB, heap=9.1GB]
[11:05:59]   ^-- Node [id=8CC259BD-98E8-4922-BBB5-8510A9B6EEA5, clusterState=ACTIVE]
1542692159714
1542692160756
1542692161760
1542692162787
1542692163791
1542692164795
1542692165798
```

Write a program to send compute to the nodes where:

- The 'data' cache is deployed
- The data nodes responsible for 'data' cache
- The client nodes accessing the 'data' cache

The program will get three ClusterGroups for cache nodes, data nodes, and client nodes:

```
public class CacheGrouping {
 public static void main(String[] args) {
 IgniteConfiguration cfg = new IgniteConfiguration();
 cfg.setPeerClassLoadingEnabled(true);
 try (Ignite ignite = Ignition.start(cfg)) {
 IgniteCluster cluster = ignite.cluster();
```

The following code snippet asks the cluster to return the nodes where the 'data' cache is deployed:

```
// All nodes on which cache with name "data" is deployed,
// either in client or server mode.
ClusterGroup cacheGroup = cluster.forCacheNodes("data");
```

The following code snippet asks the cluster to return the nodes where elements of the `'data'` cache are kept:

```
// All data nodes responsible for caching data for "data".
ClusterGroup dataGroup = cluster.forDataNodes("data");
```

The following code snippet asks the cluster to return the client nodes accessing the `'data'` cache:

```
// All client nodes that access "data".
ClusterGroup clientGroup = cluster.forClientNodes("data");
```

The following code snippet gets the reference of `IgniteCompute` for the previous three `ClusterGroups`:

```
IgniteCompute cacheGroupCompute = ignite.compute(cacheGroup);
IgniteCompute dataGroupCompute = ignite.compute(dataGroup);
IgniteCompute clientGroupCompute = ignite.compute(clientGroup);
```

The following code broadcasts the computation to the cache group nodes:

```
cacheGroupCompute.broadcast(() -> {
    System.out.println("********\r\nCache Group Only\r\n**********");
});
```

The following code broadcasts the computation to the data group nodes:

```
dataGroupCompute.broadcast(() -> {
    System.out.println("*********\r\nData Group Only\r\n************");
});
```

The following code broadcasts the computation to the client group nodes:

```
    clientGroupCompute.broadcast(() -> {
      System.out.println("*********\r\n Client Group Only\r\n*******");
    });
  }
 }
}
```

Now, run the program; it will print the client group message to the client code console. The client node keeps the local cache, so it is also a Cache Group node, hence the console will print two messages:

```
<terminated> ClientAccessCache [Java Application] C:\Sujoy\Java\jdk1.8.0_91\bin\javaw.exe (Nov 20, 2018, 11:08:22 AM)
1542692318196
1542692319199
[11:08:39] New version is available at ignite.apache.org: 2.6.0
1542692320202
1542692321207
[11:08:41] Topology snapshot [ver=8, servers=3, clients=1, CPUs=8, offheap=19.0GB, heap=16.0GB]
[11:08:41]   ^-- Node [id=930B0792-1C7C-4D9C-9317-B74400E496A3, clusterState=ACTIVE]
1542692322211
********
Cache Group Only
***********
*********
 Client Group Only
*******
[11:08:42] Topology snapshot [ver=9, servers=2, clients=1, CPUs=8, offheap=13.0GB, heap=9.1GB]
[11:08:42]   ^-- Node [id=930B0792-1C7C-4D9C-9317-B74400E496A3, clusterState=ACTIVE]
```

The CacheGrouping code's console will print **Cache Group Only** and **Data Group Only**. As we started the program as a server node, it's a cache group and a data group (data is being distributed in this node):

```
<terminated> CacheGrouping [Java Application] C:\Sujoy\Java\jdk1.8.0_91\bin\javaw.exe (Nov 20, 2018, 11:08:31 AM)
[11:08:42]   ^-- Disable processing of calls to System.gc() (add '-XX:+DisableExplicitGC' to JVM
[11:08:42] Refer to this page for more performance suggestions: https://apacheignite.readme.io/d
[11:08:42]
[11:08:42] To start Console Management & Monitoring run ignitevisorcmd.{sh|bat}
[11:08:42]
[11:08:42] Ignite node started OK (id=92820694)
[11:08:42] Topology snapshot [ver=8, servers=3, clients=1, CPUs=8, offheap=19.0GB, heap=16.0GB]
[11:08:42]   ^-- Node [id=92820694-B0FD-47A5-A7A8-EBD457C952B0, clusterState=ACTIVE]
[11:08:42] Data Regions Configured:
[11:08:42]   ^-- default [initSize=256.0 MiB, maxSize=6.4 GiB, persistenceEnabled=false]
********
Cache Group Only
***********
*********
Data Group Only
************
[11:08:42] Ignite node stopped OK [uptime=00:00:00.293]
```

When you look at the Apache Ignite server's console, it will print **Cache Group** and **Data Group**:

```
[11:08:41]    ^-- default [initSize=2 [11:08:41] Data Regions Configured:
********                              [11:08:41]    ^-- default [initSize=256.0 MiB,
Cache Group Only                      ********
***********                           Cache Group Only
*********                             ***********
Data Group Only                       ********
***********                           Data Group Only
[11:08:42] Topology snapshot [ver=9,  ***********
[11:08:42]    ^-- Node [id=A78CFD6D-0 [11:08:42] Topology snapshot [ver=9, servers=2,
[11:08:42] Data Regions Configured:   [11:08:42]    ^-- Node [id=DCA59C98-D70B-4758-A5
```

Grouping by attributes

You can configure a node with specific attributes, similar to passing arguments to a JVM. The Apache Ignite clustering API provides a method to find cluster groups where a specific user-defined attribute is set. Now, launch a node with an attribute, `'FOO'`, and value, `'BAR'`, and set it in `IgniteConfiguration`:

```
public class NodeAttributeFoo {
    public static void main(String[] args) throws InterruptedException {
        IgniteConfiguration cfg = new IgniteConfiguration();
        cfg.setPeerClassLoadingEnabled(true);
        HashMap<String, Object> userAttrb = new HashMap<>();
        userAttrb.put("FOO", "BAR");
        cfg.setUserAttributes(userAttrb);
        try (Ignite ignite = Ignition.start(cfg)) {
            while(true) {
                Thread.sleep(1000);
            }
        }
    }
}
```

Create a program to send compute to the nodes where the attribute `'FOO'` and its value `'BAR'` is set:

```
public class AttributeGrouping {
 public static void main(String[] args) {
 IgniteConfiguration cfg = new IgniteConfiguration();
 cfg.setPeerClassLoadingEnabled(true);
 try (Ignite ignite = Ignition.start(cfg)) {
 IgniteCluster cluster = ignite.cluster();
```

The `cluster.forAttribute` takes the attribute name and its value to find all of the nodes in the cluster where the key-value pair matches:

```
ClusterGroup fooBarGroup = cluster.forAttribute("FOO", "BAR");
IgniteCompute fooBarGroupCompute = ignite.compute(fooBarGroup);

// broadcast the computation to fooBar nodes
fooBarGroupCompute.broadcast(() -> {
  System.out.println("********\r\nFOO BAR group\r\n**********");
});
      }
    }
  }
```

Run the program; it will only send the computation to the `NodeAttributeFoo` node:

```
NodeAttributeFoo [Java Application] C:\Sujoy\Java\jdk1.8.0_91\bin\javaw.exe (Nov 20, 2018, 11:12:02 AM)
[11:12:12]   ^-- default [initSize=256.0 MiB, maxSize=6.4 GiB, persistenceEnab:
[11:12:22] New version is available at ignite.apache.org: 2.6.0
[11:12:41] Topology snapshot [ver=12, servers=4, clients=0, CPUs=8, offheap=26
[11:12:41]   ^-- Node [id=506544A3-48CC-4283-9A37-512CFA7000BD, clusterState=A(
[11:12:41] Data Regions Configured:
[11:12:41]   ^-- default [initSize=256.0 MiB, maxSize=6.4 GiB, persistenceEnab:
********
FOO BAR group
**********
```

Grouping by node age

You can send computations to the oldest or youngest node. The following code snippet sends computations to the oldest and youngest nodes:

```
package com.packt;
import org.apache.ignite.Ignite;
import org.apache.ignite.IgniteCluster;
import org.apache.ignite.IgniteCompute;
import org.apache.ignite.Ignition;
import org.apache.ignite.cluster.ClusterGroup;
import org.apache.ignite.configuration.IgniteConfiguration;

public class OldestAndNewest {
 public static void main(String[] args) {
     IgniteConfiguration cfg = new IgniteConfiguration();
     cfg.setPeerClassLoadingEnabled(true);
```

```
        try (Ignite ignite = Ignition.start(cfg)) {
            IgniteCluster cluster = ignite.cluster();

            //Get the oldest node
            ClusterGroup forOldest = cluster.forOldest();

            //Get a compute task for the oldest servers
            IgniteCompute compute = ignite.compute(forOldest);

            //broadcast the computation to the oldest node
            compute.broadcast(() -> {
                System.out.println("**************\r\nOld is
    Gold!!!\r\n*******************");
            });


            //Get the youngest node
            ClusterGroup forYoungest = cluster.forYoungest();

            //Get a compute task for the youngest node
            compute = ignite.compute(forYoungest);

            //broadcast the computation to the youngest node
            compute.broadcast(() -> {
                System.out.println("************\r\nYoung
    blood!!!\r\n************");
            });
        }
    }
}
```

The oldest ignite instance will print the text **Old is gold**. Verify that the other server instance didn't print anything:

```
[11:14:24] Data Regions Configured:    [11:14:24] Topology snapshot [ver=15, se
[11:14:24]    ^-- default [initSize=25 [11:14:24]    ^-- Node [id=A78CFD6D-046D-
[11:14:25] Topology snapshot [ver=16, [11:14:24] Data Regions Configured:
[11:14:25]    ^-- Node [id=DCA59C98-D7[11:14:24]    ^-- default [initSize=256.0
[11:14:25] Data Regions Configured:    *******************
[11:14:25]    ^-- default [initSize=25 Old is Gold!!!
                                        ******************* *****
                                        [11:14:25] Topology snapshot [ver=16, se
                                        [11:14:25]    ^-- Node [id=A78CFD6D-046D-
```

As the program itself is the youngest server node, it will print **Young blood**:

```
<terminated> OldestAndNewest [Java Application] C:\Sujoy\Java\jdk1.8.0_91\bin\javaw.exe
[11:14:25]
[11:14:25] Ignite node started OK (id=0956e6b3)
[11:14:25] Topology snapshot [ver=15, servers=3, clients=0, CPUs=8, o
[11:14:25]   ^-- Node [id=0956E6B3-9DE0-4C59-99DE-910A5751C432, clust
[11:14:25] Data Regions Configured:
[11:14:25]   ^-- default [initSize=256.0 MiB, maxSize=6.4 GiB, persis
****************** ***
Young blood!!!
****************** ********
[11:14:25] Ignite node stopped OK [uptime=00:00:00.145]
```

Local nodes

To work with the local node, you need to get the local ClusterGroup:

```java
public class LocalNodes {
  public static void main(String[] args) {
      IgniteConfiguration cfg = new IgniteConfiguration();
      cfg.setPeerClassLoadingEnabled(true);
          try (Ignite ignite = Ignition.start(cfg)) {
              IgniteCluster cluster = ignite.cluster();

              //Get local server group
              ClusterGroup forLocal = cluster.forLocal();

              //Get a compute task for local servers
              IgniteCompute compute = ignite.compute(forLocal);

              //broadcast the computation to local nodes
              compute.broadcast(() -> {
                  System.out.println("********\r\nLocal Only\r\n*********");
              });
          }
      }
  }
```

It prints the message to the local program console only:

```
<terminated> LocalNodes [Java Application] C:\Sujoy\Java\jdk1.8.0_91\bin\javaw.exe
[11:17:15]
[11:17:15] Ignite node started OK (id=28c6aafc)
[11:17:15] Topology snapshot [ver=17, servers=3, clients=0, CPUs
[11:17:15]   ^-- Node [id=28C6AAFC-348D-419E-9C56-D26828885DF2,
[11:17:15] Data Regions Configured:
[11:17:15]   ^-- default [initSize=256.0 MiB, maxSize=6.4 GiB,
*******************
Local Only
*************************
[11:17:15] Ignite node stopped OK [uptime=00:00:00.062]
```

Client and server nodes

Client and server nodes can be accessed through the predefined forClients() and forServers() methods of IgniteCluster. First, get the IgniteCluster:

```
IgniteCluster cluster = ignite.cluster();
```

Invoke the forClients() method of the cluster to get all client nodes:

```
ClusterGroup clientGroup = cluster.forClients();
```

Invoke the forServers() method of the cluster to get all server nodes:

```
ClusterGroup serverGroup = cluster.forServers();
```

Custom nodes

You can filter cluster nodes based on the node's metric values. The `ClusterMetrics` class offers a bucket-load of methods to examine node statistics such as CPU load. Some of the metric methods are as follows:

You can filter cluster nodes based on metric values such as this:

```
ClusterGroup workerNodes = cluster.forPredicate((node) ->
node.metrics().getAverageCpuLoad() < 0.5);
```

Caching topology

The Apache Ignite caching API provides three caching modes to distribute cache elements:

- Local
- Partitioned
- Replicated

Local

The local mode is similar to JVM caching using a HashMap. Data is local to the node and not distributed to any other nodes of the cluster. The following are the benefits of the local mode:

- Fastest data access as there is no need for network operations
- Fastest data modification

The main drawback of this approach is if there is more than one JVM that needs to access the same data, then more than one local cache will be created. A local cache is useful for read-only data access where the JVM doesn't need to update any cache elements. Still, a local cache is way better than hashmap-based JVM caches as the local mode offers all the features of an Ignite cache, such as the following:

- Data expiry
- Data eviction
- ANSI SQL query
- Transaction management

Partitioned

The default cache mode is partitioned mode. This mode is designed for achieving high scalability. In partitioned mode, the cache data is divided equally into a number of partitions, defined in the configuration, and the partitions are distributed equally between participating nodes. By default, the partition count is 2: one primary and one backup. You can modify the backup copy count.

The following diagram describes the concept. We have three participating JVMs and one cache. The cache has three keys, **Key 1**, **Key 2**, and **Key 3**, and the cache configuration is set with a default `backup=1`. The distributed cache mode keeps a primary copy of **Key 1** in **JVM 1** and a backup of of **Key 1** in **JVM 2**. Similarly for **Key 2** and **Key 3**; it keeps a backup and a primary copy. If we add another key, **Key 4**, it will be distributed within the 3 JVMs. It could keep the primary copy of **Key 4** in any of the available JVMs, say in **JVM 2**, then the backup copy of **Key 4** will be kept in either **JVM 1** or **JVM 3**:

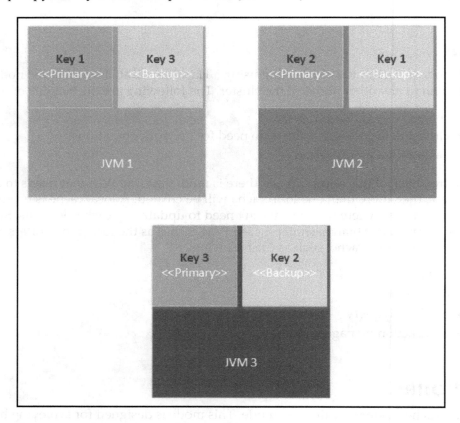

So, if we add more JVMs, then we can store more data. The distribution of data is transparent to the nodes. If a new node is added or a node goes down, the cluster redistributes the data.

The drawback of this approach is that if you connect to a node where the data (Key) is not present, then the cluster has to make two hops to fetch you the key.

Apache Ignite recommends that you use partitioned mode when you are working with a huge dataset and updating the data very frequently, so that the cluster can distribute the data and offer you high scalability. When you update a value, it doesn't have to propagate the change to all the nodes of the cluster; it just needs to update the backup copies, hence the write performance is better in this mode.

Replicated

In replicated mode, each piece of data (key) is replicated to every node of the cluster. As the key is available in all nodes, this approach offers really high availability.

The following diagram shows the data replication. Here, each JVM is holding either a primary copy or a backup copy of each key. **JVM 1** has the primary copy of **Key 1** and a backup copy of **Key 2** and **Key 3**. So, now, if we add another key (**Key 4**) to the cache, it will add the **Key 4** primary copy to any of these three JVMs and keep two backups in the other two JVMs:

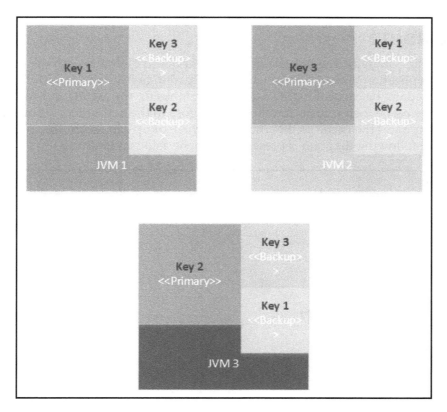

This approach offers the highest availability and read performance, but when you modify data or add a new key, it has to propagate the change to every node of the cluster. The write performance will slow down. This mode is not scalable, as adding a new node will not allow you to store more data.

Apache Ignite recommends that you use the replicated mode when the cache footprint is small and the data is updated infrequently.

Caching strategy

Apache Ignite offers three strategies to access data from a distributed cache:

- Cache aside
- Read-through and write-through
- Write behind

Cache aside

In the cache aside strategy, the Apache Ignite cluster doesn't interact with the persistence storage; the application takes the responsibility to read data from the persistence storage and update the cache. First, the application looks up the cache for data if the data is available in the cache then returns it; otherwise, it goes to the persistence storage to fetch the data and updates the cache so that the next cache lookup can return the value from the cache. The following diagram represents the cache aside architecture:

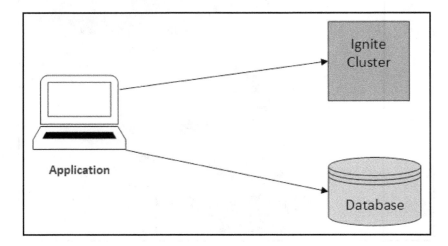

The application updates the cache when any of the following happens:

- The cache lookup is missed and the application has to query the persistence storage
- The application updates a persistence storage value
- The application inserts a value into the persistence storage

The cache aside approach is very useful for fast data access, but forces us to write boilerplate code to maintain two data sources: the database and cache.

Read-through and write-through

In the read-through and write-through strategy, the application doesn't talk to the persistence storage, it interacts with the cache. The cache is responsible for updating the persistence storage.

Read-through is when the application needs a value, it looks it up in the cache; if the value is present in the cache, then that value is returned; otherwise, the cache looks up the persistence storage, updates the cache, and returns the value.

Write-through is when the application needs to update a value, it updates the cache and the cache updates the persistence storage. The write performance is slow as the writing thread waits for the persistence storage and cache updates:

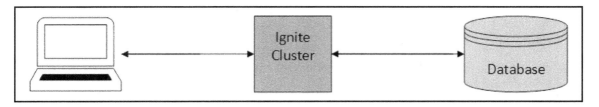

Read-through and write-through offer the flexibility to work with the cache only. The application doesn't need to worry about maintaining two data sources. The cache maintenance overhead of the cache aside strategy is no longer needed for read-through and write-through.

Write-behind

The write-behind strategy allows us to improve the write performance of the write-through approach. In write-behind, the application updates the cache and returns, while the Ignite cluster is responsible for propagating the change to the persistence store. Write-behind settings asynchronously update the persistence store with a bulk amount of data. The following diagram represents the write-behind strategy:

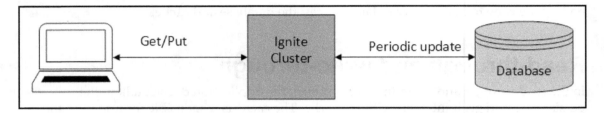

Apache Ignite supports numerous persistence stores. We will explore these persistence stores and write-behind settings in Chapter 6, *Sharpening Ignite Skills*.

Summary

In this chapter, we looked at the Apache Ignite caching architecture. We started by explaining the CAP theorem for distributed data stores and how Apache Ignite can be tuned to use AP or CP. Apache Ignite has an efficient clustering API; we looked at the various clustering configurations such as node discovery, node deployment, and node grouping.

This chapter also explored the caching modes used to distribute data. We looked at local, partitioned, and replicated cache modes and how scalability, availability, and read/write performance can be tuned using the caching modes.

This chapter concluded with the caching strategies: cache aside, read-through and write-through, and write-behind. The next chapter will explain the data grid concept and explore the web session clustering technique.

Working with Data Grids

3

So far we learned about Apache Ignite architecture, caching styles, and clustering topology. Caching can be used in the UI layer to serve static content, and a JVM-level local cache can be configured to access the frequently used objects or query results. However, a distributed cache can act as an in-memory data store and move the data closer to the application. The data grid is an abstraction of a distributed cache as a data store. In this chapter, we will explore Apache Ignite's data grid concept and build a highly available web application with Ignite Session Clustering. All user sessions will be stored in a data grid and we will use the Ignite tools to view the user sessions in the grid. The following topics will be covered:

- Exploring the Data Grid
- Configuring the Data Grid
- Web Session Clustering

Exploring the Data Grid

Apache Ignite data grids adhere to the JCache specification JSR 107. The JSR 107 specification defines five core interfaces to work with caches:

- `CachingProvider`: Defines the API to create, manage and configure `CacheManagers`
- `CacheManager`: Defines APIs to create, manage and configure *Cache*s
- `Cache`: Stores key-value pairs
- `Entry`: Single key-value pair stored in a cache
- `ExpiryPolicy`: Each cache *Entry* has a time to live. During this time, you can access, update, or remove the entry, but after that, the entry expires. The `ExpiryPolicy` defines when an Entry will expire.

The JCache API defines the following interfaces to customize cache operations: EntryProcessor, CacheEntryListener, CacheLoader, and CacheWriter.

Let's create a cache and store objects in a data grid.

Create a Java class, Key, as a key to a cache and Pojo as a value:

```
class Key implements Serializable{
 private Integer key;

 public Key(Integer key) {
   super();
   this.key = key;
 }

@Override
 public int hashCode() {
   final int prime = 31;
   int result = 1;
   result = prime * result + ((key == null) ? 0 : key.hashCode());
   return result;
 }

@Override
 public boolean equals(Object obj) {
   if (this == obj)
   return true;
   if (obj == null)
   return false;
   if (getClass() != obj.getClass())
   return false;
   Key other = (Key) obj;
   if (key == null) {
   if (other.key != null)
   return false;
   } else if (!key.equals(other.key))
   return false;
   return true;
   }
   public Integer getKey(){
     return key;
   }
 }
```

Key is serializable and overrides the equals/hashCode methods. You have to override the equals/hashCode as Key will be used to look up a Pojo. I generated the *equals* and hashCode using the Eclipse tool.

`Pojo` needs to be a `Serializable` class, as it will be transferred over the network. It just wraps a string value:

```
class Pojo implements Serializable{

 private String value;
 public Pojo(String value) {
     super();
     this.value = value;
 }
  @Override
 public String toString() {
   return "Pojo [value=" + value + "]";
 }
 public String getValue() {
   return value;
 }
}
```

Create a class to configure the `pojoCache`:

```
public class DataGridTest {

    private static final String POJO_CACHE = "pojoCache";
    public static void main(String[] args) throws InterruptedException {
        IgniteConfiguration cfg = new IgniteConfiguration();
        cfg.setPeerClassLoadingEnabled(true);
        CacheConfiguration<Key, Pojo> pojoCacheConfig = new
         CacheConfiguration<>();
         pojoCacheConfig.setName(POJO_CACHE);
         pojoCacheConfig.setCacheMode(CacheMode.REPLICATED);
         pojoCacheConfig.setAtomicityMode(CacheAtomicityMode.ATOMIC);
         pojoCacheConfig.setOnheapCacheEnabled(true);
         pojoCacheConfig.setEvictionPolicyFactory(new
         LruEvictionPolicyFactory<Key, Pojo>(8));

        cfg.setCacheConfiguration(pojoCacheConfig);
        try (Ignite ignite = Ignition.start(cfg)) {
            IgniteCache<Key, Pojo> cache =
            ignite.getOrCreateCache(POJO_CACHE);
            for (int i = 0; i < 10; i++){
                cache.put(new Key(i), new Pojo(String.format("Value
                %s", i)));
            }
            for (int i = 0; i < 10; i++) {
                System.out.println("Fetched -> key=" + i + ", value =
                " + cache.get(new Key(i)));
            }
```

```
            Thread.sleep(999999999);
        }
    }
}
```

We have configured the `pojoCache` with a name, cache mode REPLICATED (entries will be replicated in all nodes), atomicity mode ATOMIC (cache operations won't be transactional), Eviction policy set to LRU (the Least Recently Used eight objects will be stored in memory and other objects will expire). When we set the eviction policy, we need to enable onHeapCache.

The program will output the following result:

```
DataGridTest [Java Application] C:\Sujoy\Java\jdk1.8.0_91\bin\javaw.exe (Nov 20, 2018, 2:40:36 PM)
Fetched -> key=0, value = Pojo [value=Value 0]
Fetched -> key=1, value = Pojo [value=Value 1]
Fetched -> key=2, value = Pojo [value=Value 2]
Fetched -> key=3, value = Pojo [value=Value 3]
Fetched -> key=4, value = Pojo [value=Value 4]
Fetched -> key=5, value = Pojo [value=Value 5]
Fetched -> key=6, value = Pojo [value=Value 6]
Fetched -> key=7, value = Pojo [value=Value 7]
Fetched -> key=8, value = Pojo [value=Value 8]
Fetched -> key=9, value = Pojo [value=Value 9]
[14:40:55] New version is available at ignite.apache.org: 2.6.0
```

We can filter cache events and take action based on our logic. The `CacheConfiguration` API has a method to add a cache entry listener configuration. You can listen to create, update, or remove `CacheEntry` events and filter them using the `CacheEntryEventFilter` interface. We are going to change our code to filter the cache created events where the following predicate gets evaluated to true $key \% 2 == 0$.

Create a factory of `CacheEntryListener` and print the filtered events. In `CacheEntryListener` you can monitor events and filter specific entries to take special actions. For instance (if you are working in the finance sector) you can monitor cache entries and write a listener to send alerts to admins where a new cache entry is created with a value of 10,000 USD or more:

```
Factory<CacheEntryListener<Key, Pojo>> cacheEntryCreatedListenerFactory =
new Factory<CacheEntryListener<Key,Pojo>>() {
  private static final long serialVersionUID = 1L;

    @Override
    public CacheEntryListener<Key, Pojo> create() {
      CacheEntryCreatedListener<Key, Pojo> listener = new
```

```
CacheEntryCreatedListener<Key, Pojo>() {
    @Override
    public void onCreated(Iterable<CacheEntryEvent<? extends Key, ?
      extends Pojo>> events)
        throws CacheEntryListenerException {
        System.out.println("In Created Events Listener");
        events.forEach(e -> { System.out.println("Created event is
        = " +e.getValue());});
    }
};
return listener;
}
};
```

Now, create a `CacheEntryEventFilter` to filter the keys where `key.getKey() %2 ==0`. Each `CacheEntryEvent` passes through this filter; the filter has an `evaluate` method that takes a `CacheEntryEvent`. If the `evaluate` method returns `true`, the event is filtered and sent to the listener. We are going to get the *Key* from the event and return true only when the predicate `key.getKey() %2 ==0` gets evaluated to true:

```
Factory<CacheEntryEventFilter<Key, Pojo>> filterFactory = new
Factory<CacheEntryEventFilter<Key,Pojo>>() {
    private static final long serialVersionUID = 1L;
    @Override
    public CacheEntryEventFilter<Key, Pojo> create() {
        CacheEntryEventFilter<Key, Pojo> filter = new
          CacheEntryEventFilter<Key, Pojo>() {
            @Override
            public boolean evaluate(CacheEntryEvent<? extends Key, ?
              extends Pojo> event)
                throws CacheEntryListenerException {

                Key key = event.getKey();
                boolean filtertedTrue = key.getKey() %2 ==0;
                if(filtertedTrue) {
                    System.out.println("Filtered key= "+key.getKey());
                }else {
                    System.out.println("Excluding key=
                    "+key.getKey()+" from Filter");
                }
                return filtertedTrue;
            }
        };
    return filter;
    }
};
```

Configure the `pojoCacheConfig` with the filter and listener.
The `MutableCacheEntryListenerConfiguration` takes four
arguments, `CacheEntryFilterFactory`,
`CacheEntryEventFilter`, `isOldValueRequired`, and `isSynchronous`. You can filter
the events asynchronously as well by setting `isSynchronous = false`:

```
pojoCacheConfig.addCacheEntryListenerConfiguration(new
MutableCacheEntryListenerConfiguration<>(cacheEntryCreatedListenerFactory,
filterFactory, true, true));
```

Stop all Ignite instances, build the project, and put the jar in the IGNITE_HOME/lib
directory. Start a new Ignite instance and run the program. In Eclipse console, you can see
the updated values only for the following 5 filtered objects—2,4,6, 8 and 10 :

```
<terminated> DataGridTest [Java Application] C:\Sujoy\Java\jdk1.8.0_91\bin\javaw.exe
[14:42:55]   ^-- default [initSize=256.0 MiB, maxSize=6.4 GiB,
Excluding key=  1 from Filter
Filtered key=  2
In Created Events Listener
Created event is  = Pojo [value=2 updated]
Excluding key=  3 from Filter
Filtered key=  4
In Created Events Listener
Created event is  = Pojo [value=4 updated]
Excluding key=  5 from Filter
Filtered key=  6
In Created Events Listener
Created event is  = Pojo [value=6 updated]
Excluding key=  7 from Filter
Filtered key=  8
In Created Events Listener
Created event is  = Pojo [value=8 updated]
Excluding key=  9 from Filter
Filtered key=  10
In Created Events Listener
Created event is  = Pojo [value=10 updated]
```

We looked at the filters and listeners, now we'll explore the EntryProcessor. An EntryProcessor can be used to perform bulk cache operations and reduce the network calls:

```
Set<Key> keys = new HashSet<>();
for (int i = 1; i <= 10; i++) {
Key key = new Key(i);
//cache.put(key, new Pojo(String.format("Value %s", i)));
keys.add(key);
}

cache.invokeAll(keys, new CacheEntryProcessor<Key, Pojo, Object>() {
 private static final long serialVersionUID = 1L;
 @Override
 public Object process(MutableEntry<Key, Pojo> entry, Object...
 arguments)
            throws EntryProcessorException {
     Pojo value = new Pojo(entry.getKey().getKey()+" updated");
     entry.setValue(value);
     return value;
    }
});
```

The following is the program output:

```
<terminated> DataGridTest [Java Application] C:\Sujoy\Java\jdk1.8.0_91\
Created event is  = Pojo [value=10 updated]
Fetched -> key=1, value = Pojo [value=1 updated]
Fetched -> key=2, value = Pojo [value=2 updated]
Fetched -> key=3, value = Pojo [value=3 updated]
Fetched -> key=4, value = Pojo [value=4 updated]
Fetched -> key=5, value = Pojo [value=5 updated]
Fetched -> key=6, value = Pojo [value=6 updated]
Fetched -> key=7, value = Pojo [value=7 updated]
Fetched -> key=8, value = Pojo [value=8 updated]
Fetched -> key=9, value = Pojo [value=9 updated]
Fetched -> key=10, value = Pojo [value=10 updated]
[14:43:01] Ignite node stopped OK [uptime 00:00:05.087]
```

We'll explore the CacheLoader and CacheWriter in Chapter 6, *Sharpening Ignite Skills*.

Viewing cache elements

Ignite caches can be viewed using the ignitevisor command-line tool:

1. Run the `DataGridTest` program we developed earlier, and open Command Prompt.
2. Go to the `IGNITE_HOME\bin` folder and launch the `ignitevisorcmd.bat`.
3. Type `open` and hit *Enter*. It will show you a list of Ignite configurations. The default is `[0]`; hit Enter to choose the default configuration:

```
C:\Windows\System32\cmd.exe - ignitevisorcmd.bat
| 18 | examples\src\main\java\org\apache\ignite\examples\misc\springbean\spring-bean.xml    |
| 19 | platforms\cpp\examples\compute-example\config\compute-example.xml                      |
| 20 | platforms\cpp\examples\continuous-query-example\config\continuous-query-example.xml    |
| 21 | platforms\cpp\examples\odbc-example\config\example-odbc.xml                            |
| 22 | platforms\cpp\examples\put-get-example\config\example-cache.xml                        |
| 23 | platforms\cpp\examples\query-example\config\query-example.xml                          |
+--------------------------------------------------------------------------------------------+

Choose configuration file number ('c' to cancel) [0]:
```

4. It will start an Ignite node and show you the useful commands:

```
Some useful commands:
+----------------------------------------------+
| Type 'top'    | to see full topology.        |
| Type 'node'   | to see node statistics.      |
| Type 'cache'  | to see cache statistics.     |
| Type 'tasks'  | to see tasks statistics.     |
| Type 'config' | to see node configuration.   |
+----------------------------------------------+

Type 'help' to get help.

+--------------------------------------------------------+
| Status              | Connected                        |
| Ignite instance name | <default>                       |
| Config path         | C:\Sujoy\apache-ignite-fabric-2.5.0-bin |
| Uptime              | 00:00:00                         |
+--------------------------------------------------------+
visor>
```

5. Type `cache -a` and hit Enter. It will show you the statistics of all available caches:

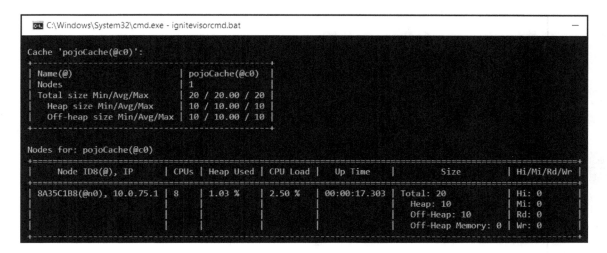

In `Chapter 4`, *Exploring the Compute Grid and Parallel Processing*, we will explore the SQL API of Apache Ignite and learn about the tools to query caches and visualize the entries.

Configuring the DataGrid

In this section, we are going to store objects in an Ignite cache and examine application performance. First, we will create a database-backed RESTful web service to store and fetch soccer players. Next, we will add a caching layer on top of the database layer to improve the query performance:

1. Install MySQL (version 8.0.11 or higher version) from the following Oracle URL: `https://dev.mysql.com/downloads/installer/`. Configure it using the the steps mentioned here: `https://youtu.be/UgHRay7gN1g`. Include MySQL workbench.

2. Launch MySQL workbench and create a new database (schema), `football`:

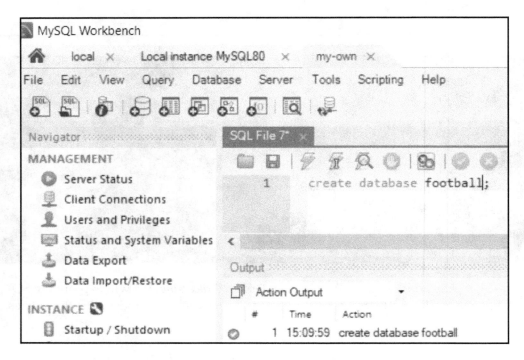

3. In query editor, execute the `use` SQL command to select our newly created database. The following is the SQL command—`use football;` (don't forget the semicolon `;`).

4. Execute the following script to create a table, `club`. `clubno` is the primary key and `cname` is the club's name:

```
create table club(
  clubno integer,
  cname varchar(200),
  constraint pk_club primary key (clubno)
);
```

5. Now, create a table, `player`. `playerno` is the primary key, `pname` represents a player's name, `wages` is a player's weekly wages ,and the `clubno` column maps a player to a club:

```
create table player(
  playerno integer,
  pname varchar(200),
```

```
wages integer,
clubno integer,
constraint pk_player primary key (playerno),
constraint fk_clubno foreign key (clubno) references club
(clubno)
);
```

6. MySQL workbench should not throw an error:

7. Insert a few rows into the `club` table:

```
insert into club values(1, 'Manchester United');
insert into club values(2, 'Real Madrid');
insert into club values(3, 'Manchester City');
insert into club values(4, 'FC Barcelona');
```

8. Launch `http://start.spring.io/` and create a Gradle project, `chapter3-datagrid`, with the following dependencies: `web`, `jpa`, `mysql`, and `devtools`:

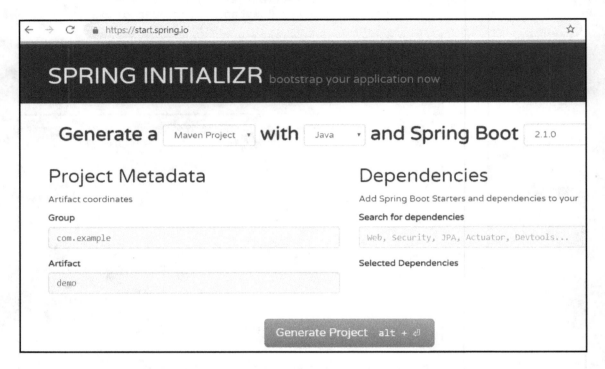

9. Unzip the downloaded zip file and import it into your IDE (`Eclipse/STS/IntelliJ`—your favorite IDE). The project structure in Eclipse will look like this:

```
v 🔧 > ignite-spring [boot] [devtools] [apache-
   v 📦 > src/main/java
      v 🗂 > com.datagrid
         > 📄 DatagridApplication.java
      > 🗂 > com.datagrid.controller
      > 🗂 > com.datagrid.entity
      > 🗂 > com.datagrid.repository
   > 📦 > src/main/resources
   > 📦 src/test/java
   > 📚 JRE System Library [JavaSE-1.8]
   > 📚 Project and External Dependencies
   > 📁 > bin
   > 📁 > gradle
   > 📁 > src
      📄 build.gradle
      📄 gradlew
      📄 gradlew.bat
      📄 settings.gradle
```

10. Now, edit the `application.properties` to enable the mySQL data source. Edit the mySQL password before saving the application.properties. The `format_sql` flag will instruct Spring Boot to generate the formatted query in the Eclipse console:

```
spring.datasource.url=jdbc:mysql://localhost:3306/football
spring.datasource.username=root
spring.datasource.password=password
spring.jpa.properties.hibernate.dialect =
org.hibernate.dialect.MySQLDialect
spring.jpa.properties.hibernate.id.new_generator_mappings = false
spring.jpa.properties.hibernate.format_sql = true
logging.level.org.hibernate.SQL=DEBUG
logging.level.org.hibernate.type.descriptor.sql.BasicBinder=TRACE
```

11. Now, create two entity classes, club and player. These classes will be annotated with a set of JPA (`javax.persistence`) annotations such as these:

- All our domain models will be annotated with the `@Entity` annotation, to mark the classes as a persistent Java class.
- *The* `@Table` annotation maps the table to this entity. You don't have to mention the table name (even the annotation) if the entity name and the table name are the same.
- *The* `@Id` annotation defines the primary key. Additionally, we can specify the ID generation type or generator, such as auto incremental ID.
- *The* `@Column` annotation defines the properties of the table column that will be mapped to the annotated field, such as `name`, `length`, `nullable`, and so on.

The following is the code snippet of the Club class:

```
package chapter3.datagrid.entity;
import javax.persistence.Column;
import javax.persistence.Entity;
import javax.persistence.Id;
import javax.persistence.Table;
@Entity
@Table(name = "club")
public class Club {
  @Id
  @Column
  int clubno;

  @Column(name = "cname")
  String name;

  //Getters/setters are omitted for brevity
}
```

The following is the code snippet of the Player class:

```
@Entity
@Table(name = "player")
public class Player {
  @Id
  @Column
  int playerno;

  @Column(name = "pname")
  String name;
```

```
@Column
int wages;

@ManyToOne(optional=false)
@JoinColumn(name="clubno",referencedColumnName="clubno")
Club club;
//Getters/setters are omitted for brevity
}
```

The @ManyToOne annotation is used to map many players to a club. The @JoinColumn is used to join two tables. The name attribute of @JoinColumn refers to the column in the source table and the referencedColumnName refers to the column referenced in the destination table. In our case, both the tables, player and club, have same column name, clubno.

Create JPA repositories for the following:

- For Player:

```
@Repository
public interface PlayerRepository extends JpaRepository<Player,
Integer>{
}
```

- For club:

```
@Repository
public interface ClubRepository extends JpaRepository<Club,
Integer>{
}
```

The beauty of Spring data is if you follow the convention, you don't have to write any code to access the database. Write a controller class to access player details.

@RestController: Represents a Spring Rest controller

@RequestMapping: Maps the path to this resource

@Get/Post/Put/DeleteMapping annotations represent the HTTP operation:

```
import org.springframework.beans.factory.annotation.Autowired;
import org.springframework.http.ResponseEntity;
import org.springframework.web.bind.annotation.*;
import chapter3.datagrid.entity.Player;
import chapter3.datagrid.repository.PlayerRepository;

@RestController
```

```
@RequestMapping("/rest")
public class PlayerController {

 @Autowired
 PlayerRepository playerRepository;

 @GetMapping("/players")
 public List<Player> getAllPlayers() {
 return playerRepository.findAll();
 }

 @PostMapping("/player")
 public Player createPlayer(@Valid @RequestBody Player Player) {
 return playerRepository.save(Player);
 }

 @GetMapping("/players/{id}")
 public Player getPlayerById(@PathVariable(value = "id") Integer id) {
 return playerRepository.findById(id).orElse(null);
 }

@PutMapping("/players/{id}")
 public Player updatePlayer(@PathVariable(value = "id") Integer playerId,
@Valid @RequestBody Player details) {
  Player player = playerRepository.findById(playerId)
 .orElseThrow(() -> new RuntimeException("Player" + playerId + " not
found"));

  player.setClub(details.getClub());
  player.setName(details.getName());
  player.setWages(details.getWages());

  Player updatedPlayer = playerRepository.save(player);
  return updatedPlayer;
 }

 @DeleteMapping("/players/{id}")
 public ResponseEntity<?> deletePlayer(@PathVariable(value = "id") Integer
id) {
 Player Player = playerRepository.findById(id)
 .orElseThrow(() -> new RuntimeException("Player:" + id + " not found"));
   playerRepository.delete(Player);

   return ResponseEntity.ok().build();
 }
}
```

Now, the project structure looks as follows:

```
v ⊞ > src/main/java
    v ⊞ > com.datagrid
        v ⊞ > controller
            > ⧉ PlayerController.java
        v ⊞ > entity
            > ⧉ Club.java
            > ⧉ Player.java
        v ⊞ > repository
            > ⧉ ClubRepository.java
            > ⧉ PlayerRepository.java
        > ⧉ DatagridApplication.java
v ⊞ > src/main/resources
    ⊞ templates
    ⊳ static
    ⧉ application.properties
> ⊞ src/test/java
```

Launch the `DatagridApplication.java` and open postman to create a player:

```
POST ∨          http://localhost:8080/rest/player


1 ▾ {
2       "playerno":3,
3       "name": "Paul Labile Pogba",
4       "wages":10000,
5       "club" :
6 ▾       { "clubno" : 1,
7             "name" : "Manchester United"
8         }
9   }
```

Now, search Paul Pogba using his `id=3`:

```
{"playerno":3,"name":"Paul Labile Pogba","wages":10000,"club":{"clubno":1,"name":"Manchester United"}}
```

The Spring Boot application will invoke a `SELECT JOIN` query to fetch the details:

```
2018-11-20 21:20:25.896 DEBUG 11288 --- [nio-8080-exec-1] org.hibernate.SQL
    select
        player0_.playerno as playerno1_1_0_,
        player0_.clubno as clubno4_1_0_,
        player0_.pname as pname2_1_0_,
        player0_.wages as wages3_1_0_,
        club1_.clubno as clubno1_0_1_,
        club1_.cname as cname2_0_1_
    from
        player player0_
    inner join
        club club1_
            on player0_.clubno=club1_.clubno
    where
        player0_.playerno=?
2018-11-20 21:20:25.907 TRACE 11288 --- [nio-8080-exec-1] o.h.type.descriptor.
```

Configuring Ignite caching

Our RESTful service makes a database call to fetch the player data. You can see the formatted SQL join logs in the Eclipse console, but we can configure a Hibernate query and L2 caching in an Apache Ignite cache. It will bypass the database and return the response from the cache.

Hibernate supports three levels of caching:

- **1st level cache**: 1st level or session caching is enabled by default. Every database request goes through the JVM level session cache; if the requested object is stored in the session cache, then that object is returned.
- **2nd level cache**: Hibernate supports additional 2nd level caching in a cache store. You need to configure Hibernate properties to enable the 2nd level cache. It stores key-value pairs in a cache store, such as in ehCache or Apache Ignite. The key is the object's id (annotated with @Id) and the value is the object itself. The L2 cache spans between sessions; when you query an object by its id, then hibernate looks up the L2 cache by the object's id and then returns the object, and queries the database if the object is not found in the cache.
- **3rd level cache**: The L2 cache can be used only for object id lookup, but it doesn't store the query results, such as when you execute a SQL query to get all the names where 'John' word is present in the record-"where name like 'John'". The 3rd level Hibernate query cache lets you store the results of the query in a cache store.

We will configure our spring boot app to store hibernate query results in the Apache Ignite cache.

Configuring L2 Caching

First, we need to modify our Spring boot project dependency to add Apache Ignite support. Edit the `build.gradle` and add the following dependencies:

```
compile group: 'org.apache.ignite', name: 'ignite-core', version: '2.5.2'
compile group: 'org.apache.ignite', name: 'ignite-spring', version:
'2.5.2'
compile group: 'org.apache.ignite', name: 'ignite-indexing', version:
'2.5.2'
compile group: 'org.apache.ignite', name: 'ignite-hibernate_5.1', version:
'2.5.2'
compile group: 'com.h2database', name: 'h2', version: '1.4.195'
```

The `ignite-hibernate_5.1` is required for L2 caching, but this jar is not available in Maven central due to a licensing issue. We need to add the gridgain Maven repo in our `build.gradle` to bring this jar. Modify the repositories section in your `build.gradle` and add the following **highlighted** lines:

```
repositories {
    maven{
       url
"http://www.gridgainsystems.com/nexus/content/repositories/external/"
    }
   mavenCentral()
}
```

The `ignite-hibernate_5.1` supports hibernate 5.1, but Spring boot brings in hibernate 5.2 jars, so we need to instruct Gradle to only consider hibernate 5.1 jars. Add the following hibernate dependencies:

```
//Ignite 2.5 supports hibernate 5.1, but spring boot brings in 5.2
dependencies
 compile group: 'org.hibernate', name: 'hibernate-core', version:
'5.1.0.Final'
 compile group: 'org.hibernate', name: 'hibernate-entitymanager', version:
'5.1.0.Final'
 compile group: 'org.hibernate', name: 'hibernate-validator', version:
'5.1.0.Final'
 compile group: 'org.hibernate.common', name: 'hibernate-commons-
annotations', version: '5.0.4.Final'
```

Hibernate properties need to be set to enable the query and L2 cache. Spring boot's way of setting properties is to define them in `application.peroperties`. Add the following properties to `application.properties` under the `resources` folder:

```
spring.jpa.properties.hibernate.cache.use_second_level_cache=true
spring.jpa.properties.hibernate.cache.use_query_cache=true
spring.jpa.properties.hibernate.cache.region.factory_class=org.apache.ignit
e.cache.hibernate.HibernateRegionFactory
```

The *second_level_cache=true* enables the 2nd level cache, the *use_query_cache=true* enables the query cache, and finally
the `region.factory_class=org.apache.ignite.cache.hibernate.HibernateRegi onFactory` sets Ignite's implementation as the hibernate region factory. You need to tell ignite about the access type and the name of the ignite instance where the hibernate objects will be stored:

```
spring.jpa.properties.org.apache.ignite.hibernate.default_access_type=READ_
ONLY
spring.jpa.properties.org.apache.ignite.hibernate.ignite_instance_name=MyGr
id121
```

Before running the application, we need to start the Ignite instance `MyGrid121`. Modify the `DatagridApplication` and add the following lines to start the ignite node and also configure the caches where the objects will be stored.

The name of each cache should be the fully qualified class name, such as `com.datagrid.entity.Club`:

```
@SpringBootApplication
public class DatagridApplication {

    public static void main(String[] args) {
        //Start the ignite node MyGrid121
        try {
            IgniteConfiguration cfg = new IgniteConfiguration();
            cfg.setIgniteInstanceName("MyGrid121");
            Ignite ignite = Ignition.start(cfg);

ignite.getOrCreateCache("org.hibernate.cache.spi.UpdateTimestampsCache");
ignite.getOrCreateCache("org.hibernate.cache.internal.StandardQueryCache");

            CacheConfiguration<Integer, Club> clubConfig = new
            CacheConfiguration<>();
            clubConfig.setAtomicityMode(CacheAtomicityMode.TRANSACTIONAL);
            clubConfig.setIndexedTypes(Integer.class, Club.class);
            clubConfig.setName("com.datagrid.entity.Club");
            ignite.getOrCreateCache(clubConfig);

            CacheConfiguration<Integer, Player> playerConfig = new
            CacheConfiguration<>();
            playerConfig.setAtomicityMode(CacheAtomicityMode.TRANSACTIONAL);
            playerConfig.setIndexedTypes(Integer.class, Player.class);
            playerConfig.setName("com.datagrid.entity.Player");
            ignite.getOrCreateCache(playerConfig);
        } catch (Exception e) {
        }
```

```
        SpringApplication.run(DatagridApplication.class, args);
    }
}
```

The `clubConfig` and `playerConfig` are the used to define the cache configuration. An Ignite cache can store a key-value pair. CacheConfiguration<Integer, Club> clubConfig defines a cache configuration for an integer key and a Club object value. Default the cache atomicity mode is atomic but to make it transactional (ACID compliant), we need to pass the atomicity mode. Index types are used to create faster object queries. Finally, the cache is created using the `getOrCreateCache` method of ignite.

We also need to annotate the entity class (both Player and Club) with two annotations:

- `@Cacheable`: Enables hibernate caching.
- `@Cache`: Defines the concurrency strategy; available options are READ, READ_WRITE, and TRANSACTIONAL. Ignite's CacheConfiguration atomicity must be transactional to set the concurrency mode—READ_WRITE, a trasaction manager needs to be defined to set the concurrency mode TRANSACTIONAL.

The Player class will be changed as follows:

```
@Entity
@Table(name = "player")
@Cacheable
@Cache(usage = CacheConcurrencyStrategy.READ_WRITE)
public class Player {
```

Now, start the spring boot application and hit the REST endpoint to fetch a player's details. It will make a database query to fetch them. Check that it took 329 milliseconds to fetch the data from the database:

The Eclipse console will show the query:

```
2018-11-20 21:23:08.961 DEBUG 3324 --- [nio-8080-exec-1] org.hibernate.SQL
    select
        player0_.playerno as playerno1_1_0_,
        player0_.clubno as clubno4_1_0_,
        player0_.pname as pname2_1_0_,
        player0_.wages as wages3_1_0_,
        club1_.clubno as clubno1_0_1_,
        club1_.cname as cname2_0_1_
    from
        player player0_
    inner join
        club club1_
            on player0_.clubno=club1_.clubno
    where
        player0_.playerno=?
2018-11-20 21:23:08.971 TRACE 3324 --- [nio-8080-exec-1] o.h.type.descriptor
```

Now, hit the same endpoint again; it will take less time: 26 ms is taken to return the object from the cache. You can compare the times: 329 ms to 26 ms. You can verify that in the Eclipse console, you wont find any SQL trace:

That's the beauty of L2 caching with Apache Ignite. You can use Apache Ignite as a hibernate L2 cache store and improve the performance of your application.

Web session clustering

Traditional web applications can scale out and handle user loads using a load balancer. A load balancer can be configured to route the user requests to the next available server. Various algorithms are there to route the user requests, such as by busyness, round robin, and so on.

The following diagram depicts the traditional web application topology with a load balancer. The user requests are intercepted by a router/load balancer, the balancer knows which web server can handle the user request, and it routes the user to that server. The user loads are evenly distributed across the cluster nodes, so if you add more servers, then the cluster can handle more user requests:

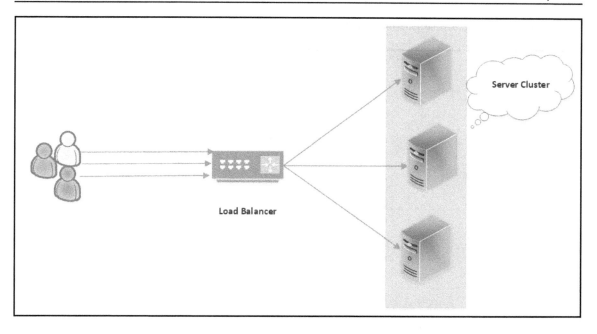

However, this introduces a new problem for stateful applications that store web sessions. The user sessions are stored in a web/app server, so the **Load Balancer** must ensure that requests from the same user are handled by the same web server instance, so that the user state is always available. This load balancing pattern is known as **sticky session**, but this is not scalable; it doesn't distribute the load evenly. Another issues is that, if a server goes down, then all user sessions of that server will be lost, as the load balancer will route all user requests of that server to a new web server, but the new server doesn't know about the user state/data.

The following diagram demonstrates the user session problem:

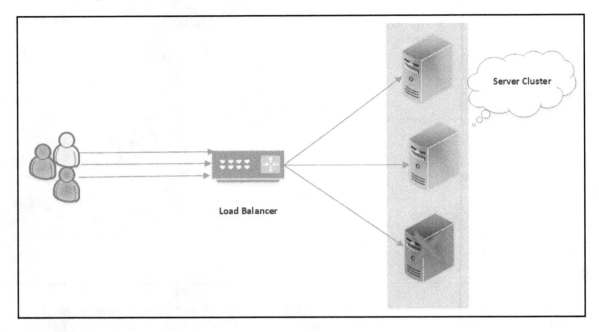

To handle this user session issue, commercial application servers provide session replication options, but session replication has its own performance and scalability problems.

Some of the known patterns to solve this problem are as follows:

- **Stateless services pattern (SSP)**: The services are stateless; user data is not stored in sessions or services. SSP is hard to implement.
- **Session datastore pattern (SDP)**: The user session is stored in a datastore. The datastore can create a single point of failure, slowness, or bottleneck for the application. Not a recommended pattern to handle user sessions.
- **Session clustering pattern (SCP)**: The user session is stored in a distributed cache cluster. This is the recommend pattern to handle user sessions.

The following diagram shows session clustering with an Ignite cluster. All user sessions are stored in a distributed Ignite cluster, and the load balancer can route user requests to any server based on the availability of the servers. This approach is highly scalable (user loads are distributed evenly) and highly available (any server can process the user requests, no session stickiness is required): .

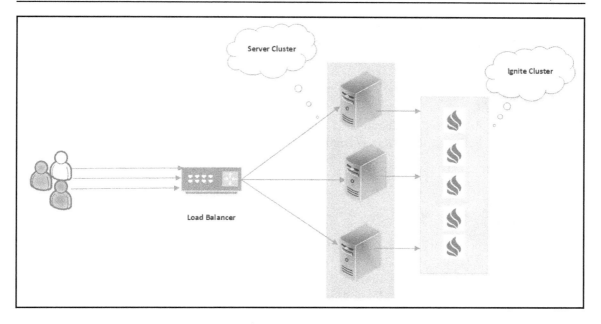

Let's create a Spring web application and store the user sessions in an Ignite cache. You don't have to write a client or call a RESTful API to store the sessions in a cache; your application only needs to add few lines of Apache Ignite configuration code in web.xml. We'll launch two Tomcat instances with our code and crash one server, but still the other server will respond to our requests. No need to set up a load balancer to route our requests; rather, we'll just change the web app URL ports to simulate the load balancing.

When you type a web URL into a browser, the following activities are performed by the server:

1. It creates a new HTTP session object.
2. It builds a http response and sets a cookie with a name = JSESSIONID and value = unique identifier of the newly created session.
3. It stores the session object in the server's RAM; the session remains active while the user is interacting with the web app, and expires after the predefined session timeout. The JSESSIONID cookie is shared among all requests in the same session.
4. After session expiration, either by timeout or log off (session.invalidate()), the web server removes the session object from its memory and any subsequent request from the same browser creates a new session.

The default value of session timeout is **30 minutes** on most containers, though you can configure it in web.xml using the following syntax:

```
<session-config>
 <session-timeout>10</session-timeout>
 </session-config>
```

First, create a web app using Gradle and edit the build.gradle. The following code snippet will tell Eclipse that this is going to be a web application:

```
apply plugin: 'java-library'
apply plugin: 'war'
apply plugin: 'eclipse'

repositories {
 jcenter()
}
war {
 baseName = 'session-clustering'
 version = '1.0.0-BUILD-SNAPSHOT'
}
```

Add spring and ignite dependencies:

```
dependencies {
 // This dependency is exported to consumers, that is to say found on their
 compile classpath.
 api 'org.apache.commons:commons-math3:3.6.1'

 // This dependency is used internally, and not exposed to consumers on
 their own compile classpath.
 implementation 'com.google.guava:guava:21.0'

 // Use JUnit test framework
 testImplementation 'junit:junit:4.12'

 compile "org.springframework:spring-webmvc:4.3.2.RELEASE"
 compile "javax.servlet:javax.servlet-api:3.1.0"
 compile "javax.servlet.jsp:javax.servlet.jsp-api:2.3.1"
 compile "javax.servlet:jstl:1.2"
 compile "org.apache.ignite:ignite-core:2.5.0"
 compile "org.apache.ignite:ignite-web:2.5.0"
 compile "org.apache.ignite:ignite-log4j:*"
 compile "org.apache.ignite:ignite-spring:2.5.0"
 compile "com.h2database:h2:1.4.196"
 }
```

Create a `Player.java` class with getters, setters, and a `toString` method. Here, we ignore the getter/setters for brevity:

```
public class Player implements Serializable{
  private static final long serialVersionUID = 1L;
  private Long id;
  private String name;
  private double wages;
  //add getters & settes here ...

  public String toString() {
      return "Player[ id="+ id+", name=" + name + ", wages=" + wages + "]";
  }
}
```

Create a spring controller with three endpoints:

```
@Controller
@RequestMapping("/")
public class PlayerController {
  AtomicLong idGenerator = new AtomicLong(100);
```

The */player* POST endpoint request mapping accepts a *player*'s details, generates a unique player identifier, and stores the *player* object in sessions with key = `playerId` and value = `player` object. The following code snippet doesn't contain any ignite framework/API code; It simply stores the `newPlayer` in session and opens the `player.jsp` page to show the newly created *player*'s id:

```
@PostMapping("/player")
public String createPlayer(HttpSession session, Model model, Player
  newPlayer) {
      Long playerId = idGenerator.incrementAndGet();
      newPlayer.setId(playerId);
      session.setAttribute(playerId.toString(), newPlayer);
      model.addAttribute("model", String.format("Player ID= %s
      added", playerId));
      return "player";
  }
```

The */player* GET request endpoint accepts a `playerId` as a request parameter, such as `/player?id=101`. If the `playerId` is found in session, the endpoint returns an HTML response with the player's details, but otherwise returns an error message explaining that the `playerId` is not found in session. Each response contains the server response time and the message:

```
@GetMapping(value = "/player")
 public String showDetails(@RequestParam("id") String playerId, Model
model,HttpSession session ) {
     Object player = session.getAttribute(playerId);
     String response = "[@%s] %s";
     if(player == null) {
         response = String.format(response, new Date(), "<font
color='red'>Player Not found</font>");
     }else {
         response = String.format(response, new Date(), player);
     }
     model.addAttribute("model", response);
     return "player";
 }
```

The initial `'/'` mapping creates a brand new session and routes users to a page (`index.jsp`) to enter player details:

```
@GetMapping(value = "/")
 public String showForm(Model model, HttpServletRequest request) {
   request.getSession(true);
   model.addAttribute("player", new Player());
   return "index";
  }
}
```

Under `src/main`, create a directory, webapp, and create a sub-directory, `WEB-INF`. Inside `WEB_INF`, create a directory, views. In the `src/main/resources` directory, create a folder, `META-INF`. The project structure will look as follows:

```
∨ 🗂 > session-clustering [apache-ignite master]
   > 📘 Deployment Descriptor: Apache Ignite We
   ∨ 🕸 Java Resources
      ∨ 🗁 src/main/java
         ∨ 🔳 com.datagrid
            ∨ 🔳 controller
               > 📄 PlayerController.java
            ∨ 🔳 dto
               > 📄 Player.java
      > 🗁 src/test/java
      ∨ 🗁 src/main/resources
         ∨ 🗁 META-INF
            📄 cache-config.xml
      > 📚 Libraries
   > 🗁 > bin
   > 🗁 gradle
   ∨ 🗁 src
      ∨ 🗁 main
         > 🗁 java
         > 🗁 resources
         ∨ 🗁 webapp
            ∨ 🗁 WEB-INF
               ∨ 🗁 views
                  📄 index.jsp
                  📄 player.jsp
               📄 spring-servlet.xml
               📄 web.xml
```

The `src/webapp/WEB-INF/views` folder contain the JSP files. The `index.jsp` shows the player entry form and maps the details to a player object. When the form is submitted, the HTTP method is POST, and the `/session-clustering/player` URL maps the request to the `createPlayer` method of the `PlayerController`:

```
<%@ taglib prefix="form" uri="http://www.springframework.org/tags/form"%>
<html>
<body>
 <h3>Welcome, Enter Player Details</h3>
     <form:form method="POST"
         action="/session-clustering/player" modelAttribute="player">
         <table>
             <tr>
```

```
                    <td><form:label path="name">Name</form:label></td>
                    <td><form:input path="name"/></td>
            </tr>
            <tr>
                    <td><form:label path="wages">Wages</form:label></td>
                    <td><form:input path="wages"/></td>
            </tr>
            <tr>
             <td><input type="submit" value="Submit"/></td>
            </tr>
        </table>
    </form:form>
</body>
</html>
```

The player.jsp just renders the model set by the PlayerController methods showDetails(...) and createPlayer(..):

```
<%@ page language="java" contentType="text/html; charset=ISO-8859-1"
 pageEncoding="ISO-8859-1"%>
<html>
<head>
<meta http-equiv="Content-Type" content="text/html; charset=UTF-8">
<title>Web session clustering</title>
</head>
<body>
 ${model}
</body>
</html>
```

The interesting part of storing sessions in Apache Ignite is the web.xml file. The web.xml file needs to be configured with Apache Ignite filters and spring. Define a spring dispatcher servlet to handle the web requests; spring configuration should be loaded from WEB-INF/spring-servlet.xml. It intercepts all web requests:

```
<servlet>
 <servlet-name>dispatcher</servlet-name>
 <servlet-class> org.springframework.web.servlet.DispatcherServlet
</servlet-class>
 <init-param>
   <param-name>contextConfigLocation</param-name>
   <param-value>/WEB-INF/spring-servlet.xml</param-value>
 </init-param>
     <load-on-startup>1</load-on-startup>
 </servlet>

<servlet-mapping>
```

```
<servlet-name>dispatcher</servlet-name>
<url-pattern>/</url-pattern>
</servlet-mapping>
```

This section boots up the Ignite session filtering. First, define a `org.apache.ignite.cache.websession.WebSessionFilter` filter and configure it to handle all requests (`url-patter = /*`). This filter performs all the magic:

```
<filter>
 <filter-name>IgniteWebSessionsFilter</filter-name>
 <filter-class>org.apache.ignite.cache.websession.WebSessionFilter</filter-
class>
 </filter>
 <filter-mapping>
 <filter-name>IgniteWebSessionsFilter</filter-name>
 <url-pattern>/*</url-pattern>
 </filter-mapping>
```

Define an Ignite servlet context listener to start a node during JVM startup and communicate with the Ignite cluster. The context parameters are used to configure Ignite. We are going to set two context parameters and a context listener:

- `IgniteConfigurationFilePath`: The spring configuration file path relative to the Ignite home or the `META-INF` folder. We created `cache-config.xml` under `META-INF`. It contains the `IgniteConfiguration` spring bean.
- `IgniteWebSessionsCacheName`: The name of the Ignite cache where the HTTP sessions will be stored. Our sessions will be stored in `web-session-cache`.
- Additionally, you can configure a parameter, `WebSessionsGridName`. This is the name of the Ignite instance where the `IgniteWebSessionsCacheName` will be stored. We don't need this for our example:

```
<listener>
<listener-
class>org.apache.ignite.startup.servlet.ServletContextListenerStartup</list
ener-class>
</listener>

<context-param>
 <param-name>IgniteConfigurationFilePath</param-name>
 <param-value>cache-config.xml</param-value>
 </context-param>

<context-param>
 <param-name>IgniteWebSessionsCacheName</param-name>
 <param-value>web-session-cache</param-value>
 </context-param>
```

Let's take a look at the spring configuration. It instructs spring to load all annotated beans from the `com.datagrid.controller` package and resolve the views from the `/WEB-INF/views` folder with a default prefix of `.jsp`. It means when a controller method returns x, then spring resolves its corresponding view as `/WEB-INF/views/x.jsp`:

```
<context:component-scan base-package="com.datagrid.controller" />
<mvc:annotation-driven />

<bean
class="org.springframework.web.servlet.view.InternalResourceViewResolver">
    <property name="prefix">
        <value>/WEB-INF/views/</value>
    </property>
    <property name="suffix">
        <value>.jsp</value>
    </property>
</bean>
```

The `META-INF/cache-config.xml` needs to enable `peerClassLoading`, start the Ignite node as a client, and configure the web session cache as the **REPLICATED** cache. Also, it defines the eviction policy as LRU with the max session objects to store as 5555. The 5555 doesn't have any significance, you can configure it based on the user load:

```
<bean id="ignite.cfg"
class="org.apache.ignite.configuration.IgniteConfiguration">
    <property name="peerClassLoadingEnabled" value="true"/>
    <property name="clientMode" value="true"/>
    <property name="cacheConfiguration">
     <list>
      <bean class="org.apache.ignite.configuration.CacheConfiguration">
          <property name="cacheMode" value="REPLICATED"/>
          <property name="onheapCacheEnabled"><value>true</value>
          </property>
          <!-- Cache name. -->
          <property name="name" value="web-session-cache"/>
          <property name="evictionPolicy">
            <bean
          class="org.apache.ignite.cache.eviction.lru.LruEvictionPolicy">
              <property name="maxSize" value="5555"/>
            </bean>
          </property>
      </bean>
     </list>
    </property>
</bean>
```

Configure two Tomcat instances to run on ports 8888 and 9999. Server 8888 should be configured as shown in the following screenshot. The start (in seconds) is set to 60000 as Ignite startup may take a while:

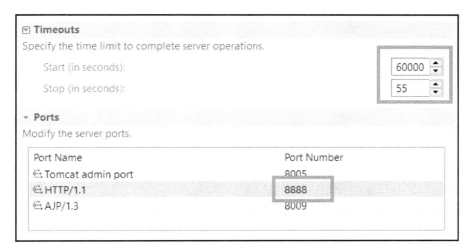

Similarly, configure server 9999. In your Eclipse editor, right-click on the project, it will open a popup menu. Click on the **Run As** sub menu and then select the "*Run On Server*" option. In **Run On Server** popup, select the server-9999. The following figure represents the **Run On Server** popup

It will start the server and start an ignite server instance from the IGNITE-HOME/bin folder. Launch Chrome, open devtools, and hit the URL at `http://localhost:9999/session-clustering/`:

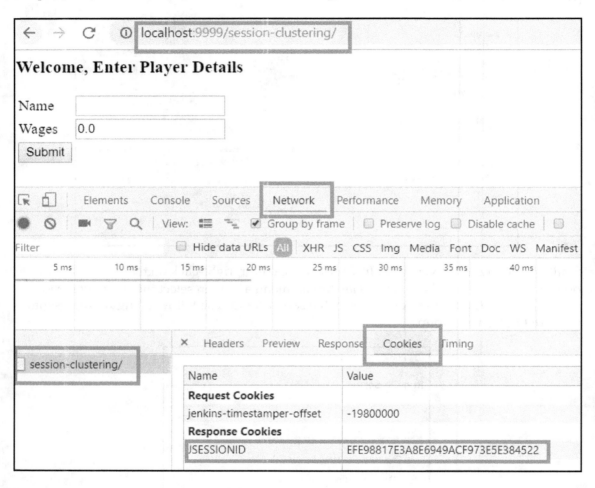

You can see a JSESSIONID cookie is sent back.

Enter player details to create a player:

It will show you player 101 added; remember the Id=101:

Try to find a player by hitting the URL
at http://localhost:9999/session-clustering/player?id=101:

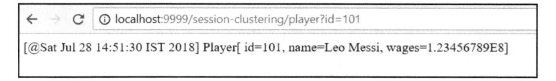

Stop server 9999. Now, if you try to access the URL
at http://localhost:9999/session-clustering/player?id=101, it will fail:

Start the 8888server. Once the 8888 server gets started, we can mock the load balancer behavior by routing our browser requests to server 8888. Had that been a normal web app, we would not have found user 101 as server 9999 is down and our session is lost. Modify the port in a web browser, and change it from 9999 to 8888:

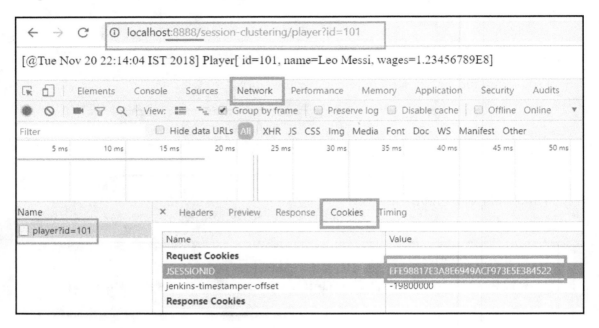

How did it work?

When we create a *player*, the controller stores the object in a session. The user sessions are stored in *web-session-cache*. You can view the web-session statistics using *ignitevisor* command line tool :

```
visor> cache -a
Time of the snapshot: 2018-11-20 22:22:08
+=================================================================================================================+
|      Name(@)      |    Mode    | Nodes | Entries (Heap / Off-heap) |   Hits   |  Misses  |   Reads  |  Writes  |
+=================================================================================================================+
| web-session-cache(@c0) | REPLICATED | 1 | min: 6 (3 / 3)           | min: 0   | min: 0   | min: 0   | min: 0   |
|                   |            |       | avg: 6.00 (3.00 / 3.00)   | avg: 0.00| avg: 0.00| avg: 0.00| avg: 0.00|
|                   |            |       | max: 6 (3 / 3)            | max: 0   | max: 0   | max: 0   | max: 0   |
+-----------------------------------------------------------------------------------------------------------------+

Cache 'web-session-cache(@c0)':
+----------------------------------------------------+
| Name(@)                | web-session-cache(@c0)    |
| Nodes                  | 1                         |
| Total size Min/Avg/Max | 6 / 6.00 / 6              |
|   Heap size Min/Avg/Max | 3 / 3.00 / 3             |
|   Off-heap size Min/Avg/Max | 3 / 3.00 / 3         |
+----------------------------------------------------+
```

After stopping server `9999`, when we tried to access port `8888`, the browser sent the JSESSIONID to the server. The server looked up the session from the Ignite cache `web-session-cache` using the session filters. In the real world, during a server failure, the load balancer will route the user requests to an available server, but still the user's sessions won't be lost. This way, your application will be more scalable and highly available.

Summary

This chapter covered Apache Ignite data grid concepts. It started with the JSR 107 specification, and covered cache configuration, cache events, listeners, and filters. We explored how the Hibernate L2 cache can be stored in Apache Ignite to improve application performance.

Web session clustering is used to store user sessions in Apache Ignite Cluster to improve system availability, scalability, and performance. This chapter explored web session clustering with Apache Ignite.

In `Chapter 4`, *Exploring the Compute Grid and Query API*, we'll learn about the Apache Ignite compute grid, parallel processing, and the Query API.

4
Exploring the Compute Grid and Query API

In Chapter 3, *Working with Data Grids*, we learned to populate and fetch Apache Ignite cache entries using the key-value pair API. This data access API is really fast, but it lacks querying capability. The next section explains the Apache Ignite Query API, used to efficiently manipulate cached entries.

This chapter covers two important components of Apache Ignite architecture: Apache Ignite Query API and distributed computing using the Apache Ignite Compute Grid. The following topics will be covered:

- Query API
- Compute grid

Query API

Apache Ignite offers an elegant query API with the following components: predicate-based ScanQuery, ANSI 99-compliant SQL query, and Lucene index-based text query. In this section, we will examine the query API.

ScanQuery

Apache Ignite's key-value pair API is used to store objects in a cache and retrieve values using keys. Apache Ignite's query API lets us query objects using expressions. The ScanQuery API allows us to execute distributed queries over cache objects. We are going to create a cache, populate it with a collection of objects, and then use ScanQuery to retrieve them. Follow these steps to try out the ScanQuery API:

1. Create a class, `Player`, with the following members:

```
public class Player implements Serializable {
private static final long serialVersionUID = 1L;
private Long id;
private String name;
private String team;
private double salary;
public Player(Long id, String name, String team, double salary) {
this.id = id;
this.name = name;
this.team = team;
this.salary = salary;
}
@Override
public String toString() {
return "Player [id=" + id + ", name=" + name + ", team=" + team +
", salary=" + salary + "]";
}
//Getters/setters here
}
```

2. Add a class, `ScanQueryTest`, create a cache with the name `Player_Scan_Cache`, and populate it with some players:

```
IgniteConfiguration cfg = new IgniteConfiguration();
 cfg.setPeerClassLoadingEnabled(true);
 try (Ignite ignite = Ignition.start(cfg)) {
    IgniteCache<Long, Player> playerCache =
 Ignition.ignite().getOrCreateCache(PLAYER_SCAN_CACHE);
    long id = 1l;
    playerCache.put(id, new Player(id++, "Leo Messi",
 "Barcelona", 996999995.00d));
    playerCache.put(id, new Player(id++, "Christiano Ronaldo",
 "Juventus", 2000000.00d));
    playerCache.put(id, new Player(id++, "Paul Pogba",
 "Manchester United", 1000000.00d));
    playerCache.put(id, new Player(id++, "Neymar", "PSG",
 99699999.00d));
```

```
playerCache.put(id, new Player(id++, "Luis Suárez",
"Barcelona", 578699.00d));
```

3. Now, query the cache using ScanQuery. `IgniteCache` has a method to pass Query and it returns `QueryCursor`. ScanQuery is an implementation of Query; it takes `IgniteBiPredicate` as an argument. `IgniteBiPredicate` takes two parameters and returns a *Boolean*. We are going to use a Java 8 lambda expression to represent `IgniteBiPredicate`. The i represents the key of the cache and p is the value or Player. Our `IgniteBiPredicate` returns `true` only if any player stored in the cache qualifies to the expression `player.getTeam()` EQ `Barcelona`. The result is returned as a `QueryCursor`; it stores all qualified entries (key-value pairs). We are going to use a Java 8 lambda to loop through the entries and print their details:

```
System.out.println("Barcelona Soccer Players");
QueryCursor<Entry<Long, Player>> barcelonaPlayersCursor =
playerCache
 .query(new ScanQuery<Long, Player>((i, p) ->
p.getTeam().equalsIgnoreCase("Barcelona")));

barcelonaPlayersCursor.forEach(e -> {
 System.out.println(e.getValue());
});
```

4. Fetch all players who earn more than 1,000,000 USD . The query could be simple `(i, p) -> p.getSalary() > 1000000`:

```
System.out.println("Rich Soccer Players");
QueryCursor<Entry<Long, Player>> richPlayers = playerCache
 .query(new ScanQuery<Long, Player>((i, p) -> p.getSalary() >
1000000));

richPlayers.forEach(e -> {
System.out.println(e.getValue());
});
```

When we run the previous program, it prints the following output:

```
Barcelona Soccer Players
Player [id=1, name=Leo Messi, team=Barcelona, salary=9.96999995E8]
Player [id=5, name=Luis Suárez, team=Barcelona, salary=578699.0]
Rich Soccer Players
Player [id=1, name=Leo Messi, team=Barcelona, salary=9.96999995E8]
Player [id=2, name=Christiano Ronaldo, team=Juventus, salary=2000000.0]
Player [id=4, name=Neymar, team=PSG, salary=9.9699999E7]
[10:09:30] Ignite node stopped OK [uptime=00:00:00.200]
```

The next section explores text-based full search.

TextQuery

The TextQuery API allows us to run full text search on stored objects. The ScanQuery goes over each cache entries and apply the predicate, which is not a very efficient way to query objects. The TextQuery works on Lucene indexes; Elasticsearch and Apache Solr use `Lucene` for indexing text. It is always advisable to use indexes for querying entries, but one drawback is an index itself takes up space and slows down the data modification (create and update) as every time you modify an entry, the index needs to be rebuilt.

You need to define the metadata to tell Apache Ignite which fields to be indexed. The `@QueryTextField` annotation enables indexing. But, your cache configuration also needs to enable indexing by setting the `setIndexedTypes`.

Let's explore the TextQuery API. These are the steps:

1. Modify the `Player` class; annotate the `name` and `team` fields with the `@QueryTextField` annotation:

    ```
    @QueryTextField()
    private String name;
    @QueryTextField
    private String team;
    ```

2. Add a class, `TextQueryTest`, and configure the cache:

    ```
    private static final String PLAYER_TEXT_CACHE =
    "Player_Text_Cache";

    public static void main(String[] args) {
    ```

```
IgniteConfiguration cfg = new IgniteConfiguration();
cfg.setPeerClassLoadingEnabled(true);
CacheConfiguration<Long, Player> playerCacheConfig = new
CacheConfiguration<>();
playerCacheConfig.setName(PLAYER_TEXT_CACHE);
playerCacheConfig.setIndexedTypes(Long.class, Player.class);
cfg.setCacheConfiguration(playerCacheConfig);
```

3. Populate the cache with a few players:

```
try (Ignite ignite = Ignition.start(cfg)) {
  IgniteCache<Long, Player> playerCache =
  Ignition.ignite().getOrCreateCache(PLAYER_TEXT_CACHE);
  long id = 11;
  playerCache.put(id, new Player(id++, "Leo Messi", "Barcelona",
    996999995.00d));
  playerCache.put(id, new Player(id++, "Christiano Ronaldo",
    "Juventus", 2000000.00d));
  playerCache.put(id, new Player(id++, "Paul Pogba", "Manchester
    United", 1000000.00d));
 playerCache.put(id, new Player(id++, "Neymar", "PSG",
    99699999.00d));
  playerCache.put(id, new Player(id++, "Luis Suárez", "Barcelona",
    578699.00d));
```

4. Search the index to find players where either name or team contains the text 'United':

```
System.out.println("United Soccer Players");
TextQuery<Long, Player> txt = new TextQuery<>(Player.class,
"United");

QueryCursor<Entry<Long, Player>> unitedPlayerCursor =
playerCache.query(txt);

unitedPlayerCursor.forEach(e -> {
System.out.println(e.getValue());
});
```

Run the program; it will print only Manchester United players:

```
[10:16:13] Data Regions Configured:
[10:16:13]   ^-- default [initSize=256.0 MiB, maxSize=6.4 GiB, persistenceEnabled=false]
United Soccer Players
Player [id=3, name=Paul Pogba, team=Manchester United, salary=1000000.0]
```

Apache Lucene can do magic, you can perform fuzzy search like Google suggestions. Fuzzy search determines whether there is any similarity between elements of the data.

If you want to fetch soccer players where the team is `'Barcelona'` or `'Barcenola'`

The step is simple

1. Add a `'~'` at the end of your search string and pass it to the `TextQuery` constructor. We are going to find the players where the text `'Barcenola'` is present, and the fuzzy search will find a match between `nola` and `lona` and return all `'Barcelona'` players:

   ```
   txt = new TextQuery<>(Player.class, "Barcenola~");

   System.out.println("Fuzzy search for 'Barcelona' as
   'Barcenola'");
   QueryCursor<Entry<Long, Player>> fuzzyCursor =
   playerCache.query(txt);

   fuzzyCursor.forEach(e -> {
   System.out.println(e.getValue());
   });
   ```

2. The output will look as follows:

   ```
   Fuzzy search for 'Barcelona' as 'Barcenola'
   Player [id=1, name=Leo Messi, team=Barcelona, salary=9.96999995E8]
   Player [id=5, name=Luis Suárez, team=Barcelona, salary=578699.0]
   ```

How about searching specific fields? The previous example looked at two indexes, name and team, to find data. We can configure our search to look at a specific index. If we are interested in `name = 'Neymar'` or `team = 'Juventus'`, it can be configured as follows:

1. You can apply Lucene search syntax in `TextQuery`. Add new code to our `TextQueryTest` class. The query would be `name:"Neymar"` OR `team="Juventus"`:

   ```
   System.out.println("multifield search for name and team");
   txt = new TextQuery<>(Player.class, "name:\"Neymar\" OR
   team:\"Juventus\"");
   QueryCursor<Entry<Long, Player>> multiField =
   playerCache.query(txt);
   ```

```
multiField.forEach(e -> {
System.out.println(e.getValue());
});
```

2. The following is the output:

```
multifield search for name and team
Player [id=2, name=Christiano Ronaldo, team=Juventus, salary=2000000.0]
Player [id=4, name=Neymar, team=PSG, salary=9.9699999E7]
[10:16:13] Ignite node stopped OK [uptime=00:00:00.346]
```

Next, we will explore the ANSI SQL query.

SqlQuery

The SQLQuery API supports ANSI-99 SQL queries against caches. This API allows SQL joins against collocated entries on the same node as well as non-collocated distributed joins. In replicated mode, SQL joins are easy to execute as all entries are replicated in all cluster nodes, but for partitioned mode, a few nodes may not contain the primary backup, hence distributed joins become complex. Apache Ignite recommends to use affinity keys to store related entries together, so a player and their club must be collocated for faster distributed query processing.

Apache Ignite's @QuerySqlField annotation makes fields accessible for SQL queries. We can even index the fields for a faster query by setting the annotation value: @QuerySqlField(index=true).

Collocated

In this section, we will use an affinity key to store the related objects together. We will create two caches: player_sql_cache & club_sql_cache, to store the soccer players and clubs respectively, then use SQL queries to fetch details. The following class represents a SoccerPlayer:

```
public class SoccerPlayer implements Serializable {
    private static final long serialVersionUID = 1L;
    @QuerySqlField(index=true)
    private Long id;
    @QuerySqlField
    private String name;
    @QuerySqlField
```

```
    private double salary;
    @QuerySqlField(index=true)
    private Long clubId;

    public SoccerPlayer(Long id, String name, double salary, Long clubId)
{
        super();
        this.id = id;
        this.name = name;
        this.salary = salary;
        this.clubId = clubId;
    }

    @Override
    public String toString() {
        return "Player [id=" + id + ", name=" + name + ", salary=" +
salary + ", clubId=" + clubId        + "]";
    }

//getters/setters
}
```

The fields annotated with the @QuerySqlField Java annotation can be queried using the Ignite SQL query and field query API.

The following class represents a soccer club:

```
public class SoccerClub implements Serializable {
 private static final long serialVersionUID = 1L;
 @QuerySqlField(index = true)
 private final Long id;
 @QuerySqlField
 private final String name;
 public SoccerClub(Long id, String name) {
     super();
     this.id = id;
     this.name = name;
 }
 @Override public String toString() {
    return "Club [id=" + id + ", name=" + name + "]";
 }

//getters/setters
}
```

We will collocate the clubs and players; we need to create a Key class to store the players. The key class will map a player and a club, and @AffinityKeyMapped will tell Ignite to collocate them. The SoccerPlayerKey will store a playerId and a clubId, and set the affinity on clubId. We need to override the equals and hashCode methods using the Eclipse/intelliJ plugin as the SoccerPlayerKey will be stored as a key:

```
public class SoccerPlayerKey implements Serializable {
    private static final long serialVersionUID = 1L;
    private final long playerId;
    @AffinityKeyMapped
    private final long clubId;
    public SoccerPlayerKey(long playerId, long clubId) {
        this.playerId = playerId;
        this.clubId = clubId;
    }
    //equals
    //hashcode
    //toString
}
```

Now, create a class to populate the cache with a collection of players:

```
public class SQLQueryCollocatedTest {
 private static final String CLUB_SQL_CACHE = "club_sql_cache";
 private static final String PLAYER_SQL_CACHE = "player_sql_cache";
 public static void main(String[] args) {
    IgniteConfiguration cfg = new IgniteConfiguration();
    cfg.setPeerClassLoadingEnabled(true);
```

Create a cache configuration for the players with key = SoccerPlayerKey, value = SoccerPlayer, and cache mode = PARTITIONED:

```
    CacheConfiguration<SoccerPlayerKey, SoccerPlayer> playerCacheConfig =
new CacheConfiguration<>();
    playerCacheConfig.setName(PLAYER_SQL_CACHE);
    playerCacheConfig.setIndexedTypes(SoccerPlayerKey.class,
SoccerPlayer.class);
    playerCacheConfig.setCacheMode(CacheMode.PARTITIONED);
```

Create a cache configuration for the clubs with the key = clubId (Long) and value= SoccerClub:

```
CacheConfiguration<Long, SoccerClub> clubCacheConfig = new
CacheConfiguration<>();
  clubCacheConfig.setName(CLUB_SQL_CACHE);
  clubCacheConfig.setIndexedTypes(Long.class, SoccerClub.class);
  clubCacheConfig.setCacheMode(CacheMode.PARTITIONED);
```

Set the cache configs to the Ignite configuration and start an Ignite instance:

```
cfg.setCacheConfiguration(playerCacheConfig, clubCacheConfig);
try (Ignite ignite = Ignition.start(cfg)) {
```

Create (or get if it already exists) the playerCache and clubCache:

```
IgniteCache<SoccerPlayerKey, SoccerPlayer> playerCache = Ignition.ignite()
.getOrCreateCache(PLAYER_SQL_CACHE);
IgniteCache<Long, SoccerClub> clubCache =
Ignition.ignite().getOrCreateCache(CLUB_SQL_CACHE);
```

Populate the clubCache with two clubs, Barcelona and Chelsea:

```
SoccerClub barcelona = new SoccerClub(11, "Barcelona");
SoccerClub chelsea = new SoccerClub(21, "Chelsea");
clubCache.put(barcelona.getId(), barcelona);
clubCache.put(chelsea.getId(), chelsea);
```

Create three soccer players, Suarez and Messi for Barcelona, and Eden Hazard for Chelsea:

```
long id = 1;
SoccerPlayer suarez = new SoccerPlayer(id++, "Luis Suárez", 578699.00d,
barcelona.getId());
SoccerPlayer messi = new SoccerPlayer(id++, "Leo Messi", 200000.00d,
barcelona.getId());
SoccerPlayer hazard = new SoccerPlayer(id++, "Eden Hazard", 178999.00d,
chelsea.getId());
```

Populate the playerCache with the players, and note that the for each player a SoccerPlayerKey is created with the player's IDand his club ID:

```
playerCache.put(new SoccerPlayerKey(suarez.getId(), suarez.getClubId()),
suarez);
playerCache.put(new SoccerPlayerKey(messi.getId(), messi.getClubId()),
messi);
playerCache.put(new SoccerPlayerKey(hazard.getId(), hazard.getClubId()),
hazard);
```

Now, we are ready to try out our first SQL query. The next section will explore the SqlQuery API.

Annotation-based query

SqlQuery takes a class and a SQL string. To fetch Eden Hazard's details, we need to construct a SqlQuery object with the following details:

```
SqlQuery<SoccerPlayerKey, SoccerPlayer> sqlQuery = new
SqlQuery<>(SoccerPlayer.class, "name = ?");
```

The query method of `IgniteCache` takes a `SqlQuery` object and returns `QueryCursor`. The `QueryCursor` contains a collection of Entry. An Entry represents a key-value pair. So, the SqlQuery can fetch you a collection of key-value pairs. The following code snippet queries the `playerCache` to return a collection of players where the `name="Eden Hazard"`. It returns a `QueryCursor` of `Entry<SoccerPlayerKey, SoccerPlayer>`:

```
QueryCursor<Entry<SoccerPlayerKey, SoccerPlayer>> resultCursor =
playerCache
 .query(sqlQuery.setArgs("Eden Hazard"));
```

We need to loop through the cursor to print the values. The following code prints the results using the Java 8 lambda function:

```
resultCursor.forEach(e -> { System.out.println(e.getValue());});
```

When we run the program, it prints Hazard's details:

```
[10:20:32]   ^-- Node [id=7BB141D0-C712-4290-A943-62D25AD0EBF5, clust
[10:20:32] Data Regions Configured:
[10:20:32]   ^-- default [initSize=256.0 MiB, maxSize=6.4 GiB, persis
Player [id=3, name=Eden Hazard, salary=178999.0, clubId=2]
```

How about joining tables? We'll join the player and club tables and fetch details. The following code snippet uses an ANSI-99 SQL join to fetch Barcelona players. When your SqlQuery fetches data from many tables, you can mention the first table directly, but the following tables need to be accessed by their cache name, such as `"cacheName".ClassName`:

```
System.out.println("Find Barcelona players");
 sqlQuery = new SqlQuery<>(SoccerPlayer.class, "from SoccerPlayer, \"" +
CLUB_SQL_CACHE +                   "\".SoccerClub "
    + "where SoccerPlayer.clubId = SoccerClub.id and SoccerClub.name =
?");
```

```
resultCursor = playerCache.query(sqlQuery.setArgs("Barcelona"));
resultCursor.forEach(e -> {
        System.out.println(e.getValue());
    });
```

The following SQL code is responsible for joining the tables, `SoccerPlayer.clubId = SoccerClub.id and SoccerClub.name = ?`. It prints the Barcelona players' details:

```
Find Barcelona players
Player [id=1, name=Luis Suárez, salary=578699.0, clubId=1]
Player [id=2, name=Leo Messi, salary=200000.0, clubId=1]
```

We fetched the player objects, but what if I'm interested in selecting a specific column, not the entire object? The SqlFieldsQuery API enables querying the fields.

Field based query

In the SqlQuery API, we cannot specify the SELECT query, but the SqlFieldsQuery allows us to write the SELECT query. The following `SqlFieldsQuery` selects the name field of `SoccerPlayer`:

```
System.out.println("Find name of each soccer player");
 SqlFieldsQuery fieldQry = new SqlFieldsQuery("select name from
SoccerPlayer");
```

When we query an `IgniteCache` with a `SqlFieldQuery`, it returns a `FieldsQueryCursor` with a list of selected rows, and each row contains the list of fields mentioned in the SELECT clause. The following code snippet fetches the names:

```
FieldsQueryCursor<List<?>> playerNamecursor = playerCache.query(fieldQry);
 playerNamecursor.forEach(name -> { System.out.println(name); });
```

Note that the `playerNamecursor` contains a list of names. The program prints the following output:

```
Find name of each soccer player
[Luis Suárez]
[Eden Hazard]
[Leo Messi]
```

We can use ANSI SQL-99 aggregate functions such as MIN, MAX, AVG, SUM, and COUNT in our field query. The following code snippet fetches the AVG, MAX, and MIN salary:

```
System.out.println("Find average, max, min salary of players");
 fieldQry = new SqlFieldsQuery("select avg(salary), max(salary),
min(salary) from SoccerPlayer");
 FieldsQueryCursor<List<?>> result = playerCache.query(fieldQry);
 result.forEach(r -> {
   System.out.println("avg=" + r.get(0) + " max=" + r.get(1) + " , min= " +
r.get(2));
 } );
```

The following is the program output:

```
Find average, max, min salary of players
avg=319232.6666666667 max=578699.0 , min= 178999.0
```

We can also use the SQL group by clause to fetch the max and min salary for each club. The following field query joins the player and club cache, groups the players by club name, and then finds the max and min salary for each group:

```
System.out.println("Find max, min salary of players group by club");
 fieldQry = new SqlFieldsQuery("select c.name , max(p.salary),
min(p.salary) from SoccerPlayer p, \"" + CLUB_SQL_CACHE + "\".SoccerClub c
where p.clubId = c.id group by c.name");

 result = playerCache.query(fieldQry);
 result.forEach(r -> {
 System.out.println("Club =" + r.get(0) + " max=" + r.get(1) + " , min= " +
r.get(2));
 });
```

To select data from multiple caches you need to refer the 2nd (and following) cache by its "cache". className such as "club_sql_cache".SoccerClub.

The following is the program output:

```
Find max, min salary of players group by club
Club =Barcelona max=578699.0 , min= 200000.0
Club =Chelsea max=178999.0 , min= 178999.0
[10:20:32] Ignite node stopped OK [uptime=00:00:00.208]
```

Non-collocated

Non-collocated SQL joins can create performance issues. We no longer need to use affinity keys to collocate the entries. In this section, we are going populate the player and club caches and use distributed SQL joins. The following are the steps:

1. Create a class, SQLQueryNonCollocatedTest:

```
public class SQLQueryNonCollocatedTest {

private static final String CLUB_SQL_CACHE = "club_sql_cache";
private static final String PLAYER_SQL_CACHE = "player_sql_cache";

public static void main(String[] args) {
IgniteConfiguration cfg = new IgniteConfiguration();
cfg.setClientMode(true);
cfg.setPeerClassLoadingEnabled(true);
```

2. Create the player config with—key = player id and value= player:

```
CacheConfiguration<Long, SoccerPlayer> playerCacheConfig = new
CacheConfiguration<>();
playerCacheConfig.setName(PLAYER_SQL_CACHE);
playerCacheConfig.setIndexedTypes(Long.class,
SoccerPlayer.class);
playerCacheConfig.setCacheMode(CacheMode.PARTITIONED);
```

3. Create the club config:

```
CacheConfiguration<Long, SoccerClub> clubCacheConfig = new
CacheConfiguration<>();
clubCacheConfig.setName(CLUB_SQL_CACHE);
clubCacheConfig.setIndexedTypes(Long.class, SoccerClub.class);
clubCacheConfig.setCacheMode(CacheMode.REPLICATED);
```

4. Set the cache configs to ignite config:

```
cfg.setCacheConfiguration(playerCacheConfig, clubCacheConfig);
```

5. Start an ignite instance, create or get the caches, and populate the player/club cache:

```
try (Ignite ignite = Ignition.start(cfg)) {

IgniteCache<Long, SoccerPlayer> playerCache =
Ignition.ignite().getOrCreateCache(PLAYER_SQL_CACHE);
IgniteCache<Long, SoccerClub> clubCache =
Ignition.ignite().getOrCreateCache(CLUB_SQL_CACHE);

SoccerClub barcelona = new SoccerClub(11, "Barcelona");
SoccerClub chelsea = new SoccerClub(21, "Chelsea");

clubCache.put(barcelona.getId(), barcelona);
clubCache.put(chelsea.getId(), chelsea);

long id = 1;
SoccerPlayer suarez = new SoccerPlayer(id++, "Luis Suárez",
578699.00d, barcelona.getId());
SoccerPlayer messi = new SoccerPlayer(id++, "Leo Messi",
200000.00d, barcelona.getId());
SoccerPlayer hazard = new SoccerPlayer(id++, "Eden Hazard",
178999.00d, chelsea.getId());

playerCache.put(suarez.getId(), suarez);
playerCache.put(messi.getId(), messi);
playerCache.put(hazard.getId(), hazard);
```

6. Now, apply a SQLquery join on the non-collocated cache to fetch the 'Barcelona' players:

```
System.out.println("Find Barcelona players");
SqlQuery<Long, SoccerPlayer> sqlQuery = new SqlQuery<>
(SoccerPlayer.class,
    "from SoccerPlayer, \"" + CLUB_SQL_CACHE + "\".SoccerClub "
      + "where SoccerPlayer.clubId = SoccerClub.id and
    SoccerClub.name = ?");

QueryCursor<Entry<Long, SoccerPlayer>> resultCursor =
playerCache.query(sqlQuery.setArgs("Barcelona"));

resultCursor.forEach(e -> {
  System.out.println(e.getValue());
});
```

7. Launch three ignite server instances and run the program; it will populate the remote nodes and generate the following output:

```
[10:30:17] Ignite node started OK (id=822c43c7)
[10:30:17] Topology snapshot [ver=2, servers=1, clients=1, CPUs=8, offheap=6.4GB, heap=8.1GB]
[10:30:17]   ^-- Node [id=822C43C7-5BC8-4A42-87E6-298DFA924C36, clusterState=ACTIVE]
Find Barcelona players
Player [id=1, name=Luis Suárez, salary=578699.0, clubId=1]
Player [id=2, name=Leo Messi, salary=200000.0, clubId=1]
[10:30:17] Ignite node stopped OK [uptime=00.00.00.210]
```

SQL functions

Apache Ignite supports custom SQL functions to perform utility tasks. The @QuerySqlFunction Java annotation makes a Java method a SQL function. You can call the function from your ANSI-99 SQL queries. In this section, we are going to write a custom SQL function to convert strings. The steps are as follows:

1. Add a Country class to store id, name, and population:

```
class Country {
 @QuerySqlField(index = true)
 private long id;
 @QuerySqlField(index = true)
 private String name;
 private long population;

public Country(long id, String name, long population) {
 super();
 this.id = id;
 this.name = name;
 this.population = population;
 }

@Override
 public String toString() {
 return "Country [id=" + id + ", name=" + name + ",
  population=" + population
 + "]";
 }
}
```

2. Add a test class to verify the SQL functions. We will create a cache, my_country, and store a collection of countries, then use a SQL function in our SqlFieldsQuery to fetch 'India'. Our custom SQL function will convert input strings to uppercase and compare them:

```java
public class SQLQueryFunctionTest {
  private static final String COUNTRY_CACHE = "my_country";
  public static void main(String[] args) {
      IgniteConfiguration cfg = new IgniteConfiguration();
      cfg.setPeerClassLoadingEnabled(true);
      CacheConfiguration<Long, Country> funcCacheConf = new
      CacheConfiguration<>();
      funcCacheConf.setName(COUNTRY_CACHE);
      funcCacheConf.setIndexedTypes(Long.class, Country.class);
      funcCacheConf.setCacheMode(CacheMode.REPLICATED);
```

3. In cache configuration, we need to specify the class where the SQL function is written:

```java
funcCacheConf.setSqlFunctionClasses(SQLQueryFunctionTest.class);
cfg.setCacheConfiguration(funcCacheConf);
```

4. Populate the cache:

```java
try (Ignite ignite = Ignition.start(cfg)) {
 IgniteCache<Long, Country> funcCache =
Ignition.ignite().getOrCreateCache(COUNTRY_CACHE);
 long id = 1;
 funcCache.put(id, new Country(id++, "USA", 123456));
 funcCache.put(id, new Country(id++, "India", 23489900));
 funcCache.put(id, new Country(id++, "France", 897633));
 funcCache.put(id, new Country(id++, "England", 666666));
```

5. Write a SQL field query to select country id and name; in the where clause, we are going to use our custom function, myUpperCase. This function needs to be defined in our class. myUpperCase converts country names to uppercase, which is very similar to the default SQL function upper:

```java
SqlFieldsQuery fieldQry = new SqlFieldsQuery(
  "select id, name from \"my_country\".Country where myUpperCase(name)
  = upper(?) ");
```

6. We are going to find `'iNdIa'` in the cache, but the Country object stores `'India'` so they will not match. Our `myUpperCase` will convert India to INDIA and upper will change the input iNdIa to INDIA:

```
System.out.println("Find 'iNdIa' - in cache the name is 'India',
so need to make it upper before  comp");
FieldsQueryCursor<List<?>> result =
funcCache.query(fieldQry.setArgs("iNdIa"));
result.forEach(r -> {
  System.out.println("id=" + r.get(0) + " country=" + r.get(1));
});
 }
}
```

7. Define our custom function. It has to be annotated with @QuerySqlFunction. It takes a string and calls Java String's toUpperCase. When the function is called, it will print the input and converted value:

```
@QuerySqlFunction
public static String myUpperCase(String name) {
String upperCase = name.toUpperCase();
System.out.println(String.format("Called the myUpperCase with %s,
returning %s",
name, upperCase));
return upperCase;
 }
}
```

8. Run the program and see the output:

```
<terminated> SQLQueryFunctionTest [Java Application] C:\Sujoy\Java\jdk1.8.0_91\bin\javaw.exe (Nov 21,

[10:36:13] Topology snapshot [ver=1, servers=1, clients=0, CPUs=8, offheap=6.
[10:36:13]    ^-- Node [id=C39C16A4-6400-4022-9606-7F11C748A442, clusterState=
[10:36:13] Data Regions Configured:
[10:36:13]    ^-- default [initSize=256.0 MiB, maxSize=6.4 GiB, persistenceEna
Find 'iNdIa' - in cache the name is 'India', so need to make it upper before
Called the myUpperCase with USA, returning USA
Called the myUpperCase with India, returning INDIA
Called the myUpperCase with France, returning FRANCE
Called the myUpperCase with England, returning ENGLAND
id=2 country=India
[10:36:13] Ignite node stopped OK [uptime=00:00:00.155]
```

The next section will cover the compute grid and distributed computation.

Compute Grid

In distributed computing, a task is split into multiple small chunks or sub-tasks; each individual task is executed in different nodes of the cluster in parallel. This pattern offers high scalability and high performance through parallel processing.

Splitter and Aggregator is a well known **enterprise integration pattern** (**EIP**) used to split a parent task into multiple child tasks, execute the child messages in parallel (possibly using message queues to distribute the sub-tasks), and then aggregate the results of each sub-task.

The Apache Ignite Compute Grid API is the gateway to distributed computing. In this section, we are going to cover the following compute grid topics:

- Distributed Closure
- Map Reduce and Fork-Join
- ExecutorService
- Job Scheduling

Distributed Closure

The `IgniteCompute` interface defines the following set of operations to execute in the cluster:

- `broadcast` and `broadcastAsync`: Broadcast given job to all nodes in the cluster group. The `broadcastAsync` returns an `IgniteFuture` and broadcasts asynchronously.
- `run` and `call`: The `run()` method executes an `IgniteRunnable` job on a node within the underlying cluster group and it doesn't return any results, but the `call()` method executes an `IgniteCallable` and returns the result of the execution.
- `apply` and `applyAsync`: Executes an `IgniteClosure` on a node within the underlying cluster group.
- `execute` and `executeAsync`: The `execute()` method executes a given job in the cluster. The async version returns a `ComputeTaskFuture` and executes the job asynchronously.
- `affinityRun` and `affinityCall`: These overloaded methods take an affinity key as argument, and execute the given job on the node where the data for provided affinity key is located.

Let's execute our first computation on an Ignite cluster.

Broadcasting asynchronously

The following are the steps to our first compute grid task:

1. Create a Gradle project called `'compute-grid'` and add the following dependencies. You have to define the `${igniteVersion}` at the top of the file under the ext section of the `buildScript` closure:

```
compile group: 'org.apache.ignite', name: 'ignite-core', version:
"${igniteVersion}"
compile group: 'org.apache.ignite', name: 'ignite-spring', version:
"${igniteVersion}"
compile group: 'org.apache.ignite', name: 'ignite-indexing',
version: "${igniteVersion}"
compile group: 'com.h2database', name: 'h2', version: '1.4.195'
```

2. We already explored message broadcasting in Chapter 2, *Understanding Topologies and Caching Strategies*. This example is going to examine the `broadcastAsync` API. We will create an `IgniteCallable` instance and broadcast it asynchronously to all nodes. The `IgniteCallable` call method returns an `IgniteFuture` object as result. Our `IgniteCallable` call will return the execution time. Add the following lines:

```
IgniteConfiguration cfg = new IgniteConfiguration();
    cfg.setPeerClassLoadingEnabled(true);
    try (Ignite ignite = Ignition.start(cfg)) {
      // Get a compute task
      IgniteCompute compute = ignite.compute();

      // broadcast the computation to all nodes
      IgniteCallable<String> callableJob = new
      IgniteCallable<String>() {
      private static final long serialVersionUID = 1L;

        @Override
        public String call() throws Exception {
          System.out.println("Executing in a cluster");
          return String.valueOf(System.currentTimeMillis());
        }
      };
      //broadcast async and get a future.
      IgniteFuture<Collection<String>> asyncFuture =
      compute.broadcastAsync(callableJob);
```

```
//Async process may take time. wait till the execution
is completed
while (!asyncFuture.isDone()) {
  System.out.println("Waiting for response");
}
//Get the response from all nodes
asyncFuture.get().forEach(result -> {
  System.out.println(result);
});
}
```

3. The future object returns a collection of strings, the individual responses from the cluster nodes. Now, launch an Ignite instance and run the program. The result will contain two responses: the remote ignite node and the program node. The following broadcast message got printed in the Eclipse console:

The remote Ignite server prints the broadcast message:

Our program waits for the async broadcast results, and finally prints the results collected from the nodes:

```
<terminated> Broadcast [Java Application] C:\Sujoy\Java\jdk1.8.0_91\bin\

Waiting for response
Waiting for response
1542777465871
1542777465891
[10:47:45] Ignite node stopped OK [uptime=00:00:00.146]
```

Exploring the run and call APIs

The compute grid's `run()` API works with `IgniteRunnable`. The `IgniteRunnable` extends Java's `Runnable` interface; the `run()` method is executed in the remote cluster. We are going to create a runnable and examine the run behavior. The following are the steps:

1. Create a class, `AdderRunnable`, to add two numbers remotely. Implement the `IgniteRunnable` interface and create a constructor to pass two integers. In the run method, add the numbers and print it in console:

```java
class AdderRunnable implements IgniteRunnable {
    private static final long serialVersionUID = 1L;
    private final int first;
    private final int second;

    public AdderRunnable(int first, int second) {
        super();
        this.first = first;
        this.second = second;
    }

    @Override
    public void run() {
        System.out.println(String.format("In
        IgniteRunnable Adder Adding %s and %s the
        result is =         %s ", first, second,
        (first + second)));
    }
}
```

2. Create a class, `IgniteRunnableAndCallable`, add the following code snippet to create an instance of `AdderRunnable`, and pass it to the run method of Ignite compute:

```
IgniteConfiguration cfg = new IgniteConfiguration();
cfg.setPeerClassLoadingEnabled(true);

try (Ignite ignite = Ignition.start(cfg)) {
    IgniteCompute compute = ignite.compute();
    compute.run(new AdderRunnable(1, 2));
}
```

3. When you execute the program, it will print the result either on your Eclipse console or on a remote server console. If you want to run it on a remote node, then get the compute instance for the remote cluster group using the following snippet: `ingnite.compute(ignite.cluster().forRemotes() );`

```
<terminated> IgniteRunnableAndCallable [Java Application] C:\Sujoy\Java\jdk1
[10:51:11]    ^-- Node [id=F9BF4509-5387-470E-9EEE-9DBD2BC6
[10:51:11] Data Regions Configured:
[10:51:11]    ^-- default [initSize=256.0 MiB, maxSize=6.4
In IgniteRunnable Adder Adding 1 and 2 the result is = 3
```

4. Now run it asynchronously, and call the `runAsync` method with an `IgniteRunnable` instance. `runAsync` returns a future to notify of job completion. The `run` method of `IgniteRunnable` is a `void`, so the `IgniteFuture` can only notify you of whether the job has been done or not, but can't return a result. Add the following snippet:

```
IgniteFuture<Void> runAsync = compute.runAsync(new
AdderRunnable(1, 2));
    while(!runAsync.isDone()) {
    System.out.println("Waiting for the job completion");
    }
    System.out.println("Job done");
```

5. Run the program again; it will wait for job completion and finally print `'Job done'`. `IgniteRunnable` is a good option for background processing such as when some calculate wages and update a cache:

```
<terminated> IgniteRunnableAndCallable [Java Application] C:\Sujoy\Java\
Waiting for the job completion
Waiting for the job completion
Waiting for the job completion
Waiting for the job completion
Waiting for the job completion
Waiting for the job completion
Waiting for the job completion
Waiting for the job completion
Job done
[10:57:19] Ignite node stopped OK [uptime=00:00:00.085]
```

The `call()` API is used when we need the result of a task execution. It takes `IgniteCallable<T>`; the `T` is a type to be returned.

1. Let's create an `AdderCallable` and examine the call behavior:

```java
class AdderCallable implements IgniteCallable<Integer> {
 private static final long serialVersionUID = 1L;
 private final int first;
 private final int second;

 public AdderCallable(int first, int second) {
  super();
  this.first = first;
  this.second = second;
  }
 @Override
 public Integer call() throws Exception {
    int result = first + second;
    System.out.println(
      String.format("In IgniteCallable Adder Adding %s and %s
      the result is =
      %s ", first, second,        result));
    return result;
  }
}
```

2. The `AdderCallable` class implements the `IgniteCallable<Integer>` interface; the call method returns the summation of two numbers passed in the constructor of `AdderCallable`. Add the following snippet to our existing code. Check that the `call` method blocks the thread and waits for the result:

```
Integer result = compute.call(new AdderCallable(1, 2));
System.out.println("Callable Job done with result "+result);
```

3. It prints the result immediately:

```
<terminated> IgniteRunnableAndCallable [Java Application] C:\Sujoy\Java\jdk1.8.0_91\bin\
In IgniteCallable Adder Adding 1 and 2 the result is = 3
Callable Job done with result 3
Waiting for the callable job completion
Waiting for the callable job completion
Waiting for the callable job completion
```

4. Blocking calls could be frustrating; you can execute a callable asynchronously. Add the following lines:

```
IgniteFuture<Integer> callAsync = compute.callAsync(new
AdderCallable(1, 2));
 while(!callAsync.isDone()) {
    System.out.println("Waiting for the callable job completion");
 }
System.out.println("Callable Job done with result "+callAsync.get());
```

5. The `callAsync` returns a future object; we can wait for the future to get done or cancelled using a while loop. The following is the console output:

```
Waiting for the callable job completion
Waiting for the callable job completion
Waiting for the callable job completion
Waiting for the callable job completion
Callable Job done with result 3
[11:10:59] Ignite node stopped OK [uptime=00:00:00.125]
```

Exploring the apply API

The compute grid's `apply` method receives a job argument and passes it to the closure at the time of execution. In the `call` or `run` methods, you can't pass any job argument. The `apply` method accepts two arguments: `IgniteClosure<R, T>` and argument`<T>`. In this section, we are going to create a closure to calculate the sum of a list of numbers. We'll pass a closure and a list of integers to the `apply` method. The following are the steps:

1. Create a new class, `IgniteApply`, and add the following lines:

```
IgniteConfiguration cfg = new IgniteConfiguration();
 cfg.setPeerClassLoadingEnabled(true);
 try (Ignite ignite = Ignition.start(cfg)) {
 IgniteCompute compute = ignite.compute();
 List<Integer> numbersToAdd = Arrays.asList(2, 3, 5, 6, 7);
    Integer result = compute.apply(new IgniteClosure<List<Integer>,
    Integer>() {
      @Override
      public Integer apply(List<Integer> numbers) {
          int sum = numbers.stream().mapToInt(i -> i.intValue()).sum();
          return sum;
      }
    }, numbersToAdd);

    System.out.println(String.format("The sum of %s is %s",
    numbersToAdd, result));
 }
```

2. We created an inline closure to loop through the list of integers and calculate the sum. The `compute.apply` method passes the `numbersToAdd` to the closure's apply method during the execution. Here is the result of the distributed processing:

```
<terminated> IgniteApply [Java Application] C:\Sujoy\Java\jdk1.8.0_91\bin\javaw.exe
[11:12:32]   ^-- Disable processing of calls to System.gc()
[11:12:32] Refer to this page for more performance suggestion
[11:12:32]
[11:12:32] To start Console Management & Monitoring run ignit
[11:12:32]
[11:12:32] Ignite node started OK (id=33d24b4a)
[11:12:32] Topology snapshot [ver=25, servers=2, clients=1, C
[11:12:32]   ^-- Node [id=33D24B4A-A22E-4971-9429-60B1D9B6277
[11:12:32] Data Regions Configured:
[11:12:32]   ^-- default [initSize=256.0 MiB, maxSize=6.4 GiB,
The sum of [2, 3, 5, 6, 7] is 23
[11:12:33] Ignite node stopped OK  uptime=00:00:00.104]
```

The difference between the apply and run/call method is in the call/run APIs, you cannot pass any job argument at execution time, but apply receives a job argument.

Next, we'll examine the `execute` and `affinity` APIs in the MapReduce/ForkJoin section.

Ignite MapReduce/ForkJoin

Apache Hadoop's MapReduce works well with offline batch jobs but was not designed to process in-memory datasets. In-memory data should be processed fast. Apache Ignite offers APIs to perform MapReduce or Java's ForkJoin on in-memory datasets. The Apache Ignite architecture offers two APIs for job distribution: distributed closure and MapReduce; however, the MapReduce API gives you more control over job to node mapping and error handling, such as you can write your own fail-over logic.

The `ComputeTask` interface is the gateway to the Ignite MapReduce framework. An Ignite MapReduce task's life cycle consists of the following phases:

- **STEP 1 (MAP)**: The initial phase is to map the jobs to the worker nodes. The `map(List<ClusterNode> subgrid, @Nullable T arg)` method of `ComputeTask` receives the collections of cluster nodes and the task argument. The `map` method needs to determine how many sub-tasks (we will use jobs or sub-tasks interchangeably) will be created and how to map the jobs to the worker nodes. It returns a `java.util.Map` with jobs as keys and mapped worker nodes as values. The MR framework then sends the jobs to the associated worker nodes, so the worker nodes can start processing the job

 By default, jobs are submitted to a thread pool and are executed in random order, but we can configure job ordering using the `CollisionSpi`.

- **STEP 2 (RESULT)**: This is an intermediate step, and gets invoked asynchronously when a job completes execution on a worker node or throws an exception. The `result(ComputeJobResult res, List<ComputeJobResult> rcvd)` method receives the result returned by the job and the list of all the job results received. This method returns a policy and determines the next course of action, in which the system will either wait for more results, reduce the results received so far, or failover this job to another node. We need to write our custom logic to determine the result policy. The available options are as follows:
    - **WAIT**: Wait for results if any are still expected

- **REDUCE**: Ignore all not yet received results and start reducing results
- **FAILOVER**: Fail-over job to execute on another node

- **STEP 3 (REDUCE)**: The final phase reduces (or aggregates) the results received so far into one compound result to be returned to the caller. The `reduce(List<ComputeJobResult> results)` method handles the result aggregation. If some jobs fails and could not be failed over, then the list of results will include the failed results. Otherwise, intermediate failed results (succeeded after fail-over) will not be in the list. The `getException()` method of `ComputeJobResult` returns the reason for failure.

Let's implement our first MapReduce job and calculate the total amount paid by the soccer clubs. We'll create eight soccer clubs, spawn jobs to calculate monthly expense for each club, map the jobs to the worker nodes, and finally reduce the results to calculate the final expense. The steps are as follows:

1. Create a class, `IgniteMapReduceTest`, and add the following lines to configure two caches, `club_job_sql_cache` and `player_job_sql_cache`. We'll reuse the `SoccerPlayer` and `SoccerClub` classes:

```
public class IgniteMapReduceTest {
  public static final String CLUB_JOB_CACHE = "club_job_sql_cache";
  public static final String PLAYER_JOB_CACHE =
  "player_job_sql_cache";
```

2. These are our soccer clubs:

```
public static String[] clubNames = new String[] { "FC Barcelona",
"Real Madrid", "Manchester United", "Manchester City",
"Chelsea", "Juventus", "PSG", "FC Bayern Munich" };

public static void main(String[] args) {
    IgniteConfiguration cfg = new IgniteConfiguration();
    cfg.setPeerClassLoadingEnabled(true);
```

3. Create a cache configuration for the players with the `key = SoccerPlayerKey`, `value=SoccerPlayer`, and cache `mode= PARTITIONED`:

```
CacheConfiguration<SoccerPlayerKey, SoccerPlayer>
playerCacheConfig = new          CacheConfiguration<>();
playerCacheConfig.setName(PLAYER_JOB_CACHE);
playerCacheConfig.setIndexedTypes(SoccerPlayerKey.class,
SoccerPlayer.class);
playerCacheConfig.setCacheMode(CacheMode.PARTITIONED);
```

4. Create cache configuration for the clubs with the `key` = `clubId` (`Long`) and `value= SoccerClub`:

```
CacheConfiguration<Long, SoccerClub> clubCacheConfig = new
CacheConfiguration<>();
 clubCacheConfig.setName(CLUB_JOB_CACHE);
 clubCacheConfig.setIndexedTypes(Long.class, SoccerClub.class);
 clubCacheConfig.setCacheMode(CacheMode.REPLICATED);
```

5. Set the cache configs to the Ignite configuration and start an ignite instance:

```
cfg.setCacheConfiguration(playerCacheConfig, clubCacheConfig);
try (Ignite ignite = Ignition.start(cfg)) {
```

6. Create (or get if they already exist) the `playerCache` and `clubCache`:

```
IgniteCache<SoccerPlayerKey, SoccerPlayer> playerCache = ignite
.getOrCreateCache(PLAYER_JOB_CACHE);
IgniteCache<Long, SoccerClub> clubCache =
ignite.getOrCreateCache(CLUB_JOB_CACHE);
```

7. Create a method to populate the players and clubs. It uses random numbers to determine the number of players to create for each club and their salaries. This method sums up the salaries and returns them to the caller:

```
public static double populatePlayersAndClubs(String[] clubNames,
  IgniteCache<SoccerPlayerKey, SoccerPlayer> playerCache,
  IgniteCache<Long, SoccerClub> clubCache) {
    Long clubId = 1l;
    long playerId = 1;
    double sum =0.0d;
    Random random = new Random();
    for (String clubName : clubNames) {
        SoccerClub club = new SoccerClub(clubId++, clubName);
        clubCache.put(club.getId(), club);
        int numberOfPlayersToCreate = random.nextInt(20);

        for (int i = 0; i <= numberOfPlayersToCreate+1; i++) {
            double salary = random.nextDouble() * 100000.00;
            SoccerPlayer player = new SoccerPlayer(playerId++,
                String.format("%s-player%s", clubName, i), salary,
                    club.getId());
            playerCache.put(new SoccerPlayerKey(player.getId(),
            club.getId()), player);
            sum+=salary;
        }
    }
```

```
        return sum;
    }
```

8. Call the `populatePlayersAndClubs` to populate the clubs and players:

```
double expectedExpense =populatePlayersAndClubs(clubNames,
playerCache, clubCache);
```

9. Create a `job` class, `ClubExpenseCalculatorJob`, to calculate the total expenses of a club. The job takes a club name as constructor argument, and extends from the `ComputeJobAdapter` class. In execute method queries the `playerCache` for the input club and sums up the salaries. It uses `SqlFieldQuery` and SQL join to calculate the sum. The map method of `ComputeTask` returns a map of `ComputeJob`. As the name suggests, the `ComputeJobAdapter` is an adapter for the `ComputeJob` interface. The job interface defines the `execute()` method for writing the job business logic and returning a job result, and also defines a method for cancelling `jobs.ComputeJobAdapter` is an abstract class that provides the default implementation of the `cancel()` method, and defines a bunch of other methods. We are going to concentrate on the `execute()` method:

```
public class ClubExpenseCalculatorJob extends ComputeJobAdapter {
  private final String clubName;
  private final IgniteCache<SoccerPlayerKey, SoccerPlayer>
  playerCache;
  private static final long serialVersionUID = 1L;
  public ClubExpenseCalculatorJob(String clubName) {
      this.clubName = clubName;
      playerCache = Ignition.ignite().getOrCreateCache
      (PLAYER_JOB_CACHE);
  }
  @Override
  public Object execute() throws IgniteException {
      SqlFieldsQuery fieldQry = new SqlFieldsQuery("SELECT
SUM(p.salary) from
      SoccerPlayer p, \"" +          CLUB_JOB_CACHE + "\".SoccerClub c
      where p.clubId = c.id AND c.name=?");

      FieldsQueryCursor<List<?>> result =
      playerCache.query(fieldQry.setArgs(clubName));
      double sum = 0.00D;
      Iterator<List<?>> iterator = result.iterator();
      if (iterator.hasNext()) {
        List<?> next = iterator.next();
        sum = next != null && !next.isEmpty() ?
        (double) next.get(0) : 0.0d;
        System.out.println(String.format("Sum of total salary
```

```
                 for club %s is %s", clubName, sum));
            }
        return sum;
    }
}
```

10. Now, we'll implement the `ComputeTask` interface. The `map` method will take the club names as arguments, so for each club create a `ClubExpenseCalculatorJob`, map each job to a worker node, and return the map. We are using the `@LoadBalancerResource` annotation to inject a `ComputeLoadBalancer`. It queries the `LoadBalancingSpi` to determine the best balanced node according to the load balancing policy.

We can configure the IgniteConfiguration with the following `LoadBalancingSpis`:

```
public Map<? extends ComputeJob, ClusterNode> map(List<ClusterNode>
subgrid, String[] names)
 throws IgniteException {
    Map<ComputeJob, ClusterNode> result = new HashMap<>();
    for (String clubName : names) {
        ComputeJobAdapter job = new ClubExpenseCalculatorJob(clubName);
        ClusterNode balancedNode = balancer.getBalancedNode(job, null);
        result.put(job, balancedNode);
    }
    return result;
}
```

The `map` method loops through the names, and for each name creates a `job = new ClubExpenseCalculatorJob(clubName)`. Then, it calls the balancer to find the best balanced node from the `subgrid` and maps the job to that node.

11. In the `result` method, we are going to write our custom failover logic. If the job result contains an exception, check the exception type; if it is an `IgniteExcecption`, failover to a different node; otherwise, throw the exception:

```
public ComputeJobResultPolicy result(ComputeJobResult res, List
<ComputeJobResult> rcvd)
  throws IgniteException {
      IgniteException exception = res.getException();
      if (exception != null) {
          if (exception instanceof IgniteException) {
              return ComputeJobResultPolicy.FAILOVER;
          } else {
              throw exception;
          }
       } else {
          return ComputeJobResultPolicy.WAIT;
      }
  }
```

12. The `reduce` method aggregates the results, loops through the results collection, gets the data, and adds it to the sum:

```
public Double reduce(List<ComputeJobResult> results)
throws IgniteException {
      double sum = 0;
      for (ComputeJobResult res : results)
        sum += res.<Double>getData();

      return sum;
  }
```

13. Now, get an Ignite compute and execute the `ComputeTask`. The final code will look as follows:

```
double totalCalculatedExpense = compute.execute(new
ComputeTask<String[], Double>() {...
      public Map<? extends ComputeJob, ClusterNode> map
      (List<ClusterNode> subgrid,
      String[] names)
        {...}
      public ComputeJobResultPolicy result(ComputeJobResult res,
      List<ComputeJobResult> rcvd)
        {...}
      public Double reduce(List<ComputeJobResult> results)
        {...}
    },  clubNames);
```

14. Launch two ignite servers and run this program. It will send eight jobs to two remote nodes.The following is the output from two server consoles:

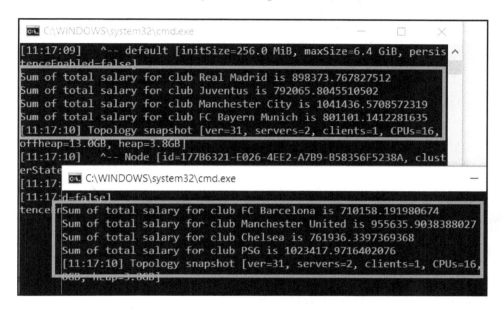

Task Adapter

We implemented the map, reduce, and result methods of the ComputeTask interface; unless we need a special failover logic, we can reuse the result logic.
The ComputeTaskAdapter class provides the default implementation of the result() method for reuse. In this section, we are going to re-implement our MapReduce job with the help of ComputeTaskAdapter.

The following are the steps:

1. Create a class, ClubExpenseTaskAdapter, which extends from ComputeTaskAdapter. As the result() method is already implemented in ComputeTaskAdapter, we'll just implement the map() and reduce(). The map method will be changed a little to use the subgrids, instead of the balancer:

```
public class ClubExpenseTaskAdapter extends
ComputeTaskAdapter<String[], Double> {
  private static final long serialVersionUID = 1L;
  @Override
```

```
public Map<? extends ComputeJob, ClusterNode> map(List<ClusterNode>
subgrid, String[] clubs)
throws IgniteException {
    Map<ComputeJob, ClusterNode> map = new HashMap<>();
    Iterator<ClusterNode> it = subgrid.iterator();
    for (final String club : clubs) {
      if (!it.hasNext())
        it = subgrid.iterator();
      ClusterNode node = it.next();
      map.put(new ClubExpenseCalculatorJob(club), node);
    }
    return map;
  }
}
```

2. The `reduce` method will be copied from the old version. The call to the `execute` method needs to be changed, as we are no longer passing any `ComputeTask` closure to the `execute` method; call the `execute` with the adapter class and `clubNames`:

```
double totalCalculatedExpense = compute.execute
(ClubExpenseTaskAdapter.class, clubNames);
```

3. Run the program; it will work as before:

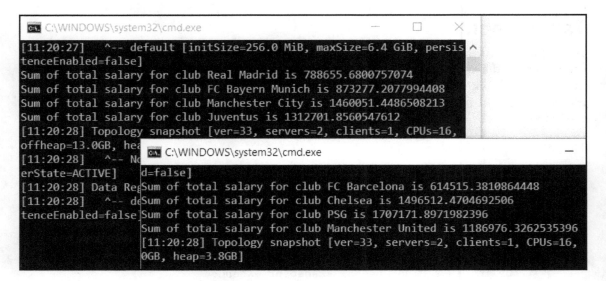

Task Split

The ComputeTaskSplitAdapter offers more flexibility over the ComputeTaskAdapter to reduce boilerplate code. This class defines a simplified adapter for ComputeTask where it implements the job mapping to available cluster nodes. We need to consider splitting tasks and returning a list of ComputeJobs. This section implements the ComputeTaskSplitAdapter:

1. Create a class, ClubExpenseTaskSplitAdapter, and extend it from ComputeTaskSplitAdapter. You need to implement the Collection<? extends ComputeJob> split(int gridSize, T arg) and reduce(List<ComputeJobResult> results) methods. The reduce logic remains the same, the *split* logic loops through the list of clubs and for each club creates a ClubExpenseCalculatorJob instance, adds it to a list, and finally returns the list of jobs:

```
public class ClubExpenseTaskSplitAdapter extends
ComputeTaskSplitAdapter<String[], Double> {
    private static final long serialVersionUID = 1L;
    @Override
    //Same as before
    public Double reduce(List<ComputeJobResult> results) throws
    IgniteException          {....}
    @Override
    protected Collection<? extends ComputeJob> split(int gridSize,
    String[] clubs) throws IgniteException {
        List<ComputeJob> jobs = new ArrayList<>();
            for (String club : clubs) {
                jobs.add(new ClubExpenseCalculatorJob(club));
            }
        return jobs;
    }
}
```

2. The call to the execute method needs to be changed. We will call the execute with the ClubExpenseTaskSplitAdapter class and clubNames. The remaining code remains unchanged:

```
double totalCalculatedExpense =
compute.execute(ClubExpenseTaskSplitAdapter.class, clubNames);
```

Task Sessions

Ignite provides an API to define a distributed session that exists for a particular task's execution; this distributed session is shared between the jobs and parent task.

The `ComputeTaskSession` interface defines a set of methods to perform the following distributed session tasks:

- `setAttribute`: A job (or the parent task) can set a session attribute; all other jobs within this task and task itself can see the attribute. This method takes a key (possible job id) and a value.
- `getAttribute`: Retrieves the session attribute value for a key.
- `waitForAttribute`: A job can call this method by passing a key and an expected value. The call is a blocking call, if this attribute is already in session, returns immediately, otherwise waits for the attribute to be set.
- `getJobSiblings`: Returns the grid jobs that are executing within the same task.
- `saveCheckpoint`: Saves the intermediate state of a job or task to storage. This is similar to a JDBC save point. You can configure the storage by implementing the `CheckpointSpi`.
- `loadCheckpoint`: Loads the saved checkpoint.

The `ComputeJobContext` interface defines the context attached to every job. The job context belongs to a job and is not shared between the jobs and the parent task. It can give you the job id and option to set/get attributes local to the job.

The `@TaskSessionResource` annotation injects a `ComputeTaskSession` resource into a job.

The `@JobContextResource` annotation injects a `ComputeJobContext` resource into a job.

You can find an example in the code bundle to use the `ComputeTaskSession` and `ComputeJobContext` to synchronize job execution. The `ClubExpenseSessionEnabledJob` class gives you the implementation. The following code snippet explains the job synchronization:

```
session.setAttribute(jobContext.getJobId(), "SUMMATION");

for (ComputeJobSibling sibling : session.getJobSiblings()) {
    try {
        System.err.println(String.format("WAITING for %s to
        complete SUMMATION", sibling.getJobId()));
        session.waitForAttribute(sibling.getJobId(), "SUMMATION", 100);
        System.err.println(String.format("DONE for %s to complete
```

```
SUMMATION",
        sibling.getJobId()));
        } catch (InterruptedException e) {
        e.printStackTrace();
    }
}
```

Each job sets the attribute value SUMMATION against its job ID as key, then it loops through the sibling jobs and checks whether they are done with the SUMMATION steps. The waitForAttribute times out after 100 milliseconds.

When we run the job, it prints the following output:

```
<terminated> JobSessionTest [Java Application] C:\Sujoy\Java\jdk1.8.0_91\bin\javaw.exe (Nov 21, 2018, 4:14:21 PM)
Going to compute max salary for job= d01fed53761-ad6f7c2b-bf79-401a-b584-6b61080619ed
WAITING for 311fed53761-ad6f7c2b-bf79-401a-b584-6b61080619ed to complete SUMMATION
DONE for 311fed53761-ad6f7c2b-bf79-401a-b584-6b61080619ed to complete SUMMATION
WAITING for 411fed53761-ad6f7c2b-bf79-401a-b584-6b61080619ed to complete SUMMATION
DONE for 411fed53761-ad6f7c2b-bf79-401a-b584-6b61080619ed to complete SUMMATION
Going to compute max salary for job= e01fed53761-ad6f7c2b-bf79-401a-b584-6b61080619ed
DONE for 311fed53761-ad6f7c2b-bf79-401a-b584-6b61080619ed to complete SUMMATION
WAITING for 411fed53761-ad6f7c2b-bf79-401a-b584-6b61080619ed to complete SUMMATION
DONE for 411fed53761-ad6f7c2b-bf79-401a-b584-6b61080619ed to complete SUMMATION
Going to compute max salary for job= 111fed53761-ad6f7c2b-bf79-401a-b584-6b61080619ed
Richest player of club Chelsea is 97956.38523681213
Richest player of club FC Bayern Munich is 79403.22619119182
Richest player of club Real Madrid is 85117.6623863205
{Juventus=96607.25, FC Barcelona=81345.98, FC Bayern Munich=79403.23, PSG=89049.72, Real
3289332.11
[16:14:32] Ignite node stopped OK [uptime=00:00:00.663]
```

Ignite Executor Service

The IgniteCompute API enables us to execute jobs on a cluster; the ExecutorService implementation of Apache Ignite also allows us to execute jobs directly on cluster nodes. The ExecutorService considers the ignite nodes as threads and distributes jobs on the cluster. We'll launch two Ignite nodes (one server and our program) and submit 10 jobs to an executor. The following are the steps to distribute jobs using the ExecutorService API:

- Create a class, ExecutorServiceTest, start an ignite server instance, ask ignite to create an ExecutorService instance, and submit 10 jobs to it:

```
IgniteConfiguration cfg = new IgniteConfiguration();
    cfg.setPeerClassLoadingEnabled(true);
        try (Ignite ignite = Ignition.start(cfg)) {
```

```
ExecutorService executorService =
ignite.executorService();
IntStream.range(1, 10).forEach( i->
        executorService.execute(new Runnable() {
                public void run() {
System.out.println(String.format("Executing
                                using
                                ExecutorService - Index %s",
i));
                            }
                })
        );
    }
```

- When we execute the program, it load balances the jobs, and executes some jobs on a remote server node and some on the local program node. The following jobs are executed on a remote node:

```
C:\WINDOWS\system32\cmd.exe

[16:44:23] Data Regions Configured:
[16:44:23]    ^-- default [initSize=256.0 MiB, maxSize=6.4 GiB, persist
Executing using ExecutorService - Index 3
Executing using ExecutorService - Index 5
Executing using ExecutorService - Index 7
Executing using ExecutorService - Index 9
Executing using ExecutorService - Index 1
[16:44:24] Topology snapshot [ver=9, servers=1, clients=0, CPUs=8, off
[16:44:24]    ^-- Node [id=B08C5FCA-579C-479C-A353-B76741F8FAE3, clust
[16:44:24] Data Regions Configured:
[16:44:24]    ^-- default [initSize=256.0 MiB, maxSize=6.4 GiB, persist
```

- The following jobs are executed on our program local node:

```
<terminated> ExecutorServiceTest [Java Application] C:\Sujoy\Java\jdk1.8.0_91\bin\
[16:44:23]
[16:44:23] To start Console Management & Monitoring run ignite
[16:44:23]
[16:44:23] Ignite node started OK (id=43d77b48)
[16:44:23] Topology snapshot [ver=8, servers=2, clients=0, CPU
[16:44:23]   ^-- Node [id=43D77B48-A3D7-471F-A45C-0B83C136BCAA
[16:44:23] Data Regions Configured:
[16:44:23]   ^-- default [initSize=256.0 MiB, maxSize=6.4 GiB,
Executing using ExecutorService - Index 2
Executing using ExecutorService - Index 6
Executing using ExecutorService - Index 4
Executing using ExecutorService - Index 8
[16:44:24] Ignite node stopped OK [uptime=00:00:00.296]
```

Ignite Job Scheduler

We configured closures and jobs, and executed them on remote nodes using the MapReduce/distributed closure API. Apache Ignite's job scheduler API can execute remote jobs periodically. The `IgniteScheduler.scheduleLocal()` method can be configured to execute periodically on a local node using the UNIX cron syntax. The **IgniteScheduler** APIs operate on **Runnable** and **Callable**. The following are the `IgniteScheduler` methods:

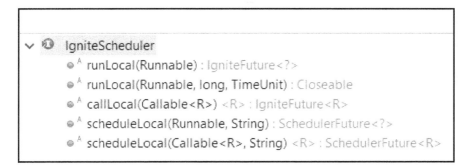

In this section, we will examine local job scheduling. If you want to execute a code snippet after N secs/minutes/hours and so on, the steps are as follows:

- Add a class, RunLocalSchedulerTest, start a local ignite instance, and call the runLocal on an IgniteScheduler instance. In runLocal pass a runnable closure, 10, and TimeUnit.MICROSECONDS. It will schedule the runnable to execute after 10 microseconds:

```
IgniteConfiguration cfg = new IgniteConfiguration();
 cfg.setPeerClassLoadingEnabled(true);
 try (Ignite ignite = Ignition.start(cfg)) {
  ignite.scheduler().runLocal(
    new Runnable() {
      @Override
          public void run() {
          System.out.println("now executed @"+new Date());
      }
    },
   10, TimeUnit.MICROSECONDS);

 Thread.sleep(1000);
 }
```

- When we run the program, it prints the following output:

```
<terminated> RunLocalSchedulerTest [Java Application] C:\Sujoy\Java\jdk1.8.0_91\bin
[16:49:36] Ignite node started OK (id=d52f134a)
[16:49:36] Topology snapshot [ver=10, servers=2, clients=0, CPU
[16:49:36]    ^-- Node [id=D52F134A-121D-4065-A943-02AA79134C1D,
[16:49:36] Data Regions Configured:
[16:49:36]    ^-- default [initSize=256.0 MiB, maxSize=6.4 GiB,
now executed @Wed Nov 21 16:49:36 IST 2018
[16:49:37] Ignite node stopped OK [uptime=00:00:01.074]
```

UNIX cron supports minimum scheduling time unit 1 minute. We'll schedule a local job to execute every 1 minute. The following are the steps:

- We need to add an ignite-schedule dependency to our build.gradle:

```
compile group: 'org.apache.ignite', name: 'ignite-schedule',
version: '1.2.0-incubating'
```

- Create a class, `LocalPeriodicSchedulerTest`, and add the following lines to schedule a local job every 1 minute with the cron expression * * * * *:

```
IgniteConfiguration cfg = new IgniteConfiguration();
 cfg.setPeerClassLoadingEnabled(true);
 try (final Ignite ignite = Ignition.start(cfg)) {
 ignite.scheduler().scheduleLocal(new Runnable() {
    @Override public void run() {
        System.out.println(String.format("Executing at %s",
        new Date()));
    }
 }, "* * * * *");

 System.in.read();
 }
```

- The `System.in.read()` waits for the user input and lets the scheduler run in background. When we run the job, it keeps printing the local time until we hit *Enter*:

```
LocalPeriodicSchedulerTest [Java Application] C:\Sujoy\Java\jdk1.8.0_91\bin\javaw.exe
[16:50:41]    ^-- Node [id=76C19CA8-C593-4704-9C69-5F9C4D5C34B1
[16:50:41] Data Regions Configured:
[16:50:41]    ^-- default [initSize=256.0 MiB, maxSize=6.4 GiB,
[16:50:51] New version is available at ignite.apache.org: 2.6.
Executing at Wed Nov 21 16:51:00 IST 2018
Executing at Wed Nov 21 16:52:00 IST 2018
Executing at Wed Nov 21 16:53:00 IST 2018
Executing at Wed Nov 21 16:54:00 IST 2018
```

We can broadcast our local job to all cluster nodes and schedule it using cron, but the remote nodes must be configured with the ignite-schedule dependency.

The following is the code to broadcast our job to remote nodes and schedule it to execute periodically, every 1 minute:

- Add a new class, `BroadcastScheduleTest` and add the following lines:

```
ignite.compute().broadcast(new IgniteCallable<Object>() {
    private static final long serialVersionUID = 1L;
    @IgniteInstanceResource
    Ignite ignite;
    @Override
    public Object call() throws Exception {
```

```
ignite.scheduler().scheduleLocal(new Runnable() {
    @Override public void run() {
        System.out.println(String.format("Executing at %s",
        new Date()));
    }
}, "* * * * *");
return null;
}
});
```

- Put the `ignite-schedule-1.2.0-incubating.jar` and its dependency, `cron4j-2.2.5.jar`, in the `IGNITE_HOME/libs` directory:

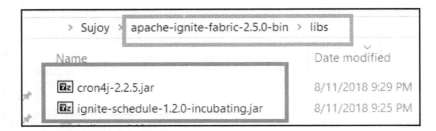

- Launch an Ignite server instance from the `IGNITE_HOME/bin` directory. It will keep printing the local time, until the server instance is stopped/killed:

```
C:\WINDOWS\system32\cmd.exe
[16:59:50]    ^-- default [initSize=256.0 MiB, max
[16:59:51] Topology snapshot [ver=16, servers=2,
[16:59:51]    ^-- Node [id=B08C5FCA-579C-479C-A353
[16:59:51] Data Regions Configured:
[16:59:51]    ^-- default [initSize=256.0 MiB, max
Executing at Wed Nov 21 17:00:00 IST 2018
Executing at Wed Nov 21 17:01:00 IST 2018
Executing at Wed Nov 21 17:02:00 IST 2018
```

We can configure remote nightly jobs to perform heavy calculations, such as a batch job to print year end bank statements or claim processing and so on. The complex event processing will explore the on the fly job execution.

Ignite AOP

Apache Ignite compute grid's AOP API can enhance a class to execute a method in a remote node. The *@Gridify* annotation can convert a method into a grid executable closure. Ignite supports three types of AOP weaving:

- **AspectJ AOP**: Remote Ignite node's classpath should contain the `aspectj` `jars`.
- **JBoss AOP**: Remote Ignite node's classpath should contain the `jboss jars`. You need to download the `jars` from Maven central and put them under Ignite's `lib` directory.
- **Spring AOP**: You need to configure `build.gradle` to include the `spring-aop` dependency. No need to put any jars in the remote Ignite node's classpath.

The following steps will convert a simple method to a grid executable closure:

- Add the following dependency to your `build.gradle` file:

```
compile group: 'org.apache.ignite', name: 'ignite-aop', version:
"${igniteVersion}"
```

- Create a class, `GridAopTest`, add the following method, and annotate it with the `@Gridify` annotation:

```
public class GridAopTest {
    @Gridify
    public void sayItLoud(String msg) {
        System.out.println("Hey " + msg + "?");
    }
}
```

- In the `main` method, add the following instructions: start an ignite instance, create an instance of the class, enhance it with `GridifySpringEnhancer`, and finally call the `sayItLoud` method on the enhanced instance of the class:

```
public static void main(String[] args) {
    IgniteConfiguration cfg = new IgniteConfiguration();
    cfg.setPeerClassLoadingEnabled(true);
    cfg.setClientMode(true);
    try (Ignite ignite = Ignition.start(cfg)) {
        GridAopTest test = new GridAopTest();
        test = GridifySpringEnhancer.enhance(test);
        test.sayItLoud("who are you!");
    }
}
```

- Now, launch an ignite server instance and run the program; it will print **Hey who are you!?** in the remote Ignite console:

```
C:\WINDOWS\system32\cmd.exe
[17:02:38] Data Regions Configured:
[17:02:38]    ^-- default [initSize=256.0 MiB, maxSize=6
[17:02:43] Topology snapshot [ver=18, servers=1, client
[17:02:43]    ^-- Node [id=B08C5FCA-579C-479C-A353-B7674
[17:02:43] Data Regions Configured:
[17:02:43]    ^-- default [initSize=256.0 MiB, maxSize=6
Hey who are you!?
[17:02:43] Topology snapshot [ver=19, servers=1, client
[17:02:43]    ^-- Node [id=B08C5FCA-579C-479C-A353-B7674
```

The enhance method applies the Spring dynamic proxy and enhances the method that has the @Gridify annotation. The enhanced method creates an instance of GridifyDefaultTask (a ComputeTaskAdapter implementation). The default task creates a GridifyJobAdapter job instance, wraps the annotated method, and executes it on a remote node.

 You can create your own task class adapter and pass it to the @Gridify annotation as a taskClass such as @Gridify(taskClass=YourClass.class).

Summary

We have examined the Apache Ignite Query API. The query API offers three styles: predicate-based, SQL-based and text-based query. This chapter covered the full text search, scan query, distributed SQL query, field query, custom SQL function, Lucene-based fuzzy query, and data affinity.

Distributed computing is an important component of the Apache Ignite architecture. The chapter concluded with the compute grid and distributed computation using the following APIs: MapReduce/ForkJoin, ExecutorService, and Job scheduling.

The Chapter 5, *Building Microservices with Service Grid*, will cover the Service Grid component of Apache Ignite and develop a microservice on top of Service Grid.

5
Building MicroServices with Service Grid

Apache Ignite provides interfaces for developing and deploying services to Ignite nodes where your data and service will collocate. In this chapter, we will build and deploy a Java service to an Ignite cluster. We will also build a data-oriented microservice and deploy it on an in-memory cluster.

We'll also examine the **complex event processing (CEP)** and **event streaming (ES)** concepts using Ignite.

The following topics will be covered:

- Service grid
- Ignite microservices
- Complex event processing

Understanding the service grid

A service grid is an Ignite cluster where we can deploy/undeploy our services. A service is a set of APIs or functionalities with a purpose, for example, you can define your order service with a set of APIs to submit or cancel an order, or list all orders.

Ignite's computation focuses on distributing computation across multiple nodes. It includes a data grid, a compute grid, and a service grid. The main difference between a data, a compute, and a service grid is the pattern and purpose of execution.

In a compute grid, a computation is split into multiple sub-tasks and executes them in multiple grid nodes in parallel. A compute grid improves scalability, availability, and the throughput of computation. The common compute grid technique is MapReduce/forkjoin. Ignite's peer class loading feature enables us to send a computation closure to a remote node.

A data grid is used to distribute data into multiple nodes in a cluster. The partitioned caching topology allows us to store more data in memory and improves scalability, whereas the replicated mode helps in making data highly available by replicating data across nodes within the cluster. A data grid's role is to store more data and allow faster data access.

The purpose of a service grid is to host services in memory and handle their life cycles. It also ensures that our services are highly available and fault-tolerant. My service may access a cache (data grid) or any other data stores for retrieving data, such as a database table or a NoSQL data store. An ignite deployed service can be invoked from a computation closure to perform some business logic.

A deployed service can be accessed using a proxy or socket API.

An ignite service grid provides the following features:

- **Distribution**: User-defined services are distributed automatically over the cluster.
- **Cluster Singletons**: Spring framework beans are singleton by default. It means only one instance of your bean serves all requests, but they are class loader/JVM-specific. Spring cannot make a bean cluster singleton or only one instance per cluster. Ignite services can be deployed as cluster singletons. Ignite ensures the singleton contract. Even if new nodes are added, or the service node is crashed, only one service instance serves the requests.
- **Fault Tolerance**: Ignite guarantees that services are continuously available, regardless of any topology change.
- **Load Balancing**: Ignite automatically manages the load balancing of services; it maintains the even distribution of services on each node within the cluster. When a new node is added or removed, Ignite automatically evaluates the deployment configuration and, if required, may redeploy an existing service on another node to maintain the even distribution of load.
- **Undeployment**: Offers APIs to undeploy any service.

- **Service Proxy**: Service grid APIs can be used to create a service proxy to access any remotely deployed service. The `@ServiceResource` Java annotation is used to auto inject a service proxy to an Ignite callable/runnable.
- **Deployment Topology**: Service grid provides APIs to get information about service deployment topology within the cluster.

Ignite's service grid provides the following two interfaces to define and deploy services in nodes—`org.apache.ignite.services.Service` and `org.apache.ignite.IgniteServices`.

To deploy a service in Apache Ignite's service grid, you need to implement the `org.apache.ignite.services.Service` interface. This interface defines the following service life cycle methods:

- `init(ServiceContext ctx)`: This is the method used for pre-initialization of services prior to execution. Here, we can initialize the resources, such as create a cache or database connection. The `ServiceContext` contains the methods and information about a specific service.
- `execute(ServiceContext ctx)`: This method is automatically invoked whenever an instance of the service is deployed on a grid node. The service remains deployed until the `cancel` methods on `org.apache.ignite.IgniteServices` are invoked explicitly or the node exits/crashes.
- `cancel(ServiceContext ctx)`: This method cancels this service. Ignite will automatically call this method whenever any of the cancel methods on `org.apache.ignite.IgniteServices` API are called.

To deploy, undeploy, or invoke a service, you need to access different methods on the `org.apache.ignite.IgniteServices` interface. It offers the following functionalities:

- It automatically deploys any number of service instances on the grid
- It automatically deploys singletons, including the cluster singleton, node singleton, or the key affinity singleton
- It automatically deploys services on node startup by specifying them in grid configuration
- It undeploys any of the services that have been deployed
- It obtains information about service deployment topology within the grid

The following relevant methods are defined in the `IgniteServices` interface:

- `deployClusterSingleton` (String name, Service svc): Deploys a cluster-wide singleton service and guarantees that there is always one instance of the service in the cluster. It can redeploy the service when the original service node crashes.
- `deployNodeSingleton` (String name, Service svc): Deploys a per-node singleton service and guarantees that there is always one instance of the service in the node.
- `deployKeyAffinitySingleton` (String name, Service svc, @Nullable String `cacheName`, Object `affKey`): Deploys one instance of this service on the primary node for a given affinity key.
- `deployMultiple` (String name, Service svc, int `totalCnt`, int `maxPerNodeCnt`): Deploys multiple instances of the service on the grid. The `totalCnt` argument signifies the maximum number of deployed services in the grid; `totalCnt` = 0 indicates unlimited. The `maxPerNodeCnt` argument signifies the maximum number of services deployed on each node. `maxPerNodeCnt` = 0 indicates unlimited services. At least one of `totalCnt` or `maxPerNodeCnt` must be greater than 0.
- `deploy(ServiceConfiguration cfg)`: Deploys multiple instances of the service on the grid according to the `ServiceConfiguration` provided.
- `deployAll(Collection<ServiceConfiguration> cfgs)`: Deploys multiple services described by the configurations provided. Depending on the parameters specified, multiple instances of the same service may be deployed.
- `cancel`(String name): If the service with the specified name is deployed in the cluster, this method undeploys the service by invoking the `cancel()` method on the `Service`.
- `cancelAll(Collection<String> names)`: Cancels services with specified names.
- `cancelAll()`: Cancels all deployed services.
- `<T> T service`(String name): Gets a locally deployed service with a specified name. `<T>` is the service interface. To access a remote service, such as calling from a client node, you need to get a service proxy.
- `<T> Collection<T>` services(String name): Gets all locally deployed services with a specified name.

- `<T> T serviceProxy(String name, Class<? super T> svcItf, boolean sticky)`: Gets a remote handle on the service. If a service is available locally, then a local instance is returned, otherwise a remote proxy is dynamically created and provided for the specified service. Once we get the service proxy, we can call the service APIs as many times as we want. The `sticky` flag indicates the stickiness of the service API calls, when `sticky= true`. Ignite should always contact the same remote service, otherwise it will try to load balance between services.

Let's create a service, deploy it within a cluster, and invoke the service remotely. The following are the steps required to create a service:

1. Create a gradle project called 'service-grid' with the following `build.gradle` dependencies:

```
buildscript {
  ext {
  igniteVersion ='2.6.0'
  }
  repositories {
  mavenCentral()
  }
}
apply plugin: 'java'
apply plugin: 'eclipse'
group = 'service-grid'
version = '0.0.1-SNAPSHOT'
sourceCompatibility = 1.8
repositories {
maven{
  url
"http://www.gridgainsystems.com/nexus/content/repositories/external/"
  }
  mavenCentral()
}

dependencies {
//Ignite deps
  compile group: 'org.apache.ignite', name: 'ignite-core', version:
    "${igniteVersion}"
  compile group: 'org.apache.ignite', name: 'ignite-spring', version:
    "${igniteVersion}"
  compile group: 'org.apache.ignite', name: 'ignite-indexing',
version:
    "${igniteVersion}"
  compile group: 'org.apache.ignite', name: 'ignite-aop', version:
```

```
        "${igniteVersion}"
    compile group: 'com.h2database', name: 'h2', version: '1.4.195'
    compile group: 'org.aspectj', name: 'aspectjweaver', version:
'1.9.1'


}
```

2. Create a Java interface called `MyDateService` using a `getTime` method to return a date:

```
public interface MyDateService {
    public Date getTime();
}
```

3. Create a `MyDateServiceImpl` class as a service implementation of `MyDateService`. The class will implement the `MyDateService` and `org.apache.ignite.services.Service` interfaces:

```
public class MyDateServiceImpl implements Service, MyDateService {
        private static final String INIT = "init@";
        private static final long serialVersionUID = 1L;
        @IgniteInstanceResource
        private Ignite ignite;
        private IgniteCache<String, Date> dateCache;
        @Override public Date getTime() {
            Date reply = dateCache.get(INIT);
            System.out.println("in getTime() method with response =
"+reply);
            return reply;
        }
        @Override public void cancel(ServiceContext ctx) {
            System.out.println("in cancel method. On node:\" +
            ignite.cluster().localNode()");
         }
        @Override public void init(ServiceContext ctx) throws Exception
{
            dateCache = ignite.getOrCreateCache("myDateCache");
            dateCache.put(INIT, new Date());
            System.out.println("in init method");
        }

        @Override public void execute(ServiceContext ctx) throws
Exception {
            System.out.println("in execute method. On node: " +
            ignite.cluster().localNode());
        }
    }
```

The @IgniteInstanceResource Java annotation injects an Ignite instance into the service class. Our class implements the Service interface methods, and the init method is called before deploying a service—in our init() method, we are creating (or getting) a cache, myDateCache, putting in a key-value pair (INIT, current time), and finally printing in init method.

The execute method is called during deployment. We print the node name where the service is getting deployed.

The cancel() method will be invoked during the undeployment of the service. Our cancel implementation just prints the node name from where the service will be cancelled.

The getTime() method returns the date stored in myDateCache during the pre-initialization of the service.

- Build the project, get the jar file, and put it in the lib directory of the Ignite installation. If the jar is not present in the Ignite server node, we wont be able to deploy it in that node.
- Let's create a Java class to deploy our service in all server nodes, as demonstrated in the following block of code:

```java
public class DeployMyService {
    public static void main(String[] args) {
        IgniteConfiguration cfg = new IgniteConfiguration();
        cfg.setPeerClassLoadingEnabled(true);
        cfg.setClientMode(true);
        try (Ignite ignite = Ignition.start(cfg)) {
            // Cluster group which includes all caching/server nodes.
            ClusterGroup cacheGrp = ignite.cluster().forServers();

            // Get an instance of IgniteServices for the cluster group.
            IgniteServices svcs = ignite.services(cacheGrp);

            // Deploy per-node singleton. An instance of the service
            // will be deployed on every node within the cluster group.
            svcs.deployNodeSingleton("myDateService", new
MyDateServiceImpl());
        }
    }
}
```

The preceding code is self-explanatory: Get an `IgniteServices` instance for all server/caching nodes, call the `deployNodeSingleton` with the name `myDateService`, and get a new instance of `MyDateServiceImpl`. And that's it! The service will be deployed in all server nodes.

- Start a server instance from Ignite installation's `bin` directory and run the `DeployMyService` class. Since the `DeployMyService` class is a client node, `myDateService` will not be deployed in that node, but the remote server nodes will initialize the service and deploy it. The following is the output from the server console. You will see the the messages in `init` method and in `execute` method...:

```
C:\WINDOWS\system32\cmd.exe
[22:05:40]    ^-- Node [id=C3BD88F3-9FFB-4236-924E-D0FAB0CE1E4A, clusterState=ACTIVE]
[22:05:40] Data Regions Configured:
[22:05:40]    ^-- default [initSize=256.0 MiB, maxSize=6.4 GiB, persistenceEnabled=fal
[22:05:40] Topology snapshot [ver=3, servers=1, clients=0, CPUs=8, offheap=6.4GB, hea
[22:05:40]    ^-- Node [id=C3BD88F3-9FFB-4236-924E-D0FAB0CE1E4A, clusterState=ACTIVE]
[22:05:40] Data Regions Configured:
[22:05:40]    ^-- default [initSize=256.0 MiB, maxSize=6.4 GiB, persistenceEnabled=fal
in init method
in execute method. On node: TcpDiscoveryNode [id=c3bd88f3-9ffb-4236-924e-d0fab0ce1e4a
, 127.0.0.1, 172.18.214.81, 192.168.0.103, 192.168.190.1, 192.168.234.1, 2002:5045:45
45:45b:1000:d02a:223e:26a1:d6b1], sockAddrs=[/192.168.190.1:47500, /192.168.234.1:475
d91:fa2f:47500, /2002:5045:45b:1000:d02a:223e:26a1:d6b1:47500, /192.168.0.103:47500,
.0.75.1:47500, /0:0:0:0:0:0:0:1:47500, /127.0.0.1:47500, /172.18.214.81:47500], discP
tExchangeTime=1543250140556, loc=true, ver=2.6.0#20180710-sha1:669feacc, isClient=fal
```

- Now, invoke the service and undeploy it. The following class is designed to call the date service and undeploy it:

```java
public class InvokeMyService {
    public static void main(String[] args) {
        IgniteConfiguration cfg = new IgniteConfiguration();
        cfg.setPeerClassLoadingEnabled(true);
        cfg.setClientMode(true);
        try (Ignite ignite = Ignition.start(cfg)) {
            MyDateService myDateService =
                ignite.services().serviceProxy("myDateService",
                MyDateService.class, false);

            System.out.println(myDateService.getTime());
            System.out.println("Now undeploy the service");
            ClusterGroup cacheGrp = ignite.cluster().forServers();
```

```
            IgniteServices svcs = ignite.services(cacheGrp);
            svcs.cancel("myDateService");
        }
    }
}
```

The `serviceProxy` method of `IgniteServices` is called to get
the `myDateService` method, and then the `getTime()` method is called on the
remote service proxy. Finally, the service is undeployed/cancelled from all server
nodes using the `cancel ('myDateService ')` method of the `IgniteServices`
interface. The program outputs the service date and then undeploys the service.
The following is the program's output:

```
<terminated> InvokeMyService [Java Application] C:\Sujoy\Java\jdk1.8.0_91\b
[22:08:23] Topology snapshot [ver=4, servers=1, clients=1
[22:08:23]    ^-- Node [id=FD3FF9AE-7925-4BC2-A9E7-D5FC542
Mon Nov 26 22:05:40 IST 2018
Now undeploy the service
[22:08:24] Ignite node stopped OK [uptime=00:00:00.148]
```

The following is the Ignite server node's output. Note that it prints in
`getTime()`... when the remote service proxy calls the `getTime()` method. **in
cancel...** is printed when the service is undeployed:

```
[22:08:23]    ^-- default [initSize=256.0 MiB, maxSize=6.4 GiB, persisten
in getTime() method with response = Mon Nov 26 22:05:40 IST 2018
in cancel method. On node:" + ignite.cluster().localNode()
[22:08:23] Topology snapshot [ver=5, servers=1, clients=0, CPUs=8, offhe
[22:08:23]    ^-- Node [id=C3BD88F3-9FFB-4236-924E-D0FAB0CE1E4A, clusterS
```

Now run the '`InvokeMyService`' program again. It will print the following
error message as the service is already undeployed. The remote service proxy
throws an exception as it fails to find the deployed '`myDateService`' service:

```
[22:12:03]    ^-- Node [id=5C25C5B4-AAB5-437C-975B-B8E580044A6F, clusterState=ACTIVE]
[22:12:03] Ignite node stopped OK [uptime=00:00:00.064]
Exception in thread "main" class org.apache.ignite.IgniteException: Failed to find deployed service: myDateService
        at org.apache.ignite.internal.processors.service.GridServiceProxy.invokeMethod(GridServiceProxy.java:174)
        at org.apache.ignite.internal.processors.service.GridServiceProxy$ProxyInvocationHandler.invoke(GridService
        at com.sun.proxy.$Proxy22.getTime(Unknown Source)
        at com.service.grid.InvokeMyService.main(InvokeMyService.java:18)
```

The following section will talk about microservices and how can we interact with multiple services.

Deploying microservices on Ignite

Before we proceed with the deployment, we must ask the question: what are microservices?

Microservices is a pattern or style to decompose a monolithic application into multiple loosely coupled services. Each service has a business responsibility, focuses on solving a business domain problem, is independently deployable, and communicates with other services in order to delegate work.

The microservices pattern evolved to solve the following problems with the monoliths:

- Monolithic apps are not easy to refactor, changes are not local, and they are very tightly coupled.
- Understanding the application is difficult. Adding a new feature requires cascading changes.
- Deploying multiple instances requires resources, such as RAM and CPU, and so you need more hardware to spin off multiple instances of your monolithic app.
- Adopting new technologies, frameworks, or languages is difficult, such as being unable to develop one module in Java and another in Golang.
- Scaling is difficult. You cannot deploy multiple instances of a module when required. Suppose you have two modules, A and B, and the bulk of the client requests are only accessing module B's services. You cannot deploy B separately, since A and B are packaged together. If we deploy multiple copies of the app, then A will unnecessarily eat up space and resources, and we will need more hardware and instances to handle the scalability and availability required.

Loosely coupled microservices can be developed separately with the following benefits:

- Each service is responsible for one specific task, so it is easy to understand and refactor
- They are easy to deploy
- They are easy to scale, as you can spin off the required services
- It is easy to adopt new frameworks, languages, data stores, and so on (polyglot architecture), since the change is only local to that specific service

There is no silver bullet that will solve all the design-related issues, and the microservices architecture has the following drawbacks:

- Alhough scalability is increased, deployment of the system as a whole is complex
- The microservices pattern forces interservice communication and adds additional complexity to handle the communication failures
- The unavailability of one service can bring down the system, and additional complexity is required to handle the availability issues
- Distributed transactions are slow and prone to failure, so complex patterns (such as Sagas) need to be applied to handle it
- A request can span multiple services, and this requires special attention in terms of traceability and monitoring

There are several design patterns for decomposing a monolithic app into multiple services and balance the forces. You can get details of microservices at `https://microservices.io/`.

Apache Ignite can be used to build a fault-tolerant, performant, and scalable microservice application. Ignite-based deployment offers the following advantages over traditional microservices deployment:

- The service grid can handle the microservice's life cycle and inter-service communication (service injection)
- The service grid is capable of automatically balancing the service deployments to achieve high scalability
- The grid manages the microservice's availability—even for the singleton cluster deployment, availability is not compromised
- The performance of microservices running on Apache Ignite grid is faster than the application server-based deployment, as the services run on in-memory
- Accessing a data node for application data or service nodes to delegate a task is faster, since all nodes are interconnected and running on in-memory

Building microservices

We'll create two microservices—conference and registration—and deploy them on an in-memory cluster. The conference service will create conferences with details, such as name, capacity, registration count, and dates. The registration service will register users to a conference; it takes a conference ID and a registrant's email ID. Internally, it communicates with the conference service to validate the conference ID and registration counts.

The *Registration* service will be deployed to the nodes where the `registration.node` attribute is set. Similarly, the `Conference` service will be deployed to the nodes where the `conference.node` attribute is present. These services will internally use Apache Ignite's data nodes to store data.

We will create two ignite caches—`conferenceCache` and `registrationCache`—and distribute data on the nodes where the `cache.node` attribute is present.

The steps are as follows:

1. Create a class to store conference details in the cache:

```java
public class Conference implements Serializable {
  private static final long serialVersionUID = 1L;

  @QuerySqlField(index = true)
  private Long id;

  @QuerySqlField
  private final String name;

@QuerySqlField
  private final long capacity;

  @QuerySqlField
  private long noOfRegistration;

  @QuerySqlField
  private final Date startDate;

  @QuerySqlField
  private final Date endDate;

//constructor and getters are omitted for brevity
}
```

2. Create an interface, `ConferenceService`, to create conferences with the following methods:

```java
public interface ConferenceService {

  public static final String SERVICE_NAME = "ConferenceService";
  public static final String CACHE_NAME = "conferenceCache";

  public Long create(Conference conference);
  public boolean update(Long confId, Conference conference);
  public boolean delete(Conference conference);
```

```
public Conference find(Long id);
}
```

3. Create a deployable microservice class, `ConferenceServiceImpl`. This class implements the life cycle methods `init()`, `cancel()`, and `execute()`, of the `Service` interfaces and business methods of the `ConferenceService` interface.

   The business methods—`create`, `update`, `find`, and `delete`—work with `conferenceCache` to manipulate `Conferences`. `conferenceCache` is instantiated in the `init()` method and cleared in the `cancel()` method. `@IgniteInstanceResource` injects an instance of ignite for cache lookup:

```
public class ConferenceServiceImpl implements Service,
ConferenceService {
    private static final long serialVersionUID = 1L;

    @IgniteInstanceResource
    private Ignite ignite;

    private static Long id;

    private IgniteCache<Long, Conference> conferenceCache;

    @Override
    public Long create(Conference conference) {
        conference.setId(id++);
        conferenceCache.put(conference.getId(), conference);
        return conference.getId();
    }

    @Override
    public boolean delete(Conference conference) {
        return conferenceCache.remove(conference.getId());
    }

    @Override
    public Conference find(Long id) {
        return conferenceCache.get(id);
    }

    @Override
    public void cancel(ServiceContext ctx) {
        conferenceCache.clear();
        System.out.println("in cancel method. On node:" +
        ignite.cluster().localNode());
```

```
        }

        @Override
        public void init(ServiceContext ctx) throws Exception {
            conferenceCache =
ignite.getOrCreateCache(ConferenceService.CACHE_NAME);
            System.out.println("initializing Conference Service");
        }

        @Override
        public void execute(ServiceContext ctx) throws Exception {
            id = 11;
            System.out.println("In execute method. On node: " +
            ignite.cluster().localNode());
        }

        @Override
        public boolean update(Long confId, Conference conference) {
            conferenceCache.put(confId, conference);
            return true;
        }
    }
```

- Once a `conference` is created, attendees can register to it.
  `RegistrationService` is the contract to register to a conference. This service
  needs to work with a model—`Registration`, to store attendee information,
  such as email ID, type of registration, and conference ID. The following is the
  `Registration class` snippet:

```
public class Registration implements Serializable {
    private static final long serialVersionUID = 1L;
    @QuerySqlField(index = true) private String id;
    @QuerySqlField(index = true) private final Long conferenceId;
    @QuerySqlField private final String email;
    @QuerySqlField private final String type;
    //constructor and getters are omitted for brevity
}
```

- We also need an `enum` for the registration type:

```
public enum RegistrationType {
    Speaker, Sponsor, General, Corporate
}
```

- The `RegistrationService` defines only one method for user registration:

```
public interface RegistrationService {
    public static final String SERVICE_NAME = "RegistrationService";
    public static final String CACHE_NAME = "registrationCache";
    public String register(Registration registration);
}
```

- The `RegistrationServiceImpl` class implements the `Service` life cycle interface and `RegistrationService` business interface. This service needs to interact with `ConferenceService` to validate the conference IDs and the registration capacity limit, and to update the conference attendee count. The `@ServiceResource` ignite annotation is used for the injection of Ignite services by a specified service name. If more than one service is deployed on a server, then the first available instance will be returned. This is the beauty of Ignite's microservices platform; you don't need to add complexity to your code in order to locate a service and invoke (JMS, RESTful API, RPC, and so on) it. The service is located and injected automatically by the framework. The following code block demonstrates the `RegistrationServiceImpl` class:

```
public class RegistrationServiceImpl implements Service,
RegistrationService {
    private static final long serialVersionUID = 1L;

    @IgniteInstanceResource
    private Ignite ignite;

    @ServiceResource(serviceName = ConferenceService.SERVICE_NAME)
    private ConferenceService conferenceService;

    private IgniteCache<String, Registration> registrationCache;

    @Override
    public void cancel(ServiceContext ctx) {
        registrationCache.clear();
        System.out.println("in cancel method. On node:" +
        ignite.cluster().localNode());
    }

    @Override
    public void init(ServiceContext ctx) throws Exception {
        registrationCache =
ignite.getOrCreateCache(RegistrationService.CACHE_NAME);
        System.out.println("initializing Registration Service");
    }

    @Override
```

```
        public void execute(ServiceContext ctx) throws Exception {
            System.out.println("In execute method. On node: " +
            ignite.cluster().localNode());
        }
```

The `register()` method invokes `find()` on the injected `conferenceService` to find the conference ID passed in with the `registration` object. If the conference ID is invalid, or if the conference capacity is exceeded, then it throws an exception. Otherwise, it generates a registration ID, puts the registration object in the cache, and increments the registration count in conference. In the real world, if more than one service instance updates the registration count in parallel, it will create data inconsistency. Later, we will look at transaction management and locking to handle such scenarios:

```
        @Override
        public String register(Registration registration) {
            Conference conference =
                conferenceService.find(registration.getConferenceId());
            if (conference == null) {
                throw new RuntimeException(
                    String.format("No Conference found for ID = %s",
                    registration.getConferenceId()));
            }

            if (conference.getNoOfRegistration() + 1 >=
conference.getCapacity()) {
                throw new RuntimeException(String.format("Capacity exceeded
for conf =
                %s, total capacity =            %s ",
registration.getConferenceId(),
                conference.getCapacity()));
            }

            String registrationId = UUID.randomUUID().toString();
            registration.setId(registrationId);
            registrationCache.put(registrationId, registration);
            conference.setNoOfRegistration(conference.getNoOfRegistration() +
1);

            conferenceService.update(conference.getId(), conference);

            return registrationId;
        }
    }
```

Now, our microservices are ready for deployment. We need to find a strategy to deploy the services and caches. Caches will be deployed on nodes where the node attribute `cache.node` is present and its value is *true*. `RegistrationService` will be deployed on nodes where the `registration.node` attribute is `true`, and `ConferenceService` will be deployed on nodes where the `conference.node` attribute is `true`. This way, we can scale the services independently. If we need more instances of the registration service, we will spin off some ignite server nodes with the `registration.node` attribute set to `true`. Similarly, if we need to store greater volumes of data, then we can spin off a few server nodes with the `cache.node` attribute set to `true`. Ignite cache configuration and service configuration allows us to pass `IgnitePredicate` filters to determine on what nodes the cache or service should be started. We will use these node filters to start the services and caches. Let's create a node filter:

- `NodeAttributeFilter` implements the `IgnitePredicate<ClusterNode>`. When a cluster node is started, it invokes the `apply` method on the filter to determine whether the node should start the service/cache. The `NodeAttributeFilter` constructor takes an attribute name and, in the `apply` method, it checks whether the cluster node has the attribute `true`. The following is the class:

```
public class NodeAttributeFilter implements
IgnitePredicate<ClusterNode>{
    private static final long serialVersionUID = 1L;
    private final String attributeName;

    public NodeAttributeFilter(String attributeName) {
        super();
        this.attributeName = attributeName;
    }

    public boolean apply(ClusterNode node) {
        Boolean attributeValue = node.attribute(attributeName);
        return attributeValue != null && attributeValue;
    }
}
```

- Create an `IgniteConfiguration` with the `cache.node` attribute and the value `true`, define `CacheConfiguration` for conference and registration, set node filters to check the cluster node attribute `cache.node`, and start an Ignite server instance with `IgniteConfiguration`:

```
public class StartCacheNodes {
    private static final String CACHE_NODE = "cache.node";
    public static void main(String[] args) {
```

```
            IgniteConfiguration cfg = new IgniteConfiguration();
            cfg.setPeerClassLoadingEnabled(true);
            HashMap<String, Object> userAttrs = new HashMap<>();
            userAttrs.put(CACHE_NODE, true);
            cfg.setUserAttributes(userAttrs);

            CacheConfiguration<Long, Conference> conferenceConfig = new
            CacheConfiguration<Long, Conference>  ();
            conferenceConfig.setTypes(Long.class, Conference.class);
            conferenceConfig.setName(ConferenceService.CACHE_NAME);
            conferenceConfig.setNodeFilter(new
    NodeAttributeFilter(CACHE_NODE));

            CacheConfiguration<String, Registration> registrationConfig = new
            CacheConfiguration<>();
            registrationConfig.setName(RegistrationService.CACHE_NAME);
            registrationConfig.setNodeFilter(new
    NodeAttributeFilter(CACHE_NODE));
            cfg.setCacheConfiguration(conferenceConfig, registrationConfig);

            Ignition.start(cfg);
        }
    }
```

- Run the program to start a cache node:

```
StartCacheNodes [Java Application] C:\Sujoy\Java\jdk1.8.0_91\bin\javaw.exe (Nov 26, 2018, 10:38:30 PM)
[22:39:02] Ignite node started OK (id=ab58f811)
[22:39:02] Topology snapshot [ver=8, servers=2, clients=0, CPUs=8, offheap=13.0GB, heap=8.1GB]
[22:39:02]   ^-- Node [id=AB58F811-66D3-4CD8-A3CA-4C197AB86B2D, clusterState=ACTIVE]
[22:39:02] Data Regions Configured:
[22:39:02]   ^-- default [initSize=256.0 MiB, maxSize=6.4 GiB, persistenceEnabled=false]
```

- Create a program to start the service nodes:

```
public class DeployServices {
  private static final String REGISTRATION_NODE = "registration.node";
  private static final String CONFERENCE_NODE = "conference.node";

  public static void main(String[] args) {
    IgniteConfiguration cfg = new IgniteConfiguration();
    cfg.setPeerClassLoadingEnabled(true);
```

- Create an Ignite configuration with two attributes—`registration.node` and `conference.node`:

```
HashMap<String, Object> userAttrs = new HashMap<>();
userAttrs.put(CONFERENCE_NODE, true);
userAttrs.put(REGISTRATION_NODE, true);
cfg.setUserAttributes(userAttrs);
```

- Create a service configuration for the conference service, and set the node filter to look for the node attribute `conference.node`. Also, set the name of the service to bind, cache name, pass an instance of the service to deploy, and finally configure the total number of services to deploy and the maximum number of services per node:

```
ServiceConfiguration confServiceConfig = new
ServiceConfiguration();
confServiceConfig.setCacheName(ConferenceService.CACHE_NAME);
confServiceConfig.setService(new ConferenceServiceImpl());
confServiceConfig.setName(ConferenceService.SERVICE_NAME);
confServiceConfig.setNodeFilter(new
NodeAttributeFilter(CONFERENCE_NODE));
confServiceConfig.setMaxPerNodeCount(1);
confServiceConfig.setTotalCount(3);
```

- Create a service configuration for the registration service, set the node filter to look for the node attribute `registration.node`. Also, set the name of the service to bind, cache name, pass an instance of the registration service to deploy, and finally configure the total number of services to deploy and the maximum number of services per node:

```
ServiceConfiguration regisServiceConfig = new ServiceConfiguration();
regisServiceConfig.setCacheName(RegistrationService.CACHE_NAME);
regisServiceConfig.setService(new RegistrationServiceImpl());
regisServiceConfig.setName(RegistrationService.SERVICE_NAME);
regisServiceConfig.setNodeFilter(new
NodeAttributeFilter(REGISTRATION_NODE));
regisServiceConfig.setMaxPerNodeCount(1);
regisServiceConfig.setTotalCount(3);
```

- Set the configurations for the services to be deployed on the grid:

```
cfg.setServiceConfiguration(confServiceConfig, regisServiceConfig);
```

- Start the node. The services will be deployed automatically as the node has both the attributes set:

```
Ignition.start(cfg);
  }
}
```

- Run the program. It will log the service life cycle method's print statements:

```
DeployServices [Java Application] C:\Sujoy\Java\jdk1.8.0_91\bin\javaw.exe (Nov 26, 2018, 10:40:53 PM)
[22:41:17] Nodes started on local machine require more than 20% of physical RAM what
initializing Conference Service
In execute method. On node: TcpDiscoveryNode [id=445a8d8f-f412-494e-a044-c1bb902e548a
initializing Registration Service
In execute method. On node: TcpDiscoveryNode [id=445a8d8f-f412-494e-a044-c1bb902e548a
[22:41:17] Performance suggestions for grid  (fix if possible)
[22:41:17] To disable, set -DIGNITE_PERFORMANCE_SUGGESTIONS_DISABLED=true
[22:41:17]    ^-- Enable G1 Garbage Collector (add '-XX:+UseG1GC' to JVM options)
```

- Now is the time to test the microservices. The following program creates a service proxy for the ConferenceService and invokes the create method to create a conference. It then creates another service proxy for the RegistrationService to register an attendee:

```
public class TestMicroServices {
  public static void main(String[] args) {
  IgniteConfiguration cfg = new IgniteConfiguration();
  cfg.setPeerClassLoadingEnabled(true);
  cfg.setClientMode(true);

  try (Ignite ignite = Ignition.start(cfg)) {
  ConferenceService conferenceSvc =
    ignite.services().serviceProxy(ConferenceService.SERVICE_NAME,
  ConferenceService.class, false);

  Long confId = conferenceSvc.create(new Conference("Microservices with
Ignite", 5,
  new Date(), new Date()));
  System.out.println(String.format("The conf id is %s", confId));

  RegistrationService registrationSvc =
  ignite.services().serviceProxy(RegistrationService.SERVICE_NAME,
  RegistrationService.class, false);

   String registeredId = registrationSvc
  .register(new Registration(confId, "sujoy@yopmail.com",
```

```
            RegistrationType.General.name()));

            System.out.println(String.format("The registration id is %s",
registeredId));
        }
      }
    }
```

- Internally, the registration service will communicate with the conference service over the cluster to validate data. Run the program. It will print the conference and registration IDs:

```
<terminated> TestMicroServices [Java Application] C:\Sujoy\Java\jdk1.8.0_91\bin\javaw.exe

[22:44:00] Topology snapshot [ver=10, servers=3, clients=1, CPUs=8,
[22:44:00]    ^-- Node [id=F4107F85-6675-4B20-9C0C-07741A3C5D57,
The conf id is 1
The registration id is b0b23714-e2ea-4fe5-a7ac-f59070dc0462
[22:44:00] Ignite node stopped OK [uptime=00:00:00.208]
```

If we restart the data nodes and service nodes, the program will start again with a conference ID of 1. In the following chapter, we are going to look at data persistence and transaction management to handle data inconsistency, synchronization, and data loss issues.

The next section covers an important aspect of modern event-driven architecture: complex event processing.

Processing complex events

Complex Event Processing, or CEP, is a real-time low latency processing of events to provide insight into what is happening or going to happen—predicting opportunities or threats.

An **event** is a change of state of something, such as when you deposit or withdraw money from your account. Here, this is the amount of money. Another example is a change in a room thermostat reading when the temperature in the room changes.

An **event stream** is a continuous, never-ending flow of events, such as airplane or car **electronic control units (ECU)** emitting millions of events per second.

A complex event processor filters, enriches, aggregates, and detects patterns from an event stream. Apache Ignite enables in-memory, real-time, never-ending event stream processing in a scalable manner.

Apache Ignite's CEP is comprised of the following components:

- **Capture events**: events from different sources can be streamed to the Ignite cluster. Apache Ignite event streamers are used to ingest data from different event sources, such as JMS, Kafka, Camel, and Twitter on Ignite caches.
- **Process events**: You can filter, enrich, or aggregate event data using Ignite indexing and Ignite SQL, text, and predicate-based cache queries, to query into the streaming data. The Ignite `StreamReceiver` (`StreamTransformer` and `StreamVisitor`) APIs are used for viewing, filtering, and enriching events.
- **Take action**: You can invoke an ignite service or update an alert cache value to inform the owners.

The next section will explore the *IgniteDataStreamer* and Ignite *JMS Streamer* to stream data into Ignite cluster.

Streaming events

Apache Ignite integrates with major stream providers, including the following:

- IgniteDataStreamer
- JMS Streamer
- Kafka Streamer
- Camel Streamer
- MQTT Streamer
- Storm Streamer
- Flink Streamer
- Flume sink
- Twitter
- RocketMQ

In this section, we are going to understand data streaming using a data streamer and some of the major stream providers.

The `addData (Object, Object)` method of IgniteDataStreamer adds data for streaming on a remote node. IgniteDataStreamer is responsible for streaming external data to a cache. The streamer doesn't send the streamed data to in-memory data grids immediately, instead buffering internally for better performance and network utilization. The `perNodeBufferSize (int)` method allows us to pre-configure the node buffer size. Once the buffer size limit is exceeded, the data is sent to remote nodes. The default buffer size is `512`.

When data streaming works faster than putting objects into the cache, the streamer sends the buffered data to remote nodes in multiple parallel threads and creates uneven memory utilization in the cluster. The `perNodeParallelOperations` setting limits the maximum number of permitted parallel buffering operations on remote nodes. When the limit is exceeded, then the `addData (Object, Object)` method is blocked to control uneven memory utilization.

The `allowOverwrite (Boolean)` method is a flag to overwrite existing cache values; by `default`, the flag is `false`. The data streamer works faster when the flag is disabled or false, since then it doesn't have to keep track of the data versioning.

In the following section, we are going to simulate a stock data streaming scenario. Alpha vantage offers a free API to gather stock data. Register and claim your free API key and then download **OHLC (Open-High-Low-Close)** data for a symbol from `https://www.alphavantage.co/documentation/`.

The following are the steps required to stream data and detect patterns:

- Put the downloaded `csv` file directly under the `service-grid\src\main\java` folder.
- Add a new Java class, StockStatus, to represent the OHLC of a stock symbol:

```
public class StockStatus implements Serializable {
  private static final long serialVersionUID = 1L;
  @QuerySqlField(index = true)
  private String symbol;
  @QuerySqlField(index = true)
  private Date timestamp;
  @QuerySqlField(index = true)
  private double open;
  @QuerySqlField(index = true)
  private double high;
  @QuerySqlField(index = true)
  private double low;
  @QuerySqlField(index = true)
  private double close;
```

```java
@QuerySqlField(index = true)
private long volume;

public String getSymbol() {
return symbol;
}

public void setSymbol(String symbol) {
this.symbol = symbol;
}

public Date getTimestamp() {
return timestamp;
}

public void setTimestamp(Date timestamp) {
this.timestamp = timestamp;
}

public double getOpen() {
return open;
}

public void setOpen(double open) {
this.open = open;
}

public double getHigh() {
return high;
}

public void setHigh(double high) {
this.high = high;
}

public double getLow() {
return low;
}

public void setLow(double low) {
this.low = low;
}

public double getClose() {
return close;
}

public void setClose(double close) {
this.close = close;
}
```

```
    public long getVolume() {
     return volume;
     }

    public void setVolume(long volume) {
     this.volume = volume;
     }

    @Override
    public String toString() {
     return "Stock [symbol=" + symbol + ", timestamp=" + timestamp + ",
open=" + open
      + ", high=" + high + ", low="
      + low + ", close=" + close + ", volume=" + volume + "]";
     }
    }
```

- Create a data streamer to continuously read the downloaded OHLC data for a stock symbol and pump the data to a cluster node. Create a cache configuration and set an expiration policy of five seconds. We want to keep only recent data. Then, create a data streamer for the OHLC_CACHE by calling the ignite.dataStreamer (OHLC_CACHE) API, and then, in an infinite loop, read the OHLC data, create an OHLC object, and stream it to the cache by calling mktStmr.addData(ohlc.getSymbol(), ohlc):

```
public class DataStreamerTest {
    public static final String OHLC_CACHE = "ohlc_status";
    static DateFormat format= new SimpleDateFormat("yyyy-MM-dd
hh:mm:ss");

    public static void main(String[] args) throws IOException,
URISyntaxException,
    Exception {
     URI uri = new
DataStreamerTest().getClass().getClassLoader().getResource
     ("intraday_1min_AAPL.csv").toURI();

     IgniteConfiguration cfg = new IgniteConfiguration();
     cfg.setPeerClassLoadingEnabled(true);

     CacheConfiguration<String, StockStatus> config = new
CacheConfiguration<>();
     config.setExpiryPolicyFactory(FactoryBuilder.factoryOf(new
     CreatedExpiryPolicy(new Duration(TimeUnit.SECONDS, 5))));
     config.setName(OHLC_CACHE);
     config.setIndexedTypes(String.class, StockStatus.class);
     cfg.setCacheConfiguration(config);
```

```
           try (Ignite ignite = Ignition.start(cfg)) {
              IgniteCache<String, StockStatus> marketDataCache =
              ignite.getOrCreateCache(config);
              try (IgniteDataStreamer<String, StockStatus> mktStmr =
              ignite.dataStreamer(OHLC_CACHE)) {
                 mktStmr.allowOverwrite(true);
                 mktStmr.perNodeParallelOperations(2);

                 while (true) {
                     try (Stream<String> stream =
Files.lines(Paths.get(uri))) {
                         stream.forEach(str -> {
                             StringTokenizer st = new
StringTokenizer(str, ",");
                             StockStatus ohlc = new StockStatus();
                             try {
ohlc.setTimestamp(format.parse(st.nextToken()));
                             } catch (ParseException e) {
                                     e.printStackTrace();
                             }
ohlc.setOpen(Double.parseDouble(st.nextToken()));
ohlc.setHigh(Double.parseDouble(st.nextToken()));
ohlc.setLow(Double.parseDouble(st.nextToken()));
ohlc.setClose(Double.parseDouble(st.nextToken()));
ohlc.setVolume(Long.parseLong(st.nextToken()));
                             ohlc.setSymbol("AAPL");
                             mktStmr.addData(ohlc.getSymbol(), ohlc);
                             System.out.println(String.format("Adding
for %s",
                             ohlc));
                         });
                  }
              }
          }
       }
   }
```

* When we run the program, it continuously prints the following log:

```
DataStreamerTest [Java Application] C:\Sujoy\Java\jdk1.8.0_91\bin\javaw.exe (Nov 26, 2018, 10:46:32 PM)
Adding for Stock [symbol=AAPL, timestamp=Fri Aug 17 14:47:00 IST 2018, open=217.06, high=217.123, low=217.06, close=217.116, volume=15447]
Adding for Stock [symbol=AAPL, timestamp=Fri Aug 17 14:46:00 IST 2018, open=217.13, high=217.15, low=217.03, close=217.07, volume=20792]
Adding for Stock [symbol=AAPL, timestamp=Fri Aug 17 14:45:00 IST 2018, open=217.11, high=217.15, low=217.06, close=217.14, volume=35993]
Adding for Stock [symbol=AAPL, timestamp=Fri Aug 17 14:44:00 IST 2018, open=217.18, high=217.21, low=217.06, close=217.104, volume=25483]
Adding for Stock [symbol=AAPL, timestamp=Fri Aug 17 14:43:00 IST 2018, open=217.06, high=217.2, low=217.06, close=217.189, volume=44444]
Adding for Stock [symbol=AAPL, timestamp=Fri Aug 17 14:42:00 IST 2018, open=217.0, high=217.068, low=216.99, close=217.064, volume=51355]
Adding for Stock [symbol=AAPL, timestamp=Fri Aug 17 14:41:00 IST 2018, open=216.92, high=217.0, low=216.88, close=217.0, volume=31223]
Adding for Stock [symbol=AAPL, timestamp=Fri Aug 17 14:40:00 IST 2018, open=217.0, high=217.09, low=216.9, close=216.93, volume=32055]
Adding for Stock [symbol=AAPL, timestamp=Fri Aug 17 14:39:00 IST 2018, open=216.989, high=217.132, low=216.97, close=216.98, volume=36640]
Adding for Stock [symbol=AAPL, timestamp=Fri Aug 17 14:38:00 IST 2018, open=216.959, high=217.09, low=216.94, close=216.989, volume=30139]
Adding for Stock [symbol=AAPL, timestamp=Fri Aug 17 14:37:00 IST 2018, open=216.94, high=217.018, low=216.877, close=216.95, volume=60774]
Adding for Stock [symbol=AAPL, timestamp=Fri Aug 17 14:36:00 IST 2018, open=217.135, high=217.184, low=216.92, close=216.936, volume=86105]
Adding for Stock [symbol=AAPL, timestamp=Fri Aug 17 14:35:00 IST 2018, open=217.23, high=217.244, low=217.13, close=217.14, volume=48172]
```

- Our OHLC cache is keeping the final five seconds of data, so let's query the cache to get the maximum value of AAPL stock during the last 5 secs. The following code snippet queries the OHLC cache to find the maximum (high) value of AAPL stock, waits for a second, and again queries the maximum value again in an infinite loop:

```java
public class DataStreamerQuery {
    public static void main(String[] args) throws IOException,
URISyntaxException,
        Exception {
        IgniteConfiguration cfg = new IgniteConfiguration();
        cfg.setPeerClassLoadingEnabled(true);
        cfg.setClientMode(true);
        try (Ignite ignite = Ignition.start(cfg)) {
            IgniteCache<String, StockStatus> marketDataCache =
Ignition.ignite().getOrCreateCache(OHLC_CACHE);
            System.out.println(marketDataCache.get("AAPL"));
            SqlFieldsQuery query = new SqlFieldsQuery("SELECT max(s.high)
from
            StockStatus s");
            while (true) {
            List<List<?>> res = marketDataCache.query(query).getAll();
            System.out.println("max for last 5 sec");
            System.out.println(res);
            Thread.sleep(1000);
            }
        }
    }
}
```

- When we run the program, it continuously prints the maximum (high) value. We can send an alert to the team responsible when the value reaches a limit:
    - We can configure other types of streamers to stream events to an Ignite cluster and then write distributed SQL query to find a pattern and finally take action, such as buy more AAPL stocks or sell them all.

Summary

This chapter explained the service grid concept and microservice deployment on Apache Ignite. We explored the core service grid APIs, the *Service* and `IgniteServices` interfaces, along with how a service can be defined, deployed, and cancelled. We also covered the importance of deploying a microservice on a service grid cluster and how the framework takes care of service availability, scalability, and inter-service communication.

This chapter also covered complex event processing, event data streaming APIs, and continuous queries. Ignite supports almost all major data streamers, such as JMS, Kafka, and Camel.

The `Chapter 6`, *Sharpening Ignite Skills*, will cover the following topics: Ignite data persistence with RDBMS and NoSQL data stores, transactional CRUD operations, locks, off-heap and native data stores, distributed data structures, including queues, sets, and ID generators, and Ignite's RESTful API.

6
Sharpening Ignite Skills

So far, we have learned about the various components of Apache Ignite's architecture – Data Grid, Compute Grid, Service Grid, Data Streaming, Caching Strategies, and Node Topology. Now is the time for us to focus on other important components of building a highly scalable and performant system. We know that traditional RDBMS are ACID compliant. However, there is a bottleneck for high scalability and performance; NoSQL databases solve this scalability problem, but they are not ACID compliant. This chapter explores how to build an ACID compliant, high performance, scalable, and highly available system.

The following topics will be covered in this chapter:

- Writing data to a persistent datastore
- Ignite's ACID-compliant transactional model
- Ignite's distributed data structure

Writing data to a persistent store

Apache Ignite's distributed clustering model and data grids move data closer to the application and help us to achieve high performance by keeping objects in memory. However, we cannot keep the entire dataset in memory because the RAM is volatile in nature. If the entire cluster goes down, we will lose our precious data. Also, keeping the entire application data in memory can affect the system performance.

The optimal design is to keep the subset of data, the most recently used or active data, in memory and the other set (inactive or not so frequently used data) can be stored in a persistent data store. Apache Ignite supports the following two persistence modes:

- Native disk-based persistence
- Third-party data store persistence: RDBMS and NoSQL

In this section, we are going to examine the default native persistence, third-party MySQL persistence, and Cassandra NoSQL persistence.

Enabling native persistence

We turn on Ignite's native persistence to store data on disk. Ignite keeps a subset of the data in memory and a superset on disk. If a cache has N entries and it is configured to keep only X objects in memory (X < N), then X-N objects are stored on disk.

The following are the advantages of native persistence:

- You can run distributed SQL queries over the full dataset, which spans both memory and disk.
- You don't have to worry about the size of the data and indexes in RAM. Ignite allows you to keep only the frequently used dataset in memory; the rest of the data can be stored on disk.
- When the entire cluster goes down and you restart it, the third-party persistence needs to preload the data and warm up the memory before it becomes operational. The native persistence cluster becomes fully operational once all the nodes are interconnected with each other.
- The native persistence keeps data and indexes in memory and on disk. But the format of in-memory data and disk data is the same. Therefore, while moving data from RAM to disk, Ignite doesn't worry about transforming data from one format to another. On the other hand, the third-party persistence needs to transform /deserialize objects from one format to another, which is an overhead.

In the following section, we'll create a cache, enable native persistence, populate the cache, restart the node, and verify the behavior. The following are the requisite steps:

1. You need to start two Ignite server nodes with the persistenceEnabled flag set to true. The examples folder contains the persistence configuration file. Open the example-persistent-store.xml file and modify the following DataStorageConfiguration to enable persistence:

```xml
<!-- Enabling Apache Ignite Persistent Store. -->
 <property name="dataStorageConfiguration">
    <bean
class="org.apache.ignite.configuration.DataStorageConfiguration">
        <property name="defaultDataRegionConfiguration">
            <bean
class="org.apache.ignite.configuration.DataRegionConfiguration">
```

```
        <property name="persistenceEnabled" value="true"/>
      </bean>
    </property>
  </bean>
</property>
```

Launch two command prompts and
run `ignite examples/config/persistentstore/example-persistent-store.xml`:

```
C:\Windows\System32\cmd.exe - ignite  examples/config/persistentstore/example-persistent-store.xml          —    □
Microsoft Windows [Version 10.0.16299.726]
(c) 2017 Microsoft Corporation. All rights reserved.

D:\demo\apache-ignite-fabric-2.6.0-bin\bin>ignite examples/config/persistentstore/example-persistent-store.xml
[20:22:56]
[20:22:56]    /  /   __/ \/ /  /.   __/
[20:22:56]   _/ // (7 7   // /  7 / /
[20:22:56]  /___/\__/ /\_/ / / / / /__/
[20:22:56]
[20:22:56] ver. 2.6.0#20180710-sha1:669feacc
[20:22:56] 2018 Copyright(C) Apache Software Foundation
[20:22:56]
[20:22:56] Ignite documentation: http://ignite.apache.org
```

2. Add a new Java class, `NativePersistenceTest,` to our service grid project to create a cache and populate it with a custom `MyPojo` class. `MyPojo` is a simple POJO class:

```java
class MyPojo implements Serializable {
private static final long serialVersionUID = 1L;
private String message;
public MyPojo(String message) {
    this.message = message;
}
  public String getMessage() {
  return message;
  }
  @Override
  public String toString() {
  return "MyPojo [message=" + message + "]";
  }
}
```

3. `NativePersistenceTest` creates a cache called `NativePersistence` and its configuration, activates the cluster as the cluster's persistence property is changed, and populates the cache with `100_000` `MyPojo` entries:

```
public class NativePersistenceTest {
    public static void main(String[] args) {
        IgniteConfiguration cfg = new IgniteConfiguration();
        cfg.setClientMode(true);

        CacheConfiguration<String, MyPojo> config = new
CacheConfiguration<>();
        config.setName("NativePersistence");
        config.setIndexedTypes(String.class, MyPojo.class);
        cfg.setCacheConfiguration(config);
        Ignite ignite = Ignition.start(cfg);
        ignite.cluster().active(true);
        IgniteCache<String, MyPojo> myPojoCache =
        ignite.getOrCreateCache(config);
        IntStream.range(1, 100000).forEach(
          i -> {
             System.out.println(String.format("putting %s in
             cache", i));
             myPojoCache.put(String.valueOf(i), new
             MyPojo(String.valueOf(i)));
          }
        );
    }
}
```

4. Run the program. It will put the objects in cache and the server nodes start persisting the elements. Go to the `<<IGNITE_HOME>>/work/db` folder. You will see the following two sub-folders: starting with `node00-` and `node01-`, representing the two server nodes we started, and a `wal` folder for the logs:

(D:) > demo > apache-ignite-fabric-2.6.0-bin > work > db	
Name	Date modified
node00-1dee469f-28f8-4cae-bbcd-097df8a06009	11/26/2018 8:27 PM
node01-242bc578-2d57-4591-bf77-5d8841ebdd2a	11/26/2018 8:27 PM
wal	11/26/2018 8:27 PM
lock	11/26/2018 8:27 PM

5. Each node folder contains a unique directory for every cache deployed on that node. If we deploy two caches, it will contain two directories. Open both node directories. They contain the `cache-NativePersistence` folder for our `NativePersistence` cache:

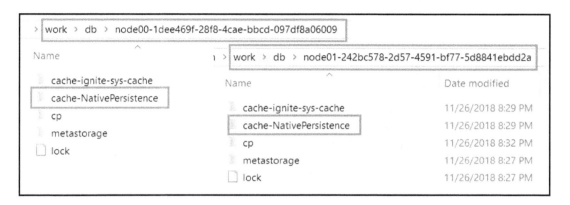

6. Open the `cache-NativePersistence` folder. You will see many `part-n.bin` (part-0, part-2, and so on) files and an `index.bin` file. A `part-n.bin` file is created for every partition that this node is either a primary or backup of. We have two nodes, so the cache entries were partitioned into two sets: `node00` contains `part-0`, `part-2`, and so on, and `node01` contains `part-1`, `part-4`, and so on. `index.bin` keeps track of the cache indexes:

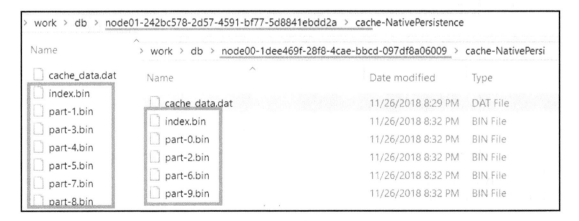

Our `NativePersistence` cache data is persisted on disk. Now restart the nodes. You should still be able to fetch the data that we stored in the cache. The following code queries the `NativePersistence` cache to get the values:

1. Create a `NativePersistenceAccessTest` class, add the following code snippet to activate the cluster, and fetch `100_000` entries from the cache:

```
public class NativePersistenceAccessTest {
  public static void main(String[] args) {
  IgniteConfiguration cfg = new IgniteConfiguration();
  cfg.setClientMode(true);
  Ignite ignite = Ignition.start(cfg);
   ignite.cluster().active(true);
   IgniteCache<String, MyPojo> myPojoCache =
   ignite.getOrCreateCache("NativePersistence");
   IntStream.range(1, 100000).forEach(i -> {
     System.out.println(myPojoCache.get(String.valueOf(i)));
   });
   }
 }
```

2. Restart the server nodes and run the program. It will print the cache entries:

```
<terminated> NativePersistenceAccessTest [Java Application] C:\Sujoy\Java\jdk1.8.0
[20:40:29] Ignite node started OK (id=c94bdc53)
[20:40:29] Topology snapshot [ver=5, servers=2, clients=3,
[20:40:29]    ^-- Node [id=C94BDC53-74FE-4E8A-B5BC-5699BD04F5
[20:40:29]    ^-- Baseline [id=0, size=2, online=2, offline=0]
MyPojo [message=1]
MyPojo [message=2]
MyPojo [message=3]
MyPojo [message=4]
MyPojo [message=5]
MyPojo [message=6]
MyPojo [message=7]
MyPojo [message=8]
MyPojo [message=9]
MyPojo [message=10]
```

One of the advantage of native persistence is that the cluster becomes fully operational once all the nodes are connected with each other.

What if one of the cluster nodes doesn't come up?

The following process examines the cluster restart and node failure behavior:

1. Kill one server node and restart the program.
2. It will throw the following exception: `org.apache.ignite.cache.CacheServerNotFoundException: Failed to map keys for cache (all partition nodes left the grid)`:

```
NativePersistenceAccessTest [Java Application] C:\Sujoy\Java\jdk1.8.0_91\bin\javaw.exe (Nov 26, 2018, 8:42:15 PM)
Exception in thread "main" org.apache.ignite.cache.CacheServerNotFoundException: Failed to map keys for cache
        at org.apache.ignite.internal.processors.cache.GridCacheUtils.convertToCacheException(GridCacheUtils.
        at org.apache.ignite.internal.processors.cache.IgniteCacheProxyImpl.cacheException(IgniteCacheProxyImp
        at org.apache.ignite.internal.processors.cache.IgniteCacheProxyImpl.get(IgniteCacheProxyImpl.java:910)
        at org.apache.ignite.internal.processors.cache.GatewayProtectedCacheProxy.get(GatewayProtectedCachePro
        at com.persistence.NativePersistenceAccessTest.lambda$0(NativePersistenceAccessTest.java:21)
        at java.util.stream.Streams$RangeIntSpliterator.forEachRemaining(Streams.java:110)
        at java.util.stream.IntPipeline$Head.forEach(IntPipeline.java:557)
        at com.persistence.NativePersistenceAccessTest.main(NativePersistenceAccessTest.java:20)
Caused by: class org.apache.ignite.internal.cluster.ClusterTopologyServerNotFoundException: Failed to map keys
```

3. Since we killed the node that contained the partition for `key =5`, it raised an exception.

It looks like native persistence has a serious problem: if a node fails to start, then the application will lose data!

The problem lies within our cache configuration, not in native persistence. We need to reconfigure our cache to keep a backup!

The following process examines this behavior:

1. Stop the server nodes.
2. Delete the `db` folder from the `<<IGNITE_INSTALLATION>>/work` directory.
3. Start two server nodes using the `ignite examples/config/persistentstore/example-persistent-store.xml` command.
4. Modify our `NativePersistenceTest`'s cache configuration to create a backup:

```
config.setName("NativePersistence");
config.setBackups(1);
config.setIndexedTypes(String.class, MyPojo.class);
```

5. Run the `NativePersistenceTest` program again.
6. Now kill all server nodes.

7. Start only one node using the
   `ignite examples/config/persistentstore/example-persistent-store.xml` command.

8. Run `NativePersistenceAccessTest` again. It should not fail, and it should print the following message:

```
<terminated> NativePersistenceAccessTest [Java Application] C:\Sujoy\Java
MyPojo [message=5885]
MyPojo [message=5886]
MyPojo [message=5887]
MyPojo [message=5888]
MyPojo [message=5889]
MyPojo [message=5890]
MyPojo [message=5891]
MyPojo [message=5892]
MyPojo [message=5893]
MyPojo [message=5894]
```

We'll learn about **Write Ahead Log (WAL)** and checkpointing in the performance tuning section.

Persisting data to MySQL

In this section, we will create a model Java class, `'conference'`, and persist it to a MySQL table. We already installed MySQL in Chapter 2, *Understanding the Topologies and Caching Strategies*. Let's reuse the MySQL instance to persist cache data.

Create a Java program, store objects into a cache, and then persist the cached data to a MySQL table. Follow this process to persist data to a MySQL table:

1. Modify the `build.gradle` file and add a dependency for the MySQL client with the `compile group: 'mysql', name: 'mysql-connector-java', version: '8.0.11'` command.

2. Create a schema called `'persistence'` and add a new table called `'conference'` with the following DDL:

```
CREATE TABLE `persistence`.`conference` (
 `id` INT(10) NOT NULL,
 `name` VARCHAR(45) NOT NULL,
 `startDateTime` DATETIME NOT NULL,
 `endDateTime` DATETIME NOT NULL,
 PRIMARY KEY (`id`));
```

3. Launch the My SQL workbench, connect to your database, expand the **Schemas** section, and right-click on **Tables**:

4. Click on the **Create table** sub-menu and create our new `Conference` table:

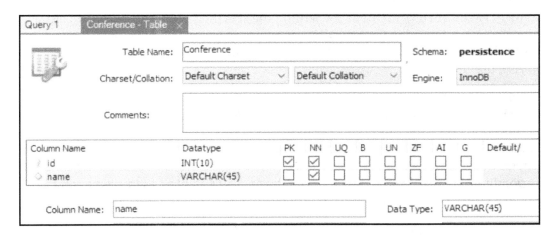

5. Create a Java model called `Conference.java` with the following fields: `id` = conference identifier, `name` = name of the conference, `startDateTime` = when the conference will start, and `endDateTime` = when the conference will end:

```
class Conference implements Serializable {
 private static final long serialVersionUID = 1L;
 private Long id;
 private String name;
 private Date startDateTime;
 private Date endDateTime;
 //getter/setters
 }
```

Ignite's `CacheStore<K, V>` interface provides APIs for cache persistent storage for read-through, write-through, and write-behind behavior. It extends the `CacheWriter` and `CacheLoader` interface.

`CacheLoader` is used to read through or load data into a cache. It has a `V load(K key)` method to load a value for a cache entry. The cache calls this method when a requested entry is not yet loaded in the cache. `Map<K, V> loadAll(Iterable<? extends K> keys)` loads multiple objects into a cache.

`CacheWriter` is used to write through to persistent storage. The persistent storage could be a filesystem, a NoSQL database, a RDBMS, or any external storage where you want to store the cache entries. It defines the `void write(Cache.Entry<? extends K, ? extends V> entry)` and `void writeAll(Collection<Cache.Entry<? extends K, ? extends V>> entries)` methods for writing the specified entries to persistent storage. The developer has to understand the difference between `insert` and `update`. The simplest way is to check the `id/key` field of the value object. If the `id` is `null` or `0`, then use `insert`; otherwise, use `update`.

The `CacheStore` interface has the following out-of-the-box implementations. Check that `CacheJdbcPojoStore` can persist a **POJO (Plain Old Java Object)** to database storage using reflection and JDBC support. `GridCacheWriteBehindStore` enables write-behind logic. `CacheStoreAdapter` is an abstract class and it provides default implementation for bulk operations, such as `loadAll`, `writeAll`, and `deleteAll`, by sequentially calling the corresponding `load`, `write`, and `delete` methods. You still need to implement the `load`, `write`, and `delete` methods.

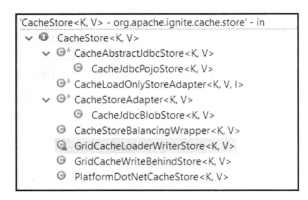

1. Create a `CacheStoreAdapter` to store the `Conference` objects to a database table. We need to implement the `load`, `write`, and `delete` methods. To persist the values to a database table we are going to need a database connection. In this example, we'll configure a Spring JDBC template bean and inject it to our `CacheStoreAdapter`.

 The `@SpringResource(resourceName=<<name>>)` annotation injects the `<<name>>` resource from Spring ApplicationContext, before injecting the resource we need to define it (the name should match) in the Spring application context of the XML configuration.

2. Add a `ConferenceCacheStore` class and extend it from the `CacheStoreAdapter` class. It will use the `@SpringResource` annotation to inject a `jdbcTemplate` for JDBC operations. We will define `jdbcTemplate` and other Spring beans shortly. It will have the following methods:

   - `load(Long key)`: Loads the `key` from the `Conference` table using the `jdbcTemplate` `queryForObject` API and the `SELECT` query.

   - `write(Entry<Long, Conference> entry)`: Inserts a `conference` object to a `Conference` table using the `update` method of `jdbcTemplate`. We can build intelligence by checking the `getId()` method on the `Conference` object. If it is `null`, then execute the `insert` query; otherwise, execute the `update` query.

   - `delete(Object key)`: Deletes the `key` from `Conference` table using SQL's `DELETE` query:

```
public class ConferenceCacheStore extends
CacheStoreAdapter<Long, Conference> {
@SpringResource(resourceName = "jdbcTemplate")
private JdbcTemplate jdbc;

@Override
public Conference load(Long key) throws CacheLoaderException
{
System.out.println(jdbc);
RowMapper<Conference> rowMapper = new
BeanPropertyRowMapper<Conference>(Conference.class);
return jdbc.queryForObject(String.format("SELECT * FROM
CONFERENCE WHERE ID=%s", key),
rowMapper);
}
@Override
public void write(Entry<? extends Long, ? extends Conference>
entry) throws CacheWriterException {
```

```
Conference conf = entry.getValue();
System.out.println(entry);
jdbc.update("INSERT INTO CONFERENCE(id, name, startDateTime,
endDateTime) VALUES(?, ?, ? ,?)" conf.getId(),
conf.getName(),
conf.getStartDateTime(), conf.getEndDateTime());
}
@Override
public void delete(Object key) throws CacheWriterException {
jdbc.update("DELETE FROM CONFERENCE WHERE ID =?", key);
    }
}
```

3. Create a spring application context XML configuration file called `cache-config.xml`, save it in the `/src/main/resourcecs/META-INF/` folder, and define the following beans:
   - A `dataSource` with a driver class, URL, username, and password.
   - A `jdbcTemplate` with the `dataSource` reference. This bean will be injected to our `CacheStoreAdapter`.
   - Configure an `IgniteConfiguration` for our `conferenceCache`. Define a `CacheConfiguration` with the following:
       - `name = 'conferenceCache'`
       - `readThrough=true`: Enables read-through. It will call the `CacheLoader`'s `load` method if an entry is not found in cache. The `Conference load(Long key)` method will be invoked.
       - `writeThroug=true`: Enables write-through. When an entry will be put or updated in the cache, internally the `void write(Entry<? extends Long, ? extends Conference>` `entry)` of `CacheWriter` (`CacheStoreAdapter`) will be called to persist the entry to an external store (a database, in this case).
       - `cacheStoreFactory` with`ConferenceCacheStore`: This attribute determines which `CacheStore` implementation will persist/load our cache entries:

```
<bean class="org.springframework.jdbc.datasource.DriverManagerDataSource"
id="dataSource">
<property name="driverClassName"
value="com.mysql.cj.jdbc.Driver"></property>
```

```xml
<property name="url"
value="jdbc:mysql://localhost:3366/persistence"></property>
<property name="username" value="root"></property>
<property name="password" value="password"></property>
</bean>
<bean id="jdbcTemplate" class="org.springframework.jdbc.core.JdbcTemplate">
<property name="dataSource" ref="dataSource"/>
</bean>

<bean id="ignite.cfg"
class="org.apache.ignite.configuration.IgniteConfiguration">
<property name="clientMode" value="true" />
<property name="cacheConfiguration">
<list>
   <bean class="org.apache.ignite.configuration.CacheConfiguration">
     <property name="name" value="conferenceCache"></property>
     <property name="readThrough" value="true"></property>
     <property name="writeThrough" value="true"></property>
     <property name="cacheStoreFactory">
    <bean class="javax.cache.configuration.FactoryBuilder"
factory-method="factoryOf">
<constructor-arg value="com.persistence.rdbms.ConferenceCacheStore"/>
</bean>
</property>
</bean>
</list>
</property></bean>
```

4. Create a Java class to read the `cache-config.xml` Spring beans and start an Ignite instance. As we have already defined the Ignite configuration to start a client node, it will launch a client instance, get the `conferenceCache` reference, and finally, put two `Conference` objects into our cache. In turn, the objects will be written to our `conference` table:

```java
public class MySQLPersistenceTest {
  public static void main(String[] args) {
    Ignite ignite = Ignition.start("cache-config.xml");
    ignite.cluster().active(true);
    IgniteCache<Long, Conference> cache =
ignite.getOrCreateCache("conferenceCache");
        cache.loadCache(null);
        cache.put(11, new Conference(11, "GOTO;", new Date(), new
Date()));
        cache.put(21, new Conference(21, "StrangeLoop;", new Date(), new
Date()));                          System.out.println("done");
    }
  }
```

5. Build the project and put the service `.jar` and `mysql` client `.jar` in the `lib` folder of our Ignite installation folder:

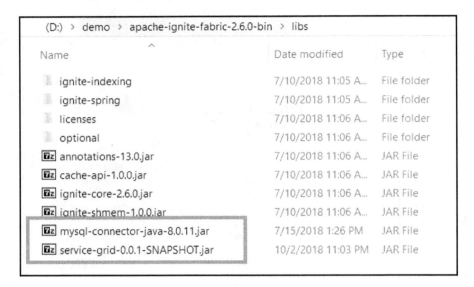

- Now we need an Ignite server instance to store the cache and write the cache entries back to our persistent store. The server instance must know about `dataSource` and `jdbcTemplate` because the service code will be executed in the server, so add the following Spring bean definitions to `example-persistent-store.xml`:

```
    <bean
class="org.springframework.jdbc.datasource.DriverManagerDataSource"
    id="dataSource">
        <property name="driverClassName" value="com.mysql.cj.jdbc.Driver">
        </property>
        <property name="url" value="jdbc:mysql://localhost:3366/persistence">
        </property>
        <property name="username" value="root"></property>
        <property name="password" value="password"></property>
    </bean>

    <bean id="jdbcTemplate"
class="org.springframework.jdbc.core.JdbcTemplate">
        <property name="dataSource" ref="dataSource"/>
    </bean>
```

6. Start the Ignite server instance with the Spring config we just added: `examples/config/persistentstore/example-persistent-store.xml`.

7. Run the program. It will save the cache entries to our MySQL table:

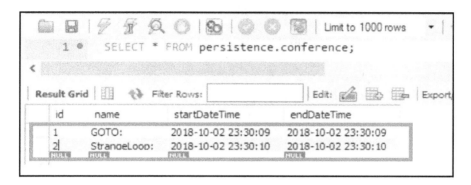

We created a persistent code to store data to a MySQL table; how about a NoSQL data store? The following section will store data to a NoSQL datastore.

Persisting data to Cassandra

We have examined Apache Ignite's write-behind with MySQL persistence. In this section, we'll persist data to a NoSQL datastore.

NoSQL data stores can be categorized into four sub-categories:

- **Key-Value pair**: DynamoDB and Redis
- **Graph DB**: Neo4j
- **Document Store**: MongoDB and Apache CouchDB
- **Column Store**: Apache Cassandra and HBase

Apache Ignite offers NoSQL integration with the document (MongoDB) and column stores (Apache Cassandra). Apache Cassandra is a peer-to-peer, distributed, high performance, linearly scalable, and fault-tolerant NoSQL open source data store. It was designed at Facebook to achieve the scalability of Amazon's DynamoDB and Google's Bigtable. Cassandra can be used to store **online transaction processing** (OLTP) as well as reporting (**OLAP**) data.

The main advantages of Cassandra are as follows:

- It was designed to scale, and supports big data scalability at the petabyte level.
- It offers linear scalability. You can add more nodes to store more data.
- There are no master-slave nodes. Peer-to-peer distributed nodes make sure that there is no single point of failure. Nodes communicate with each other, every second, using the **Gossip** protocol.
- It provides flexible schema design. You can store structured and unstructured data any time you add a new column.
- It is easy to replicate data.
- It provides automatic data partitioning.
- It also provides caching out-of-the-box. Data is first stored in memory (**memtable**). When the buffer is full, it automatically moves the data onto disk (**SStable**).
- Commits are durable, similar to Ignite's WAL. It keeps track of every commit into a log.

Before we write code to store and retrieve data from Cassandra, we need to understand the basic building blocks of Cassandra. The following are the key concepts of Cassandra:

- **Clusters**: A cluster is a collection of Cassandra nodes and contains keyspaces.
- **Keyspaces**: Keyspaces are analogous to relational databases. A keyspace is a namespace with a name and a set of attributes, such as replication strategy and replication factor. It supports two replication strategies: simple strategy and network topology strategy. It contains a set of column families.
- **Column family**: A column family is a collection of rows. Each row contains a collection of columns:
    - row 1 may contain 2 columns key → 1 value → { 'name' : 'sujoy', age: 10}
    - row 2 may contain 4 columns key →2 and value → {'name' : 'Vijay', age:30, sex:'M', married: true}
- **CQL**: **Cassandra Query Language** (**CQL**) is used to access and manipulate data.

You can download the installation media from `http://cassandra.apache.org/download/` and `untar/unzip` the media to start playing with Apache Cassandra:

1. Open a Terminal/Command Prompt.
2. Go to the `<<CASSENDRA_INSTALLATION_DIRECTORY>>/bin` folder.
3. Execute the `cassandra/cassandra.bat` file.

4. It will start Cassandra. Once the node starts, you can launch the CQL terminal to define the data models.

5. Launch `cqlsh/cqlsh.bat`.

6. It will open the `cqlsh>` prompt.

7. Type `describe keyspaces;`. It will list the existing keyspaces:

```
C:\Windows\System32\cmd.exe - cqlsh

WARNING: pyreadline dependency missing.  Install to enable
cqlsh> describe keyspaces;

system_schema    system               system_traces
system_auth      system_distributed

cqlsh>
```

8. Now create your own keyspace called `'persistence'` to verify the Cassandra persistence. Enter the `create keyspace persistence with replication = {'class': 'SimpleStrategy', 'replication_factor': 1};` CQL command:

```
C:\Windows\System32\cmd.exe - cqlsh

cqlsh> create keyspace persistence with replication = {'class':
   ... 'SimpleStrategy', 'replication_factor': 1};
```

9. It will create the new namespace. Type `describe keyspaces;` again to view our new keyspace:

```
C:\Windows\System32\cmd.exe - cqlsh

WARNING: pyreadline dependency missing.  Install to enable
cqlsh> describe keyspaces;

system_schema    system               system_traces
system_auth      system_distributed   persistence

cqlsh>
```

10. We will use this namespace to create our table:

```
C:\Windows\System32\cmd.exe - cqlsh
cqlsh>
cqlsh>
cqlsh>
cqlsh> use persistence;
cqlsh:persistence>
```

11. Create our `conference` table with `CREATE TABLE conference(id int primary key, name text, startDateTime timestamp, endDateTime timestamp);`. You must specify the primary key column.

12. It will create the table. Now view the `'persistence'` namespace by executing the following CQL: `describe persistence`:

```
C:\Windows\System32\cmd.exe - cqlsh                                                        —  □  ×
cqlsh:persistence>
cqlsh:persistence>
cqlsh:persistence> describe persistence

CREATE KEYSPACE persistence WITH replication = {'class': 'SimpleStrategy', 'replication_factor': '1'}  AND durable_writ
s = true;

CREATE TABLE persistence.conference (
    id int PRIMARY KEY,
    enddatetime timestamp,
    name text,
    startdatetime timestamp
) WITH bloom_filter_fp_chance = 0.01
    AND caching = {'keys': 'ALL', 'rows_per_partition': 'NONE'}
    AND comment = ''
    AND compaction = {'class': 'org.apache.cassandra.db.compaction.SizeTieredCompactionStrategy', 'max_threshold': '32'
'min_threshold': '4'}
    AND compression = {'chunk_length_in_kb': '64', 'class': 'org.apache.cassandra.io.compress.LZ4Compressor'}
```

Apache Cassandra, the namespace, and the table are configured. Now it's time to examine the Apache Ignite's integration with Apache Cassandra. Perform the following steps:

1. Add the following Gradle dependencies to enable Cassandra. `ignite-cassandra-store` contains the Cassandra integration classes. `cassandra-driver-core` is the datastax driver for accessing Cassandra's datastore. `ignite-cassandra-serializers` is needed for Blob persistence, where the entire object is encrypted, serialized, and stored in a Cassandra column:

```
//Cassandra
compile group: 'org.apache.ignite', name:'ignite-cassandra-store',
version: "${igniteVersion}"
```

```
        compile group: 'com.datastax.cassandra', name: 'cassandra-driver-
core',
        version: '3.0.0'
        compile group: 'org.apache.ignite', name:
        'ignite-cassandra-serializers', version: '2.6.0'
        compile group: 'commons-io', name: 'commons-io', version: '2.6'
```

2. Create a `Conference` POJO class to represent our data model. Make sure to define the default constructor. It will be invoked by the persistence settings to move data from Cassandra to POJO and POJO to Cassandra:

```
public class Conference implements Serializable {
  private static final long serialVersionUID = 1L;
  private Integer id;
  private String name;
  private Date startDateTime;
  private Date endDateTime;
  public Conference() {}
  public Conference(Integer id, String name, Date startDateTime,
  Date endDateTime) {
      super();
      this.id = id;
      this.name = name;
      this.startDateTime = startDateTime;
      this.endDateTime = endDateTime;
  }
//Getters/setters and toString
  ...
  }
```

3. Create persistence settings for the cache store factory for our `conference` table. The persistence settings must have the following attributes:
    - Keyspace and table name: `<persistence keyspace="persistence" table="conference">`
    - `<keyPersistence class='' , strategy='' , ... >` and `<valuePersistence class='' , strategy='' , ...>`
        - class (required): Java class name for the Ignite cache key

- strategy (required): One of three possible persistent strategies:
  - PRIMITIVE: Stores the key value as is by mapping it to a Cassandra table column with the corresponding type. It should only be used for simple Java types (`int`, `long`, `String`, `double`, `Date`), which can be mapped to corresponding Cassadra types.
  - BLOB: Stores the key value as a BLOB by mapping it to a Cassandra table column with the blob type. It could be used for any Java object. The conversion of a Java object to a BLOB is handled by the *serializer*, which could be specified in the `serializer` attribute.
  - POJO: Stores each field of an object as a column with the corresponding type in the Cassandra table. It provides the ability to utilize Cassandra secondary indexes for object fields.
- serializer (optional): Required for the BLOB strategy to serialize the keys/values. Here are the implementations:
  - `org.apache.ignite.cache.store.cassandra.serializer.JavaSerializer` —Java serialization
  - `org.apache.ignite.cache.store.cassandra.serializer.KryoSerializer` —uses the Kryo serialization framework
- column (optional): Specifies the column name for PRIMITIVE and BLOB strategies to store the key/value. If not specified, the column with the `key` name will be used for `keyPersistence`, and the column with the `value` name will be used for `valuePersistence`.

Working with the POJO strategy

In our example, we have a primitive integer as a `key` and the `Conference` class as `value`. In the persistence settings `.xml` file, the `keyPersistence` node represents the key of our cache. A `key` can be a concrete object, but in our case the `key` is just an integer. Therefore, we'll set the `id` as `key` in `keyPersistence`. We are using the POJO strategy, so we won't set the `column` attribute for the `valuePersistence` node. The `<field >` markup node is used to map the Java members to Cassandra columns.

1. Create a `conference-persistence-settings.xml` file and keep it in the `/src/main/resourcecs/META-INF/` folder:

```
<persistence keyspace="persistence" table="conference">
    <keyPersistence class="java.lang.Integer" strategy="PRIMITIVE" column="id"/>
    <valuePersistence class="com.persistence.cassendra.Conference" strategy="POJO">
     <field name="id" column="id"/>
     <field name="name" column="name"/>
     <field name="startDateTime" column="startdatetime"/>
     <field name="endDateTime" column="enddatetime"/>
    </valuePersistence>
  </persistence>
```

2. Create a class to configure Cassandra's data source and a cache store factory to persist the cached objects in our Cassandra datastore:

```
public class CassandraPersistencePOJOTest {
    public static void main(String[] args) throws IOException {
```

3. Configure Cassandra's `DataSource`:

```
DataSource cassandraDataSource = new DataSource();
 cassandraDataSource.setContactPoints("127.0.0.1");
 RoundRobinPolicy robinPolicy = new RoundRobinPolicy();
 cassandraDataSource.setLoadBalancingPolicy(robinPolicy);
 cassandraDataSource.setReadConsistency("ONE");
 cassandraDataSource.setWriteConsistency("ONE");
```

4. Read the persistence settings for Cassandra's key/value persistence:

```
String file = CassandraPersistencePOJOTest.class.getClassLoader()
 .getResource("META-INF//conference-persistence-settings.xml")
.getFile();
 String persistenceSettingsXml = FileUtils.readFileToString
(new File(file), "utf-8");
 KeyValuePersistenceSettings persistenceSettings = new
KeyValuePersistenceSettings(persistenceSettingsXml);
```

5. Define Cassandra's cache store factory and set the Cassandra `DataSource` and persistence settings:

```
CassandraCacheStoreFactory<Integer, Conference>
cassandraCacheStoreFactory = new CassandraCacheStoreFactory
<Integer, Conference>();
 cassandraCacheStoreFactory.setDataSource(cassandraDataSource);
cassandraCacheStoreFactory.setPersistenceSettings(persistenceSettings);
```

6. Define the cache configuration, set the `cassandraCacheStoreFactory` to `cacheStoreFactory`, and enable write-through, write-behind, and read-through:

```
CacheConfiguration<Integer, Conference> configuration =
new CacheConfiguration<>();
 configuration.setName("cassandra");
 configuration.setCacheStoreFactory(cassandraCacheStoreFactory);
 configuration.setWriteThrough(true);
 configuration.setWriteBehindEnabled(true);
 configuration.setReadThrough(true);
```

7. Set the cache configuration:

```
IgniteConfiguration cfg = new IgniteConfiguration();
 cfg.setCacheConfiguration(configuration);
```

8. Start the Ignite server with the Cassandra cache configuration:

```
Ignite ignite = Ignition.start(cfg);
 System.out.println("done");
 final IgniteCache<Integer, Conference> cache =
ignite.getOrCreateCache("cassandra");
```

9. Put a `Conference` object into the cache:

```
cache.put(1, new Conference(1, "GOTO", new Date(), new Date()));
```

10. Get the object from the cache:

```
Conference gotoConf = cache.get(1);
System.out.println("Value: " + gotoConf);
 }
}
```

11. Run the program and query the Cassandra table. The CQL is `SELECT * from conference;`:

```
C:\Windows\System32\cmd.exe - cqlsh
cqlsh:persistence>
cqlsh:persistence> SELECT * from conference;

 id | enddatetime            | name | startdatetime
----+------------------------+------+------------------------
  1 | 2018-10-21 13:01:10+0000 | GOTO | 2018-10-21 13:01:10+0000

(1 rows)
cqlsh:persistence>
```

Working with the BLOB strategy

In the BLOB strategy, we need only two columns: a column for the cache key and a column for the value object stored in the cache. The key column will contain the primitive integer and the value column will store the kyro serialized `Conference` object. The following are the steps to configure the BLOB strategy:

1. Run the following CQL to create a new table: `CREATE TABLE conference_blob(id int primary key, value blob);`.

2. Create a new persistence setting for the `conference_blob` table. Note that `keyPersistence` remains unchanged, the `valuePersistence` strategy is changed to `BLOB`, and `serializer="org.apache.ignite.cache.store.cassandra.serializer.KryoSerializer"` is set. In BLOB, the entire `Conference` object will be serialized using `KyroSerializer` and stored in the `Value` column:

```
<persistence keyspace="persistence" table="conference_blob">
 <keyPersistence class="java.lang.Integer" strategy="PRIMITIVE"
 column="id" />
 <valuePersistence class="com.persistence.cassendra.Conference"
 strategy="BLOB"
```

```
        serializer="org.apache.ignite.cache.store.cassandra.
        serializer.KryoSerializer" />
    </persistence>
```

3. Change the code to read from this new persistence file and store objects into a new cache called 'cassandra_blob':

```
public class CassandraPersistenceBLOBTest {
    public static void main(String[] args) throws IOException {
        // Configuring Cassandra's persistence
        DataSource cassandraDataSource = new DataSource();
        cassandraDataSource.setContactPoints("127.0.0.1");
        RoundRobinPolicy robinPolicy = new RoundRobinPolicy();
        cassandraDataSource.setLoadBalancingPolicy(robinPolicy);
        cassandraDataSource.setReadConsistency("ONE");
        cassandraDataSource.setWriteConsistency("ONE");

        //Read the persistence settings for Cassandra Key-Value
persistance
        String file =
CassandraPersistencePOJOTest.class.getClassLoader()
    .getResource("META-INF//conference-persistence-settings2.xml")
    .getFile();
        String persistenceSettingsXml = FileUtils.readFileToString
        (new File(file), "utf-8");
        KeyValuePersistenceSettings persistenceSettings =
        new
        KeyValuePersistenceSettings(persistenceSettingsXml);


    //Define Cassandra cache store factory, set the
    cassandra dataSource and persistence settings
    CassandraCacheStoreFactory<Integer, Conference>
cassandraCacheStoreFactory = new
CassandraCacheStoreFactory<Integer, Conference>();
        cassandraCacheStoreFactory.setDataSource(cassandraDataSource);
        cassandraCacheStoreFactory.setPersistenceSettings
        (persistenceSettings);

    //Define the cache configuration, set the
    cassandraCacheStoreFactory as cacheStoreFactory , enable
    //write through, write behind and read through
    CacheConfiguration<Integer, Conference> configuration =
    new CacheConfiguration<>();
    configuration.setName("cassandra_blob");
    configuration.setCacheStoreFactory(cassandraCacheStoreFactory);
    configuration.setWriteThrough(true);
    configuration.setWriteBehindEnabled(true);
```

```
configuration.setReadThrough(true);

// Sets the cache configuration
IgniteConfiguration cfg = new IgniteConfiguration();
cfg.setCacheConfiguration(configuration);

// Starting Ignite
Ignite ignite = Ignition.start(cfg);
System.out.println("done");

final IgniteCache<Integer, Conference> cache =
ignite.getOrCreateCache("cassandra_blob");

// Put some data
cache.put(3, new Conference(3, "Linux", new Date(), new Date()));

// Get it
Conference linuxConf = cache.get(3);
System.out.println("Value: " + linuxConf );
}
}
```

4. Run the new program. It will store data in our new table. The following CQL shows the serialized object in the `conference_blob` table. Check that the value column contains the serialized object:

Processing transactions

Apache Ignite supports atomic and ACID-compliant transactional cache operations. In ACID-compliant mode, you can perform more than one cache operation (same key, different key, different cache) together. Either all of these operations will be committed or none of them will be; there won't be any partial execution of operations.

Suppose you want to update two values:

```
cache.put(2, value1);
cache.put(3, value2);
```

If the preceding two operations are wrapped inside a transaction and the second update fails, then the first update will be rolled back.

Ignite supports two modes for cache operations: atomic and transactional. In atomic mode, each cache operation is committed individually. For example, if `cache.put(3, value2)` fails, the first update, `cache.put(2, value1)`, will still be committed.

Atomic mode performs better than transactional mode because it doesn't need to keep track of the locks and two-phase commits.

Exploring transactional mode

The `IgniteTransactions` interface defines the APIs to enable ACID-compliant semantics when working with caches. We can start a transaction by calling the `tx*****(...)` methods on the `IgniteTransactions` interface and work with one cache or across multiple caches.

Ignite transactions work on caches where the atomicity mode is `CacheAtomicityMode.TRANSACTIONAL`. By default, the atomicity mode is set to `CacheAtomicityMode.ATOMIC`.

The following example explores transactional behavior:

1. Create a class called `TransactionHelloWorld`:

```
public class TransactionHelloWorld {
    private static final String MY_ATOMIC_CACHE = "myAtomicCache";
    private static final String MY_TRANSACTIONAL_CACHE =
    "myTransactionalCache";
    public static void main(String[] args) {
```

2. Create a transactional cache config by setting the atomicity mode to `CacheAtomicityMode.TRANSACTIONAL`:

```
CacheConfiguration<Long, String> myTransactionalCacheConfig = new
CacheConfiguration<Long, String>();
    myTransactionalCacheConfig.setName(MY_TRANSACTIONAL_CACHE);
    myTransactionalCacheConfig.setAtomicityMode
    (CacheAtomicityMode.TRANSACTIONAL);
```

3. Create an atomic cache config by setting the atomicity mode
   to `CacheAtomicityMode.ATOMIC`:

   ```
   CacheConfiguration<Long, String> myAtomicCacheConfig =
   new CacheConfiguration<Long, String>();
    myAtomicCacheConfig.setName(MY_ATOMIC_CACHE);
    myAtomicCacheConfig.setAtomicityMode(CacheAtomicityMode.ATOMIC);
   ```

4. Set both the cache configurations:

   ```
   IgniteConfiguration cfg = new IgniteConfiguration();
   cfg.setCacheConfiguration(myTransactionalCacheConfig,
   myAtomicCacheConfig);
   ```

5. Start Ignite:

   ```
   Ignite ignite = Ignition.start(cfg);
   ```

6. Get the transactional cache:

   ```
   IgniteCache<Long, String> txCache =
   ignite.getOrCreateCache(MY_TRANSACTIONAL_CACHE);
   ```

7. Get the atomic cache:

   ```
   IgniteCache<Long, String> atomicCache =
   ignite.getOrCreateCache(MY_ATOMIC_CACHE);
   ```

8. Get an instance of `IgniteTransactions` and start a transaction with a default
   isolation, concurrency, timeout, and invalidation policy:

   ```
   IgniteTransactions transactions = ignite.transactions();
   Transaction tx = transactions.txStart();
   ```

9. Within the `try` block, first put two values in the transactional cache and then in
   the atomic cache, immediately throw a runtime exception. In the cache block,
   catch the runtime exception and roll back the on-going transaction. It will roll
   back the `txCache` operations wrapped inside the transaction:

   ```
   try {
       txCache.put(21, "Value1");
       txCache.put(31, "Value2");

       atomicCache.put(21, "Value1");
       atomicCache.put(31, "Value2");
       throw new RuntimeException("Failing the tx");
   } catch (Exception e) {
       System.out.println("rolling back transaction");
   ```

```
        tx.rollback();
    } finally {
        tx.close();
    }
```

10. Now look up the keys in the transactional cache as well as in the atomic cache. The transactional cache should not return any values, as the `tx` was rolled back:

```
System.out.println("key 2 in Tx Cache = "
+ txCache.get(21));
System.out.println("key 3 in Tx Cache = "
+ txCache.get(31));
```

11. The atomic cache should not have any effect on `tx.rollback()`. It should return these values:

```
System.out.println("key 2 in Atomic Cache = "
+ atomicCache.get(21));
System.out.println("key 3 in Atomic Cache = "
+ atomicCache.get(31));
    }
}
```

12. When we run the program, it prints the following output:

```
TransactionHelloWorld [Java Application] C:\Sujoy\Java\jdk1.8.0_91\bin\javaw.exe (Nov 26, 2018,
[21:11:17]   ^-- Node [id=627C8469-F88A-41EE-AA3B-9A278A7317CC, cluster
[21:11:17]   ^-- Baseline [id=0, size=2, online=2, offline=0]
[21:11:17] Data Regions Configured:
[21:11:17]   ^-- default [initSize=256.0 MiB, maxSize=6.4 GiB, persiste
rolling back transaction
key 2 in Tx Cache = null
key 3 in Tx Cache = null
key 2 in Atomic Cache = Value1
key 3 in Atomic Cache = Value2
```

Transaction concurrency and isolation

Transaction concurrency and isolation are two important aspects of Ignite transactions. In this section, we'll look at concurrency mode and isolation levels.

Concurrency mode determines when to acquire the lock on the nodes. Apache Ignite supports two concurrency modes for transactions: `TransactionConcurrency.OPTIMISTIC` and `TransactionConcurrency.PESSIMISTIC`.

In `OPTIMISTIC` mode, the lock is acquired at the transaction preparation phase. The transaction coordinator sends a prepare message to the primary node. The primary node acquires the lock and sends a prepare message to all other nodes that are participating in the transaction; participating nodes try to acquire locks. Once all participating nodes are done with acquiring locks, they send a reply to the primary node, the transaction is committed, and the locks are released.

In `PESSIMISTIC` mode, the lock is acquired at the time of data access on all cache operations, both read and write.

The transaction isolation level determines how concurrent transactions will be isolated from one another and handle operations on the same keys. Apache Ignite supports three isolation levels

- `TransactionIsolation.READ_COMMITTED`: Ongoing transactions always read data from the global store or cache. Suppose a transaction needs to read a value more than once: it may get different values between the reads, since the cache may be updated concurrently by other threads.
- `TransactionIsolation.REPEATABLE_READ`: If a value was read once within a transaction, then all consecutive reads will provide the same in-transaction value.
- `TransactionIsolation.SERIALIZABLE`: All transactions occur in a completely isolated fashion, as if all transactions in the system had executed serially, one after the other.

A transaction can be created with the concurrency mode and isolation level as follows:

```
try (Transaction tx =
  ignite.transactions().txStart(TransactionConcurrency.PESSIMISTIC,
TransactionIsolation.REPEATABLE_READ)){

}
```

Exploring distributed data structures

One of the coolest Ignite features is its distributed data structures. You can use a data structure of your choice in a distributed fashion. We use distributed key/value pair caches, database tables, or complex serialization techniques to share objects between the JVMs/applications. Ignite's distributed data structure allows us to share data structure beyond heap, between the JVMs

Ignite supports the following distributed data structures.

CountDownLatch

Java 5 introduced the `java.util.concurrent` package for concurrent programming. It contains many useful utility classes, such as the `CountDownLatch` class for synchronizing threads within a JVM. Apache Ignite's `IgniteCountDownLatch` synchronizes threads across the cluster nodes.

You can create a `IgniteCountDownLatch` using the following syntax: `IgniteCountDownLatch latch = ignite.countDownLatch(name, cnt, autoDel, create);`

The `countDownLatch` method accepts the following arguments:

- `name`: The name of the latch.
- `cnt`: The count for new latch creation. If the `create` flag is `false` (it means you want to fetch an existing), then this value is ignored.
- `autoDel`: If this flag is `true`, then the latch will be deleted from cache when its count reaches zero.
- `create`: If this flag is `true`, the latch will be created if does not exist.

This method throws `IgniteException` if the latch could not be created or fetched.

In this section, we'll create a countdown latch with a permit of 10 and spawn 10 distributed worker threads using Ignite's `ExecutorService`. Each worker thread will countdown the latch. The main program will wait for all threads to complete by invoking the `latch.await()` method. Once all threads are done processing, synchronization is complete, and the main thread completes.

The following are the steps to execute the code:

1. Create a program called `CountDownLatchTest` and start an Ignite server instance:

```
public class CountDownLatchTest {
  public static void main(String[] args) {
    IgniteConfiguration cfg = new IgniteConfiguration();
    cfg.setClientMode(false);
    cfg.setPeerClassLoadingEnabled(true);
    Ignite ignite = Ignition.start(cfg);
```

2. Create a distributed countdown latch with the name `'myLatch'`, the count `10`, auto-delete set to `false`, and create set to `true`:

```
final IgniteCountDownLatch latch = ignite.countDownLatch
("myLatch", 10, false, true);
```

3. Get an instance of Ignite's `ExecutorService`:

```
ExecutorService executorService = ignite.executorService();
```

4. Submit 10 worker jobs to the `executorService`. Each worker thread will countdown the latch value to indicate that the processing is done. In the real world, we have to put `latch.countDown()` inside a try-finally block so that the latch's `countDown` method is invoked even if we get any exception in worker processing. If any worker thread fails to countdown the latch, the main program will wait forever. The worker thread also prints the latch value:

```
IntStream.range(1, 11).forEach(i -> executorService.execute
(new Runnable() {
    @Override
    public void run() {
        System.out.println(String.format("Executing using
         ExecutorService - Index %s", i));
        int value = latch.countDown();
        System.out.println("latch value now " + value);
    }
}));
```

5. Now wait for all worker threads to complete by calling the `latch.await()` method:

```
System.out.println("Waiting for all threads to to complete");
latch.await();
System.out.println("Processing completed");
```

6. Now launch two Ignite servers and then run the program.

7. The `ExecutorService` will distribute the loads. When I ran the program, I got the following output. This server's nodes processed four worker threads. You can see that the latch value is 0. This means all threads are done:

```
[21:17:29] Topology snapshot [ver=2, servers=2, clients=0, CPUs=8, off
[21:17:29]    ^-- Node  id=D41B26E3-8FA2-4F09-918E-CA48567ECF25  cluste
[21:17:29] Data Regions configured:
[21:17:29]    ^-- default [initSize=256.0 MiB, maxSize=6.4 GiB, persist
Executing using ExecutorService - Index 4
Executing using ExecutorService - Index 10
Executing using ExecutorService - Index 7
Executing using ExecutorService - Index 1
latch value now 3
latch value now 2
latch value now 1
latch value now 0
```

8. Another server instance processed three worker threads:

```
[21:17:29] Topology snapshot [ver=2, servers=2, clients=0, CPUs=8,
[21:17:29]    ^-- Node  id=D1D8EF66-829D-4181-81CC-34F63979CF9E  clu
[21:17:29] Data Regions configured:
[21:17:29]    ^-- default [initSize=256.0 MiB, maxSize=6.4 GiB, pers
Executing using ExecutorService - Index 5
Executing using ExecutorService - Index 2
Executing using ExecutorService - Index 8
latch value now 6
latch value now 5
latch value now 4
```

9. The main program node, being a server node, processed the remaining three workers. The main thread waited for all threads to complete. Once the countdown permit became 0, `latch.await()` stopped waiting. Note that it printed Waiting for all thread... and then Processing completed:

```
CountDownLatchTest [Java Application] C:\Sujoy\Java\jdk1.8.0_91\bin\javaw.exe (Nov 26, 2018, 9:17:07 PM)
[21:17:30]
[21:17:30] Ignite node started OK (id=f9bdd179)
[21:17:30] Topology snapshot [ver=3, servers=3, clients=0, CPUs=8, offheap=19.0GB, heap=9
[21:17:30]   ^-- Node [id=F9BDD179-3482-4EFE-BD9E-DE2494F65E20, clusterState=ACTIVE]
[21:17:30] Data Regions Configured:
[21:17:30]   ^-- default [initSize=256.0 MiB, maxSize=6.4 GiB, persistenceEnabled=false]
Executing using ExecutorService - Index 3
Executing using ExecutorService - Index 6
Executing using ExecutorService - Index 9
Waiting for all threads to to complete
latch value now 9
latch value now 8
latch value now 7
Processing completed
```

Now we know how to synchronize the distributed threads across cluster
using `IgniteCountDownLatch`.

Semaphore

Semaphore is another way of synchronizing threads for solving the `producer-consumer`
problem or guarding a critical section. Ignite's distributed semaphore data structure
is `IgniteSemaphore`.

We can define a semaphore using the following syntax:

```
IgniteSemaphore semaphore = ignite.semaphore(
"mySemaphore", // semaphore name.
20, // permits.
true, // Release acquired permits if node, that owned them, left topology.
true // Create if it doesn't exist.
);
```

`IgniteSemaphore` has two important methods:

- `acquire()` and other variants, such as `acquire(int permits)`,
  `tryAcquire(int permits)`, and `acquireUninterruptibly()`. Acquires a
  permit, or a given number of permits for `acquire(int permits)`
  and `tryAcquire(int permits)`, from this semaphore, **blocking until one is
  available**.
- `release()`/`release(int permits)` Releases a permit, or a given number of
  permits, returning it/them to the semaphore.

In this section, we'll create a producer thread and a consumer thread. The producer will wait until the consumer finishes consumption. This `producer-consumer` synchronization is done through a distributed `IgniteSemaphore` object.

The following are the steps to execute the program:

1. Create a program called `SemaphoreTest` and start an Ignite server instance:

```
public class SemaphoreTest {
  private static final int MAX_RUN = 5;
  private static final String MY_SEMAPHORE = "mySemaphore";

  public static void main(String[] args) {
      IgniteConfiguration cfg = new IgniteConfiguration();
      cfg.setClientMode(true);
      cfg.setPeerClassLoadingEnabled(true);
      Ignite ignite = Ignition.start(cfg);
```

2. Create a distributed semaphore with only one permit:

```
final IgniteSemaphore semaphore = ignite.semaphore
(MY_SEMAPHORE, 1, true, true);
```

3. Create a `Producer` class. In the constructor, get the distributed semaphore object using its name. In the `run` method, acquire a semaphore permit. This call is a blocking call if no permit is available. The producer waits for the permit until the consumer releases it. The thread stops running after five iterations:

```
class Producer implements Runnable {
  private IgniteSemaphore semaphore;
  private int maxRun = 0;

  Producer(String name, int max) {
      semaphore = Ignition.ignite().semaphore(name, 0, true, false);
      this.maxRun = max;
  }
  @Override
  public void run() {
      int run = 0;
      while (true) {
          if (run != 0) {
              System.out.println("Waiting to produce ");
          }
          semaphore.acquire();
        run++;
          System.out.println("Produced "+run+" at "+
          SemaphoreTest.getCurrentTimeStamp());
```

```
        if (run >= maxRun) {
            System.out.println("Stopping production after "
            + run + " runs");
            break;
        }
        try {
            Thread.sleep(100);
        } catch (InterruptedException e) {
            e.printStackTrace();
        }
    }
  }
}
```

4. Create a `consumer` class. In the constructor, get the distributed semaphore object using its name. In the `run` method, release a semaphore permit:

```
class Consumer implements Runnable {
 private IgniteSemaphore semaphore;
 private int maxRun = 0;

 Consumer(String name, int max) {
     semaphore = Ignition.ignite().semaphore(name, 0,
     true, false);
     this.maxRun = max;
 }
@Override public void run() {
   int run = 0;
   while (true) {
       System.out.println("Waiting to consume");
       semaphore.release();
       run++;
       System.out.println("Consumed "+run+" at "
       + SemaphoreTest.getCurrentTimeStamp());
       if (run >= maxRun) {
           System.out.println("Stopping consumption after " + run
           + " runs");
            break;
       }
       try {
           Thread.sleep(100);
       } catch (InterruptedException e) {
           e.printStackTrace();
       }
    }
  }
}
```

5. Create `ExecutorService` in the main method and submit two jobs to execute in the remote cluster nodes:

```
System.out.println("available permits = "
+ semaphore.availablePermits());
 ExecutorService executorService = ignite.executorService();
 executorService.submit(new Consumer(MY_SEMAPHORE, MAX_RUN));
 executorService.submit(new Producer(MY_SEMAPHORE, MAX_RUN));
```

6. Launch two Ignite server nodes and run the program. If the `Producer` worker starts first, you can see the following output; the producer will wait for the consumer to complete, then produce the next object:

```
Produced  1 at 21:31:12.284       Waiting to consume
Waiting to produce                Consumed 1 at 21:31:12.300
Produced  2 at 21:31:12.389       Waiting to consume
Waiting to produce                Consumed 2 at 21:31:12.409
Produced  3 at 21:31:12.494       Waiting to consume
Waiting to produce                Consumed 3 at 21:31:12.519
Produced  4 at 21:31:12.599       Waiting to consume
Waiting to produce                Consumed 4 at 21:31:12.626
Produced  5 at 21:31:12.704       Waiting to consume
Stopping production after 5 runs  Consumed 5 at 21:31:12.734
                                  Stopping consumption after 5 runs
```

We have learned how to solve the producer-consumer issue in a distributed cluster. In the Lock section, we'll learn about using distributed locks to guard a critical section.

ID generator

An ID generator should sequentially generate unique IDs across the cluster. In all our examples, we created hardcoded IDs for cache keys or used a database to generate a unique ID. Sequential ID generation is an important task in distributed computing. Ignite provides the `IgniteCacheAtomicSequence` interface to generate an atomic sequence.

The following code snippet creates an `IgniteCacheAtomicSequence` interface:

```
IgniteAtomicSequence seq = ignite.atomicSequence(
  "name", // name of sequence generate
  0, // Initial value for sequence.
  true // Create if it does not exist.
);
```

In the real world, the initial value can be read from a persistent store and set in `IgniteCacheAtomicSequence`.

In this section, we'll create a sequence generator and send it across the cluster to generate IDs. The following are the requisite steps:

1. Create a program called `IdGeneratorTest` and start an Ignite instance:

```
public class IdGeneratorTest {
 public static void main(String[] args) {
    IgniteConfiguration cfg = new IgniteConfiguration();
    cfg.setClientMode(true);
    cfg.setPeerClassLoadingEnabled(true);
    Ignite ignite = Ignition.start(cfg);
```

2. Create an instance of the `IgniteAtomicSequence` generator with the initial value 0:

```
IgniteAtomicSequence seq = ignite.atomicSequence("mySeq",
0, true);
```

3. Create a semaphore with permit set to 7. The main thread will wait for worker threads to finish using this semaphore:

```
IgniteSemaphore semaphore = ignite.semaphore("mySync", 7,
true, true);
```

4. Create an `ExecutorService` instance for worker thread distribution:

```
ExecutorService executorService = ignite.executorService();
```

5. Submit seven worker jobs. In the `run` method, increment the `seq` number and release a semaphore permit for the main thread:

```
IntStream.range(1, 8).forEach(i -> executorService.execute
(new Runnable() {
 @Override
 public void run() {
    System.out.println(String.format("Thread Index %s -
    Sequence id is %s", i, seq.incrementAndGet()));
    semaphore.release();
    try {
        Thread.sleep(300);
    } catch (InterruptedException e) {e.printStackTrace();}
    }
}));
```

6. In the main thread, wait for the seven permits. Once all seven permits are released, print that the worker threads are done:

```
semaphore.acquire(7);
System.out.println("Processing done");
```

7. Launch two Ignite servers and run this program. It will print unique sequence IDs in remote nodes. The following is an example output:

```
[21:36:11]    ^-- Node [id=06B05B8E-34E9-4046-   [21:36:11] Topology snapshot [ver=5, servers=2,
[21:36:11] Data Regions Configured:               [21:36:11]    ^-- Node [id=9584A3F5-D105-4D09-AF7D
[21:36:11]    ^-- default [initSize=256.0 MiB     [21:36:11] Data Regions Configured:
Thread Index 5 - Sequence id is 2001              [21:36:11]    ^-- default [initSize=256.0 MiB, max
Thread Index 2 - Sequence id is 2002             Thread Index 4 - Sequence id is 1001
                                                 Thread Index 7 - Sequence id is 1002
[21:36:12] Ignite node started OK (id=1003       Thread Index 1 - Sequence id is 1003
[21:36:12] Topology snapshot [ver=5, server
[21:36:12]    -- Node [id=10D920E9-28 D-4535-9B22-0506F0B9F481, clusterState=ACTIVE]
Thread Index 3 - Sequence id is 1
Thread Index 6 - Sequence id is 2
Processing done
```

We can configure our atomic sequencer using `AtomicConfiguration`.

Queue and Set

Apache Ignite supports the following two distributed data structures for storing objects—Queue and Set. Queue and Set can be deployed in two modes:

- **Collocated**: All elements of the queue and set reside on the same cluster node, which is useful for small collections.
- **Non-collocated**: Useful for large collections. Elements of queue and set are equally distributed across the cluster. By default, all collections are non-collocated.

The `CollectionConfiguration` class provides the APIs to configure the collections (Set and Queue).

We can define a distributed `Set` as follows:

```
IgniteSet<T> set = ignite.set(
  "$name", // Set name.
  new CollectionConfiguration() // Collection configuration.
);
```

The queue can be defined as follows:

```
IgniteQueue<T> queue = ignite.queue(
 "$name", // Queue name.
 0, // Queue capacity. 0 for unbounded queue.
 new CollectionConfiguration() // Collection configuration.
);
```

We'll create two distributed collections: a set and a queue. Three worker threads will populate them and a printer thread will print the collection elements. We'll populate duplicate elements from different threads to verify the Set's behavior. The following are the steps to execute the code:

1. Create a `Publisher` class to populate the collections. The class takes four arguments:
   - `latchName`: Fetches a distributed latch and counts it down when the thread finishes execution. The latch is required to synchronize `Publisher` and `Printer`. The `Printer` class waits for all publishers to finish.
   - `setName`: Fetches the distributed set and populates it.
   - `queueName`: Fetches the distributed queue and populates it.
   - `elements`: Integer elements to add to our set and queue.

   The `run` method loops through the elements and adds them to the set and queue. After each `add` operation, it waits for a second and finally counts down the latch to indicate that the collection processing is done:

```
class Publisher implements Runnable{
 private final List<Integer> elements;
 private final IgniteSet<Integer> distributedSet;
 private final IgniteQueue<Integer> distributedQueue;
 private final IgniteCountDownLatch latch;

 Publisher(String latchName, String setName, String queueName,
Integer...elements
     ){
       this.elements = Arrays.asList(elements);
       this.distributedSet= Ignition.ignite().set(setName, null);
       this.distributedQueue = Ignition.ignite().queue(queueName, 0,
null);
       this.latch = Ignition.ignite().countDownLatch(latchName, 0,
false, false);
     }
     @Override
      public void run() {
```

```
        elements.forEach(i->{
            distributedSet.add(i);
            distributedQueue.add(i);
            System.out.println(String.format("Adding %s", i));
            try {
                Thread.sleep(1000);
            } catch (InterruptedException e) {e.printStackTrace();}
        });
         latch.countDown();
    }


}
```

2. Create a `Printer` class. This class waits for the latch to synchronize with the publishers. When all elements are published, it starts looping through the collections. Similar to `Publisher`, this class also takes a queue, set, and latch name:

```
class Printer implements Runnable{
 private final IgniteSet<Integer> distributedSet;
 private final IgniteQueue<Integer> distributedQueue;
 private final IgniteCountDownLatch latch;

 Printer(String latchName, String setName, String queueName ){
     this.distributedSet= Ignition.ignite().set(setName, null);
     this.distributedQueue = Ignition.ignite().queue(queueName, 0,
null);
     this.latch = Ignition.ignite().countDownLatch(latchName, 0,
false, false);
 }
 @Override
 public void run() {
     System.out.println("Wait for other threads to finish");
     latch.await();

     System.out.println("Start printing");
     for(Integer i : distributedSet) {
         System.out.println("Object found in Set - >" + i);
     }

     for(Integer i : distributedQueue) {
         System.out.println("Object found in Queue - >" + i);
     }
 }
 }
```

3. Create a class to define the collections:

```
public class QueueAndSetTest {

private static final String QUEUE_NAME = "myQueue";
 private static final String SET_NAME = "mySet";
 private static final String LATCH_NAME = "syncLatch";

public static void main(String[] args) throws InterruptedException {
 IgniteConfiguration cfg = new IgniteConfiguration();
 cfg.setClientMode(true);
 cfg.setPeerClassLoadingEnabled(true);
 Ignite ignite = Ignition.start(cfg);
```

4. Create a collection configuration:

```
CollectionConfiguration collectionConfig = new
CollectionConfiguration();
 collectionConfig.setCollocated(false);
```

5. Define the distributed collections and a latch with three permits, as we will create three publisher instances:

```
IgniteQueue<Integer> distributedQueue =ignite.queue(QUEUE_NAME, 0,
 collectionConfig);
IgniteSet<Integer> distributedSet = ignite.set(SET_NAME,
collectionConfig);
IgniteCountDownLatch latch = ignite.countDownLatch(LATCH_NAME, 3,
false, true);
```

6. Create an `ExecutorService`:

```
ExecutorService executorService = ignite.executorService();
```

7. Submit a `Printer` task. The printer thread will wait until the publishers are done publishing:

```
executorService.submit(new Printer(LATCH_NAME, SET_NAME,
QUEUE_NAME));
```

8. Submit three worker threads for populating the collections (note that the following three numbers are duplicates: 2, 3, and 55). The set should print them only once, but the queue will print them twice:

```
executorService.submit(new Publisher(LATCH_NAME, SET_NAME,
QUEUE_NAME, 1,2,3));
 executorService.submit(new Publisher(LATCH_NAME, SET_NAME,
QUEUE_NAME,
```

```
        100,2,55));
        executorService.submit(new Publisher(LATCH_NAME, SET_NAME,
QUEUE_NAME, 1000,
        5000, 55, 3));

        executorService.awaitTermination(10000, TimeUnit.MILLISECONDS);
        System.out.println("Processing done");
```

9. Launch two server nodes and run the program. It will print the similar output. Note that three threads are putting objects in our collections. The set prints seven elements with no duplicates, and the queue prints 10 elements (2, 3, and 5)twice:

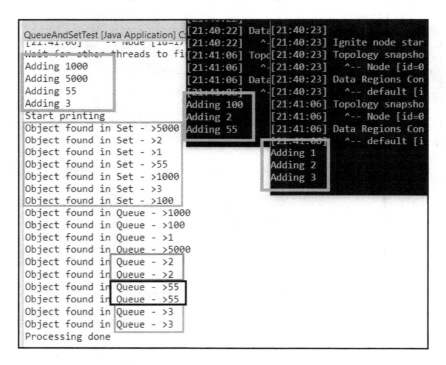

Atomic types

Ignite supports distributed atomic types, similar to Java's java.util.concurrent.atomic package, to carry out thread-safe operations on a single variable. As of version 2.6, Ignite supports four atomic types: long, reference, stamped, and sequence. We have already covered IgniteAtomicSequence in the *ID generator* section. Here, we'll take a look at the other three types.

IgniteAtomicLong

The `IgniteAtomicLong` interface provides a long variable that can be read and written atomically, and that also supports advanced atomic operations.

We can create a long value as follows:

```
IgniteAtomicLong atomicLong = ignite.atomicLong("myLong", // Atomic long
name.
 0, // Initial value.
 true // Create if it does not exist.
 );
```

All operations are atomic in nature. You can change a value as follows:

```
System.out.println("The new value is - "+atomicLong.addAndGet(2));
```

The output will look like this:

```
<terminated> AtomicTest [Java Application] C:\Sujoy\Java\jdk1.8.0_91\bin\javaw.exe (Nov 26,
[21:46:45] Data Regions Configured:
[21:46:45]    ^-- default [initSize=256.0 MiB, maxSize=6.4 GiB, persis
The new value is - 2
```

IgniteAtomicReference

The `IgniteAtomicReference` interface provides an object reference variable that can be read and written atomically.

We can define a reference with an initial value as follows:

```
IgniteAtomicReference<String> ref = ignite.atomicReference("myRef", //
atomic Reference name.
 "myValue", // Initial value for atomic reference.
 true // Create if it does not exist.
 );
```

We defined a string reference, but you can define any type of your choice. One important method of `IgniteAtomicReference` is `compareAndSet(T expVal, T newVal)`. This method conditionally sets the new value if `expVal` is equal to the current value. This behavior is similar to optimistic locking: when you update a value, you must have the most recent object. If anyone updated it after you read the value, then you can't change the value.

The following example demonstrates that behavior. We create the object with `myValue`, now trying to update the value but passing old value as `notMyValue`; hence, the existing value and my `expValue` won't match:

```
System.out.println("did it update? " + ref.compareAndSet("notMyValue", "new
Value")
 + " , the ref value is -" + ref.get());
```

Here, we have `expValue="myValue"`, which is the current reference value. Hence, the reference value will be changed to `"new Value"`:

```
System.out.println("did it update? " + ref.compareAndSet("myValue", "new
Value") + " , the ref value is -"  + ref.get());
```

Here is the output:

```
<terminated> AtomicTest [Java Application] C:\Sujov\Java\jdk1.8.0_91\bin
did it update? false , the ref value is -myValue
did it update? true , the ref value is -new Value
```

IgniteAtomicStamped

The `IgniteAtomicStamped` interface provides a rich API for working with distributed atomic stamped values. It is different from `IgniteAtomicReference`, as `IgniteAtomicStamped` keeps both an object reference and a stamp internally. The reference and stamp can both be changed using a single atomic operation.

Atomic stamped can be defined as follows:

```
IgniteAtomicStamped<String, Integer> stamp = ignite.atomicStamped("myStamp"
, //atomic stamped name
 "my init value", //initial value
  0, //initial stamp
  true // create if doesn't exist
);
```

Similar to atomic reference, stamped has the `compareAndSet(T expVal, T newVal, S expStamp, S newStamp)` method to conditionally set the new value and new stamp. It will be set if `expVal` and `expStamp` are equal to the current value and current stamp, respectively.

Run the following code to verify the `compareAndSet` behavior:

```
IgniteAtomicStamped<String, Integer> stamp =
ignite.atomicStamped("myStamp", "my init value", 0, true);
 System.out.println(stamp.get());
 stamp.set("new value", 1);
 System.out.println(stamp.get());
 System.out.println("did it update? " +stamp.compareAndSet("value", "2nd
update", 1, 2)+" , value is ="+ stamp.get());
 System.out.println("did it update? " +stamp.compareAndSet("new value",
"2nd update", 1, 2)+" , value is ="+ stamp.get());
```

The output will look like this:

```
<terminated> AtomicTest [Java Application] C:\Sujoy\Java\jdk1.8.0_91\bin\javaw.exe (Nov 26,

IgniteBiTuple [val1=my init value, val2=0]
IgniteBiTuple [val1=new value, val2=1]
did it update? false , value is =IgniteBiTuple [val1=new value, val2=1]
did it update? true , value is =IgniteBiTuple [val1=2nd update, val2=2]
[21:46:45] Ignite node stopped OK [uptime=00:00:00.222]
```

Summary

This chapter covered the art of building an ACID-compliant high performance, scalable, and highly available system. We learned about data persistence and how to persist data to a commonly-used RDBMS and NoSQL datastore, such as MySQL and Cassandra. We explored read and write operations through caching.

We examined the nitty-gritty details of using a transactional cache operation to maintain data integration and consistency.

We explained data synchronization using semaphore, countdown latch, and Ignite's distributed data structure. `Chapter 7`, *Deploying to Production*, will concentrate on fine-tuning your application, securing nodes using SSL, white- and blacklisting objects, calculating the memory footprint, benchmarking, and performance tuning.

7
Deploying To Production

Once the feature development process is complete, we prepare to deploy the application to production. This involves configuration changes, automation, security changes, performance benchmarking, and more. Let's get down to the nitty-gritty of fine-tuning our Apache Ignite application for production deployment. The following topics will be covered:

- Durable Memory Model
- Metrics
- Securing the nodes
- Performance turning
- Deployment

Apache Ignite is a RAM-intensive framework. We must understand the memory utilization of our application before doing the capacity planning, such as how many nodes do we need? How much memory should be allocated to a node? The following section will explain the memory model of Apache Ignite and how can we configure it to get the optimal result.

Understanding the memory model

Apache Ignite has a durable memory architecture for storing and accessing data and indexes. The memory architecture for in-memory and on-disk storage for native persistence is the same. The available memory is split into multiple pages (you can configure the page size) and are stored in off-heap (outside the Java heap) and on disk.

The durable memory can have multiple data regions and each data region can be configured separately to set the size, eviction policies, persistent flag and many other attributes. The following diagram depicts the durable memory architecture:

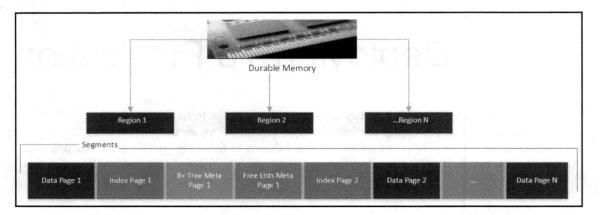

The basic components are as follows:

- **Data regions**: By default, Apache Ignite creates a single data region which can take upto 20% of available RAM. We can configure the durable memory size using the `DataStorageConfiguration` API. The following code snippet configures our durable memory to use 6 GB RAM, enables metrics, sets the page size of 2 KB (the default page size is 4 KB and you can set the page size value as minimum 1 KB and max 16 KB and the value should be power of 2—such as 1, 2, 4, 8 and 16), sets the minimum and maximum system region size, and finally sets two data region configs—`soccerRegion` and `hockeyRegion` (each region can be configured separately):

```
IgniteConfiguration cfg = new IgniteConfiguration();

DataStorageConfiguration storageCfg = new
DataStorageConfiguration();
// set max size 6GB.
storageCfg.getDefaultDataRegionConfiguration().setMaxSize(6L * 1024
* 1024 * 1024);
storageCfg.setMetricsEnabled(true);
storageCfg.setPageSize(2 * 1024);
storageCfg.setSystemRegionInitialSize(50 * 1024 * 1024);
storageCfg.setSystemRegionMaxSize(100 * 1024 * 1024) ;
storageCfg.setDataRegionConfigurations(soccerRegion, hockeyRegion);
cfg.setDataStorageConfiguration(storageCfg);

Ignition.start(cfg);
```

- **Memory segments**: A memory segment is a continuous array of physical memory bytes allocated by the OS, and each array element is a page of fixed size defined in `DataStorageConfiguration`. There four types of page—data, index, B+ tree, and free lists.
- **Data pages**: A data page holds multiple key/value pairs. When a new entry is added to the page, Ignite checks for the best page to store the key/value pair. If the entry size exceeds the page size, it spans more than one data page. Each data page is divided into four parts—a header for page metadata, entries are stored right-to-left, the offsets (pointers to the entries inside a page) are stored left-to-right, and the middle of the page is kept free to let the offset and data (key/value) grow:

Header	Off 1	Off 2	....	....	Data 2(key + value)	Data 1(key + value)

- **Index pages**: Ignite keeps a dedicated B+ tree for each SQL index and cache keys. An index page stores the information to locate a value in data page, the offset value of data page, and links to other index pages to retrieve indexed values quickly.
- **B+ tree meta-pages**: These store the root of a specific B+ tree and its layers for efficient execution of range queries. The B+ tree data structure is used for efficient data retrieval.
- **Free lists meta-pages**: This is a doubly linked list data structure and stores references to free page groups. Index and data page groups are stored separately. Each group contains references to memory pages of approximately equal free space.

The following section will explain the internal workflow of durable memory management—how Ignite manages cache operations.

Retrieving a value

Suppose you have configured `playerCache` to be created in the `soccerRegion` data region. When you try to retrieve a player's details from the cache, internally the following steps are executed:

1. You call `playerCache .get(playerId);`.
2. Ignite finds the data region associated with `playerCache`, which is the `soccerRegion` region. If you don't configure any data regions for your cache, Ignite uses the default data region to store the cache entries.
3. Once the data region is found, it needs to find the page where the `player` entry is stored. Ignite looks up the meta-pages in `"soccerRegion"` to find the root of the B+ tree associated with`"playerCache"`. The B+ tree stores the indexes of`"playerCache"` using the `hashcode` of `"playerId"` (long value for this example but could be an object as well).
4. Next, Ignite calculates the `hashcode` of the `"playerId"` and looks up the B+ tree to find the index page associated with the `hashcode`.
5. If no index page is found, that means the `"playerId"` wasn't put in the `"playerCache"` and a `null` value is returned to the caller; the process ends here.
6. Otherwise, Ignite reads the index page and retrieves data page information and the page offset for `"playerId"`.
7. It locates the data page (in RAM or on disk) and retrieves the `"player"` from the page offset.

This section explained the internal execution flow of data retrieval process. The following section will talk about the internals of storing an entry.

Storing an entry

When we store a `player` entry in `playerCache`, the following steps are executed:

1. We invoke `playerCache.put(playerId, player);`.
2. Ignite finds the `"soccerRegion"` data region where the `playerCache` is configured.
3. Ignite looks up the meta-pages in `"soccerRegion"` to find the root of the B+ tree associated with the `"playerCache"`.

4. Ignite calculates the `hashcode` of the `"playerId"` and looks up the B+ tree to find the index page associated with the `hashcode`.

5. If no index page is found in the memory or on disk, then a new index page will be requested from one of the free lists. Once the index page is provided, it will be added to the B+ tree with the `hashcode` of the `"playerId"`, but the index page doesn't know about the data page and its offset where the *player* object will be stored (it will be updated in step 8).

6. `[inserting a new player]` If the index page is new and empty, then based on the size of the entry (the `playerId` and `player` objects), a data page will be provided by one of the free lists. The cache entry is added to the data page.

7. `[updating an existing player]` If the index page refers to a data page, then the `player` object will be added to the data page.

8. The index page will be updated to store the data page reference and its offset where the `player` object is being stored.

This section explained the internal workflow of storing entries to caches, but we just can't keep adding new objects to our cache as there is a limit to everything, and the Ignite cluster has a maximum capacity too. However, Apache Ignites prevents **out of memory** (**OOM**) errors by employing its out-of-the-box eviction policy. The following section focuses on Apache Ignite's object eviction policy.

Preventing OOM

Apache Ignite can be configured to persist entries (native or third-party) by enabling the persistence flag, or it may not persist data at all. When native persistence is turned on, then Ignite stores entries in memory and on disk. When native persistence is turned off (either using a third-party persistence store or no persistence), then Ignite uses the off-heap memory to store the entries and allocates new pages in RAM when required. We know that Ignite's durable memory has a maximum limit (20% of RAM or an overridden value); when that limit is reached and Ignite cannot allocate a page, it purges some of the data to prevent OOM errors. This purging technique is known as *eviction*, and Ignite provides APIs to configure the eviction policy.

Ignite supports eviction from the following:

- Off-heap memory
- On-heap memory

The following sections will explain the off-heap and on-heap eviction policies.

Off-heap eviction

By default, the eviction policy is **disabled** and we need to configure `DataRegionConfiguration` to turn it on. When the eviction policy is pre-configured, Ignite starts purging the pages as the memory consumption of the data region gets to 90% of the allocated memory of the data region. During eviction, Ignite applies the user-configured eviction algorithm and finds the pages to purge. It can completely remove the entries from the page. However, it cannot purge the entire page when an entry is locked and actively participating in a transaction. In cases like this, Ignite removes all other entries from the page and frees up some memory.

The off-heap eviction policy supports two **least recently used** (LRU) algorithms for selecting pages.

RANDOM_LRU

Ignite keeps track of the `'last access'` timestamp of all pages in an array. When a page is accessed, the array entry is updated with the timestamp. The random LRU algorithm randomly finds five pages from the array and evicts the oldest timestamp page.

The following Java configuration sets the random LRU eviction algorithm for a data region:

```
DataRegionConfiguration region1= new DataRegionConfiguration();
region1.setName("region1");
region1.setPageEvictionMode(DataPageEvictionMode.RANDOM_LRU);
```

The corresponding XML configuration is as follows:

```
<bean class="org.apache.ignite.configuration.DataRegionConfiguration">
<property name="pageEvictionMode" value="RANDOM_LRU"/>
```

RANDOM_2_LRU

Ignite stores the two most recent timestamps of all pages in an array. During eviction, it randomly selects five array indexes and computes the minimum difference between two timestamps for these five pages, compares the five minimum differences, and removes the least recently used page. This algorithm is useful for evicting data pages that are accessed rarely but have accidentally been accessed once.

The following Java configuration sets the RANDOM_2_LRU eviction algorithm for a data region:

```
DataRegionConfiguration region1= new DataRegionConfiguration();
  region1.setName("region1");
  region1.setPageEvictionMode(DataPageEvictionMode.RANDOM_2_LRU);
```

The corresponding XML configuration is as follows:

```
<bean class="org.apache.ignite.configuration.DataRegionConfiguration">
<property name="pageEvictionMode" value="RANDOM_2_LRU"/>
```

On-heap eviction

Ignite is an off-heap memory framework, but we can configure it to enable on-heap caching by setting the setOnheapCacheEnabled flag in CacheConfiguration. On-heap caching is effective for scenarios where you need to read a lot of **hot data**.

Ignite supports the eviction of entries from on-heap memory as well. The following sections detail the on-heap eviction algorithms.

LRU

This removes the least recently used entries from the cache. You need to enable on-heap caching in the cache configuration and set LruEvictionPolicyFactory as the eviction policy. LruEvictionPolicyFactory needs to know about the maximum number of entries to keep on-heap:

```
CacheConfiguration<Long, String> cacheCfg = new CacheConfiguration<>();

// Enabling on-heap caching for this distributed cache.
 cacheCfg.setOnheapCacheEnabled(true);
 // Set the maximum cache size to 10,000 (default is 100,000).
 cacheCfg.setEvictionPolicyFactory(new LruEvictionPolicyFactory<>(10000));
```

FIFO

First-in First-out (FIFO) evicts the on-heap cache entries that have spent the longest time on the heap. FifoEvictionPolicyFactory needs to be configured to enable FIFO eviction.

SORTED

We can write our own comparator to select the entries to evict first.
The `SortedEvictionPolicyFactory` can be configured for custom sorting.

The eviction policy removes entries from the on-heap and off-heap caches to prevent OOM errors. We can also configure a *swap space* to prevent OOM errors. The following section will explain what a swap space is and how can we configure it.

Swap space

A swap space is used to prevent OOM errors. If data persistence is not enabled, eviction can create data loss for our application. However, if we don't want to enable native or third-party persistence, we can configure a physical disk location to swap data from RAM to disk. If the swap path is configured and Ignite cannot allocate any more pages, the OS swaps data from RAM to the swap location. We need to configure `DataStorageConfiguration`'s `maxSize` greater than the RAM size and set `swapPath` to enable OS data swapping.

The swap space data is available as long as the node is active. Once the node shuts down, the data is lost. We should never consider swap space as replacement to data persistence. You cannot enable both the swap path and the eviction policy.

The following code snippet enables data swapping for a data region:

```
DataRegionConfiguration region1 = new DataRegionConfiguration();
 region1.setName("region1");
 region1.setSwapPath("D:\\ignite\\swap");
```

Expiring entries

Ignite's data expiry policy specifies the amount of time that must pass before considering an entry as expired. The expiration policies count the time from any of the following three events: creation time, last access time, and last modified time.

The following are the available expiry policies:

- `AccessedExpiryPolicy`: Defines the expiry duration of a cache entry based on the last time it was accessed. It doesn't consider the update time, only the creation and last access times are considered.
- `CreatedExpiryPolicy`: Defines the expiry duration of a cache entry based on when it was created.

- `EternalExpiryPolicy`: Specifies that cache entries won't expire.
- `ModifiedExpiryPolicy`: Defines the expiry duration of a cache entry based on the last time it was updated—create and update.
- `TouchedExpiryPolicy`: Defines the expiry duration of a cache entry based on when it was last created, updated, or accessed.

When an entry is expired, it is removed from the heap/Ignite native persistence storage/swap path. However, the third-party persistence store doesn't remove it.

You can find examples of the expiration policy in `com.deploy.expire.ExpiryPolicyTest` in the `Chapter 7` code bundle.

Monitoring memory and caches

Complex distributed applications need end-to-end monitoring and management. Various **application performance monitoring** (**APM**) tools are available to proactively identify system glitches and bottlenecks. Apache Ignite offers APIs to enable, collect, and retrieve system performance. In this section, we'll take a look at the following two types of metrics:

- Memory region monitoring
- Cache monitoring

Memory region monitoring

The `DataRegionMetrics` interface is the gateway to Apache Ignite's memory region monitoring APIs. The first step to collect metrics is to enable it. The `DataStorageMetrics` interface provides methods to get metrics for data storage. The following Java code snippet enables metrics for a data region:

```
DataRegionConfiguration region1 = new DataRegionConfiguration();
  region1.setName("region1");
  region1.setMetricsEnabled(true);
```

It can also be enabled and disabled at runtime via JMX beans.

`ignite.dataRegionMetrics()` returns a collection of `DataRegionMetrics`. You can invokes methods on `DataRegionMetrics` to get different statistics.

`ignite.dataStorageMetrics()` returns a `DataStorageMetrics` instance to check the data storage metrics.

The following are the steps to create two data regions, create a data storage configuration, and collect metrics for them:

1. Create a Java class called MemoryMonitoring:

```
public class MemoryMonitoring{
  private static final int KB = 1024;
  private static final int MB = 1024 * 1024;
  private static final long GB = MB * 1024;

  public static void main(String[] args) {
```

2. Add a data region, region1, enable metrics, and set the initial and maximum size:

```
DataRegionConfiguration region1 = new DataRegionConfiguration();
region1.setName("region1");
region1.setMetricsEnabled(true);
region1.setPersistenceEnabled(true);
region1.setInitialSize(500 * MB);
region1.setMaxSize(500 * MB);
```

3. Create another region, region2, enable metrics, but don't set the initial and maximum size:

```
DataRegionConfiguration region2 = new DataRegionConfiguration();
region2.setName("region2");
region2.setPersistenceEnabled(true);
region2.setMetricsEnabled(true);
```

4. Create a data storage configuration and set the data region configurations and page size, and enable data storage metrics:

```
DataStorageConfiguration storageCfg = new
DataStorageConfiguration();
storageCfg.getDefaultDataRegionConfiguration().setMaxSize(6L * GB);
storageCfg.setMetricsEnabled(true);
storageCfg.setPageSize(2 * KB);
storageCfg.setDataRegionConfigurations(region1, region2);
```

5. Create an Ignite configuration, set the data storage configuration, and start an Ignite server instance with the configuration:

```
IgniteConfiguration cfg = new IgniteConfiguration();
cfg.setPeerClassLoadingEnabled(true);
cfg.setDataStorageConfiguration(storageCfg);
Ignite ignite = Ignition.start(cfg);
```

6. Retrieve the data region metrics collection and loop through it:

```
System.out.println("Data Region Metrics...");
Collection<DataRegionMetrics> dataRegionMetrics =
ignite.dataRegionMetrics();
dataRegionMetrics.forEach(m -> {
    System.out.println(">>>***********************************<<<<");
    System.out.println(">>> Memory Region Name: " + m.getName());
    System.out.println(">>> OffHeapSize Size: " +
    m.getOffHeapSize());
    System.out.println(">>> Physical Memory Size: " +
    m.getPhysicalMemorySize());
    System.out.println(">>>***********************************<<<<");
});
```

7. Get the data storage metrics and print the results:

```
System.out.println("Data Storage Metrics...");
DataStorageMetrics dataStorageMetrics = ignite.dataStorageMetrics();
System.out.println("_____");
System.out.println("Off-heap size = "+
dataStorageMetrics.getOffHeapSize());
System.out.println("Allocated size= "+
dataStorageMetrics.getTotalAllocatedSize());
  }
}
```

8. Run the program. It will print the metrics for data regions and data storage.

Cache monitoring

The CacheMetrics interface provides APIs for monitoring distributed caches.
The setStatisticsEnabled method of CacheConfiguration sets whether statistics
gathering is enabled on a cache or not. The metrics() method of IgniteCache returns
the whole cluster's snapshot metrics for the cache and the localMetrics() method gets
the local node's metrics snapshot for the cache.

The following code snippet will create a cache configuration, enable statistics gathering,
and monitor the whole cluster's snapshot metrics for the cache:

1. Create a class called CacheMonitoring:

```
public class CacheMonitoring {
    public static void main(String[] args) throws
    InterruptedException {
```

2. Create a cache configuration and enable statistics:

```
CacheConfiguration<Long, String> myCacheConf = new
  CacheConfiguration<>();
String randomCacheName = "My Cache " + UUID.randomUUID().toString();
myCacheConf.setName(randomCacheName);
myCacheConf.setStatisticsEnabled(true);
myCacheConf.setIndexedTypes(Long.class, String.class);
```

3. Create an Ignite configuration with `myCacheConf` and start an Ignite instance:

```
IgniteConfiguration cfg = new IgniteConfiguration();
cfg.setPeerClassLoadingEnabled(true);
cfg.setCacheConfiguration(myCacheConf);
Ignite ignite = Ignition.start(cfg);
```

4. Create or get the cache instance and populate the cache in a child thread:

```
IgniteCache<Long, String> cache =
  ignite.getOrCreateCache(randomCacheName);
ExecutorService svc = ignite.executorService();
svc.submit(new Runnable() {
        @Override
        public void run() {
            while (true) {
                int val = new Random().nextInt(50000);
                String string = cache.get(Long.valueOf(val));
                for (int i = 0; i <= val; i++) {
                    cache.put(Long.valueOf(i), "value=" + i);
                }
            }
        }
});
```

5. Get all the cluster metrics for the cache and print them periodically:

```
System.out.println("Cache Metrics...");
 while (true) {
        CacheMetrics metrics = cache.metrics();
        System.out.println("********************************");
        System.out.println("Avg Get time = " +
         metrics.getAverageGetTime());
        System.out.println("Avg Put time = " +
         metrics.getAveragePutTime());
        System.out.println("Cache Hits = " +
         metrics.getCacheHits());
        System.out.println("Cache Misses = " +
         metrics.getCacheMisses());
```

```
    System.out.println("Cache Evictions = " +
      metrics.getCacheEvictions());
  Thread.sleep(200);
    }
  }
}
```

6. Run the program. It will print cluster metrics for the cache.

JMX console monitoring

Ignite supports remote monitoring through JMX console. To start the JMX server, you need to set an environment variable called IGNITE_JMX_PORT with a valid unoccupied port number.

The following are the steps to enable JMX monitoring:

1. Let's assume that port 7788 is available (if not, then find a valid port), set IGNITE_JMX_PORT=7788, start an Ignite server instance, and rerun our CacheMonitoring example.

2. We need a JMX console viewer. Open JDK's bin directory and launch jmc:

3. In JMC, create a connection for port 7788 (or your IGNITE_JMX_PORT value):

4. Right-click on **MBean Server** for `localhost:7788` and start the JMX console.

5. It will open the overview page and show statistics of memory and CPU usage. Open the **MBean Browser.**

6. Expand the `'org.apache'` node and find our `"My Cache ...."` cache node (your cache name will be different but will start with the name `'My Cache'`):

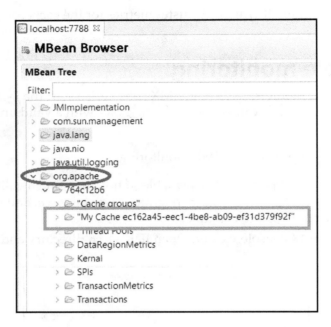

7. Click on the `CacheClusterMetricsMXBeanImpl` node to get the global cluster statistics for our cache:

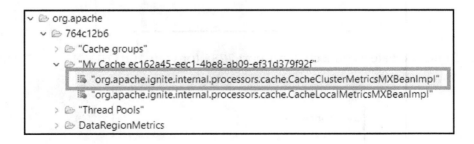

8. The **Attributes** tab will show you statistics such as
   AverageGetTime and **CacheHitPercentage**:

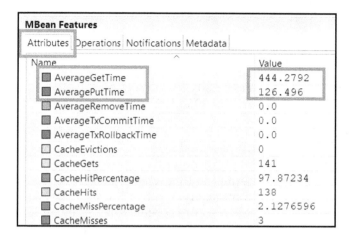

9. The **Operations** tab will show you the available JMX operations, such as
   disabling stats:

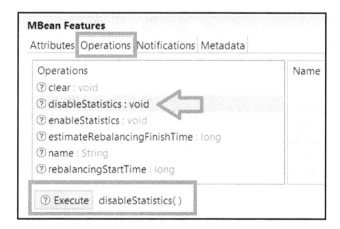

10. Execute the **disableStatistics** operation and check your Eclipse console. It will
    stop printing the stats. Now invoke the **enableStatistics** operation and check the
    Eclipse console again; it should start showing the stats.

In this section, we enabled statistics and collected cache and memory metrics. If you see any
unexpected metrics values, change your cache or data region configuration and keep
monitoring your app until you get the expected result.

We monitored system metrics using JMX console and Java code. The next section will tell you about the importance of Ignite cluster security in production, as malicious code can cause undesired effects, security breaches, or damage the system.

Securing data

Application security has become a necessity for protecting sensitive data from malicious activity. Ignite provides the following mechanism to protect our sensitive data:

1. **Inter node communication**: Ignite doesn't have a master node to communicate with other nodes. When a new node gets added or removed from the network, the cluster rebalances data transparently. Therefore, we need to secure the inter-node communication channel so that when a new node is added, it doesn't get our application data automatically. Ignite allows you to use SSL socket communication to provide a secure connection among all Ignite nodes. We can configure SSL context factory to use trusted certificates and passwords.

2. **Authentication**: Ignite allows you to secure the cluster by configuring authentication, but authentication is only supported when persistence is enabled.

3. **Trusting serialized data**: Serialized data can be compromised. If a malicious code snippet is injected into a node, then during deserialization it can cause undesired effects, security breaches, or damage the system. Ignite nodes can be configured to handle this data deserialization risk by setting the following two system properties.

IGNITE_MARSHALLER_WHITELIST: Create a whitelist file with a list of safe objects for deserialization such as com.packt.Player and com.packt.Club and set the path to the file to this system property. You can pass VM arguments or set the value programmatically. If an object is not listed in the whitelist file, then Ignite throws an exception during deserialization.

4. **Protecting the third-party data store**: Your persistent data store can be compromised and data can be damaged. You can secure the third-party data store by enforcing IP security groups. AWS and other cloud providers offer IP security groups.

IGNITE_MARSHALLER_BLACKLIST: creates a blacklist file with a list of unsafe/compromised objects such as com.packt.Admin and com.packt.Account and set the path to the file to this system property. You can pass VM arguments or set the value programmatically. If an object is listed in the blacklist file, then Ignite throws exception during deserialization.

Now we know the importance of securing Ignite cluster, the art of monitoring Ignite components, and how to configure memory and the cache to get metrics. Next, we'll look at performance improvement.

Tuning performance

Performance tuning is important for improving the user experience. Apache Ignite makes network calls, communicates with other nodes, serializes objects, swaps entries from RAM to disk, rebalances data, stores objects on-heap and off-heap, creates WAL files, and more. Therefore, we need to keep an eye on different areas to improve the overall system performance. Ignite provides the following tips (https://apacheignite.readme.io/docs/performance-tips) to tune different areas:

- Turn off back ups
- Tune durable memory
- Tune data rebalancing
- Configure thread pools
- Use collocated computations
- Use data streamer
- Batch up your messages
- Tune garbage collection
- Disable internal event notifications

Try avoiding distributed joins and take a key/value-based approach. The code bundle has an example to show you the difference between distributed SQLs and key/value-based algorithms.

The following section will take you through the Ignite deployment environments and options.

Exploring the deployment options

We have explored the Ignite memory architecture, monitored metrics, tuned performance, and secured our application. Now we are ready to deploy our code to production. Apache Ignite supports various deployment environments, such as the following:

- **Docker**: This is the de facto standard for packaging apps. Its a `"Package Once Deploy Anywhere"` [Arun Gupta] solution for our apps. Docker allows us to package Ignite deployments with all the dependencies into a standard container.
- **AWS**: You can easily set up an Ignite cluster in AWS by starting an Apache Ignite machine image in EC2. AWS is a public cloud and resolves all infrastructural (scalability, security, deployment and so on) problems.
- **Google Cloud**: Apache Ignite machine images can be installed in Google cloud to set up a cluster and get the advantages of public cloud deployment, such as elastic scaling.
- **Apache Mesos**: Ignite supports scheduling and running Apache Ignite nodes in a Mesos cluster. Apache Mesos' scheduling and task management frameworks provide efficient distribution and isolation of resources and makes large-scale deployment easier.
- **Kubernetes**: This is an *open source system for automating deployment, scaling, and management of containerized applications.* Apache Ignite can be deployed in Kubernetes, it supports stateless and stateful deployment.

Summary

This chapter covered the nitty-gritty of fine-tuning our Apache Ignite application for production deployment. It started with Ignite's memory architecture—data store configuration, data regions, and pages.

We explored all the advanced features and use cases of Apache Ignite. We went through why you should use Apache Ignite, in-memory technologies, the installation and clustering of Ignite nodes, caching topologies, and various caching strategies such as cache aside, read- and write-through, and write-behind. We delved into detailed aspects of Ignite's data grid, such as web session clustering and querying data. You also obtained hands-on experience of processing large volumes of data using compute grid and Ignite's map-reduce and executor service.

You gained experience with the memory architecture of Apache Ignite, looked at how to monitor memory and the cache, explored complex event processing, examined event streaming, and looked at time series prediction of opportunities and threats. Additionally, we covered the off-heap and on-heap caching, swapping, native and third-party persistence, and Spring framework integration with Apache Ignite.

You mastered the features of Apache Ignite 2.x and are now able to build an efficient, high-performance, scalable, and high-availability system architecture using Ignite.

References

- https://ignite.apache.org/features/
- https://apacheignite.readme.io/docs

Other Books You May Enjoy

If you enjoyed this book, you may be interested in these other books by Packt:

Big Data Analytics with Hadoop 3
Sridhar Alla

ISBN: 978-1-78862-884-6

- Explore the new features of Hadoop 3 along with HDFS, YARN, and MapReduce
- Get well-versed with the analytical capabilities of Hadoop ecosystem using practical examples
- Integrate Hadoop with R and Python for more efficient big data processing
- Learn to use Hadoop with Apache Spark and Apache Flink for real-time data analytics
- Set up a Hadoop cluster on AWS cloud
- Perform big data analytics on AWS using Elastic Map Reduce

Artificial Intelligence for Big Data
Manish Kumar, Anand Deshpande

ISBN: 978-1-78847-217-3

- Manage Artificial Intelligence techniques for big data with Java
- Build smart systems to analyze data for enhanced customer experience
- Learn to use Artificial Intelligence frameworks for big data
- Understand complex problems with algorithms and Neuro-Fuzzy systems
- Design stratagems to leverage data using Machine Learning process
- Apply Deep Learning techniques to prepare data for modeling
- Construct models that learn from data using open source tools
- Analyze big data problems using scalable Machine Learning algorithms

Leave a review - let other readers know what you think

Please share your thoughts on this book with others by leaving a review on the site that you bought it from. If you purchased the book from Amazon, please leave us an honest review on this book's Amazon page. This is vital so that other potential readers can see and use your unbiased opinion to make purchasing decisions, we can understand what our customers think about our products, and our authors can see your feedback on the title that they have worked with Packt to create. It will only take a few minutes of your time, but is valuable to other potential customers, our authors, and Packt. Thank you!

Index

www.ingramcontent.com/pod-product-compliance
Lightning Source LLC
Chambersburg PA
CBHW080634060326
40690CB00021B/4934